# The Limits of Kindness

Caspar Hare presents a novel approach to questions of what we ought to do, and why. The traditional way to approach this subject is to begin by supposing a foundational principle, and then work out its implications. Consequentialists say that we ought to make the world impersonally better, for instance, while Kantian deontologists say that we ought to act on universalizable maxims, and contractualists say that we ought to act in accordance with the terms of certain hypothetical contracts. These principles are all grand and controversial. The motivating idea behind *The Limits of Kindness* is that we can tackle some of the most difficult problems in normative ethics by starting with a principle that is humble and uncontroversial. Being moral involves wanting particular other people to be better off.

From these innocuous beginnings, Hare leads us to surprising conclusions about how we ought to resolve conflicts of interest, whether we ought to create some people rather than others, what we ought to want in an infinite world, when we ought to make sacrifices for the sake of needy strangers, and why we cannot, on pain of irrationality, attribute great importance to the boundaries between people.

# The Limits
# of Kindness

Caspar Hare

OXFORD
UNIVERSITY PRESS

# OXFORD
UNIVERSITY PRESS

Great Clarendon Street, Oxford, OX2 6DP,
United Kingdom

Oxford University Press is a department of the University of Oxford.
It furthers the University's objective of excellence in research, scholarship,
and education by publishing worldwide. Oxford is a registered trade mark of
Oxford University Press in the UK and in certain other countries

Published in the United States of America by Oxford University Press
198 Madison Avenue, New York, NY 10016, United States of America

British Library Cataloguing in Publication Data
Data available

Library of Congress Cataloging in Publication Data
Data available

ISBN 978–0–19–969199–9 (Hbk.)
ISBN 978–0–19–874802–1 (Pbk.)

# Contents

## Part II

## Part III

# Acknowledgments

I have had helpful conversations about the material I cover here with many, many people. I cannot list them all. I will single out: John Broome, Steve Darwall, Nina Emery, Peter Graham, Elizabeth Harman, Sally Haslanger, Brian Hedden, Pamela Hieronymi, Mark Johnston, Simon Keller, Julia Markovits, Melissa Mohr, Alistair Norcross, Agustin Rayo, Miriam Schoenfield, Brad Skow, Kieran Setiya, Bob Stalnaker, Judith Thomson, Jay Wallace, Steve Yablo, Helen Yeter Chappel and Richard Yeter Chappel. Thanks.

# A Stylistic Note

Throughout the body of this book I will try to avoid using items of specialist philosophical vocabulary without first explaining what I take them to mean.[1] If you are a professional philosopher, then you may find this condescending. You may feel that you do not need to be schooled in the tools of your trade. I apologize. I do it because I suspect that quite often, when professional philosophers use specialized terms, they have subtly different senses of those terms in mind.

One example, involving not-so-subtly-different senses of a not-very-specialized term: We talk a great deal about *biting the bullet*. For example, "I confronted David Lewis with my damning objection to modal realism, and he bit the bullet." I have asked a number of philosophers about what, precisely, this means, and received a startling range of replies.

Around 70 percent say that the metaphor has to do with *surgery*. When battlefield doctors in ages past were operating on a wounded soldier without anesthetic, they would give him a bullet to bite down on. Grimly, the soldier would accept and endure his operation. So, in philosophy, for you to bite the bullet is for you grimly to accept a seemingly absurd consequence of the theory you endorse. This is, I think, the most widely understood sense of the term. (Though it is not obvious that it is the original sense—the first recorded use is in Rudyard Kipling, and he did not make it clear precisely what metaphor he had in mind. And the medical history is dubious. Why would battlefield doctors have had their patients bite down on metal, rather than cloth or leather, if they cared at all about their patients' teeth?)

Some others say that the metaphor has to with *injury*. To bite a bullet is to take a bullet to the face—like biting the dust, but worse. So, in philosophy, for you to acknowledge that you are biting the bullet is for you to acknowledge that an objection has gravely wounded your theory.

Yet others say that the metaphor has to do with *food*. To bite a bullet is to be surprised to find that something unpalatable lurks within your food.

---

[1] I will be less fastidious in the footnotes.

So, in philosophy, for you to acknowledge that you are biting the bullet is for you to acknowledge that you are surprised to find that something unpalatable lurks within the consequences of your theory. One philosopher said to me that the metaphor has to do with *magic*. To bite a bullet is to catch a bullet, Houdini-style, in your teeth. So, in philosophy, for you to bite the bullet is for you elegantly to intercept a seemingly lethal objection and render it benign. For years, when people had suggested that this philosopher was "biting the bullet" on this or that point (his views concerning the existence of medium-sized objects required a lot of bullet-biting), he had taken this to be the highest of praise.

I conclude from my highly unscientific survey that, more than 30 percent of the time, when a philosopher claims to be "biting the bullet," a small gap opens up between what he or she means and what his or her reader or listener understands him or her to mean.

And I guess that these small gaps in understanding are more common than we normally think. Over the course of a long-ish book they will interact and multiply, if left alone. Best not to leave them alone.

# Introduction

## 0.1. Normative Ethics

Let us begin with some basics. This book is about *normative ethics*. What is that?

There is a natural distinction between claims like these:

"The square root of two is irrational."
"The economy is in decline."
"Proxima Centauri is our Sun's closest big neighbor."
"That really, really hurt."

and claims like these:

"You ought to be nice to your grandmother."
"Paris is beautiful."
"Lying to little children to serve your own ends is wrong."
"Television is bad for the soul."

The first sort of claim pertains only to the way things are, the second sort of claim pertains, at least in part, to the way things ought to be. In philosophy-speak: the first sort of claim is *descriptive*, the second *normative*.[1]

Some normative claims overtly concern morality. For example:

"Cyril is a dishonorable bounder."
"The administration is irredeemably corrupt."
"Harry wronged you by taking your hat."

Others do not. For example:

---

[1] I should note (the first of many qualifications) that, though the basic distinction is natural and easy to grasp, drawing a precise boundary between normative and descriptive claims is an exceptionally interesting and difficult job. We need not worry about that here.

"Eating your hair is a bad way to conserve energy."

"On clay, Roger Federer ought to adjust his backhand to compensate for the higher bounce of the ball."

*Moralists* are in the business of making normative claims of the first sort, *moral-normative* claims.[2]

*Moral theorists* are moralists with a systematic bent. They are unsatisfied with claims about particular things, like Cyril, or Harry's action-of-taking-your-hat. They have grander ambitions. They want to make very general claims about kinds of things:

"All people of kind —— are dishonorable bounders."

"All actions of kind —— wrong you."

"All punishments of kind —— are unjust."

Their idea is for these general claims to serve as the basis of a theory that will entail claims about particular things.

*Normative ethicists* are moral theorists with a special interest in individual people—in how they are, and in what they do.[3] Normative ethicists are not directly concerned with when institutional structures are fair and just, when policies are discriminatory, when aspirations are noble, when customs are deviant and contrary to nature . . . and so on and so forth. They want a theory of the conditions under which people are good or bad, honorable or dishonorable, admirable or loathsome . . . etc. And they want a theory of the conditions under which people's actions are right or wrong, permissible or impermissible, praiseworthy or blameworthy . . . etc. They are, not to mince words, high-minded busy-bodies. Their goal is to tell you how you ought, morally, to be and what you ought, morally, to do.

---

[2] Again, I should note that, though the distinction between normative claims that have a moral flavor and normative claims that do not is natural enough, there is no uncontroversial way of drawing a precise boundary between the realm of the moral and the realm of the normative-non-moral. Again, we need not worry about that here.

[3] This is how the term "normative ethics" is standardly used by philosophers (when introducing the subject, philosophers standardly say that the central questions of normative ethics are "how should we live?" "what should we do?" "how should we be?"). There is a worry that the term is misleadingly general—"the ethics of individual action" or "the ethics of life" might be better terms for what philosophers have in mind. But I am not going to try to change entrenched ways of talking here.

## 0.2. Why Normative Ethics is Hard

Suppose we try to join the high-minded busy-bodies, and set about building a theory of normative ethics. How hard can this be? Quite hard, it turns out. Let us start by addressing the morality of action. Our first job is to find some general claims about the moral status of actions to build our theory around. But this is not a simple matter. Trusting our instincts, looking for general claims that have a *plausible ring* to them, will not help, because many general claims about the moral status of actions that have a plausible ring to them turn out to be inconsistent with one another. Normative ethicists have proven to be very adept at rooting out and exposing such inconsistencies. I will discuss here, and over the coming chapters, three celebrated examples of pairs of inconsistent, right-seeming normative claims. Here is one pair:

*Betterness*
You do wrong only if things overall would have been better if you had acted in some other way.

*Violation*
It is wrong to inflict grievous physical harm on an unconsenting, innocent person who poses no threat to anybody, unless you can secure massively disproportionate benefits by doing so.

*Betterness* seems right. If I accuse you of doing something wrong, then I cannot very well say "though, of course, things would have been no better if you had done anything else." By accusing you, I seem to be committing myself to the idea that things would have been better if you had done something else. And *Violation* sounds right too. Of course, it is not okay to hurt unconsenting, innocent, unthreatening people.

But the claims are inconsistent. Consider:

Human Fuel
While piloting a steel, steam-engined boat across the bleak South Seas, you receive a distress call from Amy, who has been left to die of thirst on a nearby, bare island by cruel pirates. Knowing that you are the only boat in the area, you pick her up, and then receive another distress call from Brian and Celia, left to die of thirst on a not-so-nearby, bare island by more cruel pirates. You do not have enough coal to get to them, and no part of your steel boat will serve as fuel . . . but Amy is both large and

dehydrated . . . Knock her on the head, shove her in the furnace and you will make it over there. And nobody but you will ever know.

If *Violation* is true then it would be wrong to use Amy-power to save Brian and Celia. But, if *Betterness* is true, then, seemingly, it would not be wrong. If you knock Amy on the head, then one person will have been killed in a quick, relatively painless way. If you do not, then two people will have been killed in a lingering, relatively painful way. It is no better that two people be killed in a lingering, relatively painful way than that one person be killed in a quick, relatively painless way.[4]

Here is another celebrated example of a pair of inconsistent, right-seeming claims:

*Harm*
An action is wrong only if it harms something with morally significant interests.

*Optimizing the Health of your Child*
Whenever you have made it your business to conceive and bear a child, it is wrong to choose that your child be unhealthy, rather than healthy, unless you have strong reasons to do so.

*Harm* seems right. If I argue that you have done the wrong thing, and you reply "Where was the harm in that?," then I must answer your question or lose the argument. And *Optimizing the Health of your Child* seems right too. Of course parents ought to have some concern for the health of their children. Of course they ought to act on that concern, absent strong reasons to the contrary.

But the claims are inconsistent. Consider:

Not Postponing Conception
Mary is recovering from German measles. Her doctor recommends that she postpone her efforts to conceive a child for a couple of months. If she conceives a child in the next couple of months, then the child will, most likely, have significant health problems. Mary has no strong reasons to conceive a child immediately, but she does have a mild preference for *getting on with it.* She gets on with it. Nine and a half

---

[4] This problem goes by various names. It is sometimes referred to as "Scheffler's Paradox," after an influential treatment of it in Scheffler (1992), sometimes referred to as "Foot's Problem" after an influential treatment of it in Foot (1985). But philosophers were aware of some form or other of the problem well before that. See, e.g., McCloskey (1963). I will discuss the problem in more detail in Chapter 7.

months later baby Mariette is born, with significant health problems. This is not a disaster—Mary is a woman of means, so Mariette's health problems do not impose a burden on wider society, and, on balance, Mariette has a rewarding life. But it is not great either—Mariette's health problems are a chronic source of anxiety, pain, and frustration to her.

If *Optimizing the Health of your Child* is true, then it would seem that Mary did wrong by conceiving her child immediately. But, if *Harm* is true, then it would seem that she did no wrong. If Mary had not conceived a baby immediately, then she would, most likely, have conceived a baby some time later, as genetically different from the actual Mariette as typical non-twin siblings are genetically different. On any plausible view of essence (of the conditions under which particular people would or would not have existed), that child would not have been Mariette. On any plausible view of harm, you do not harm somebody whose life is, on balance, rewarding, by making it the case that he or she exists rather than not.[5] So Mary did not harm Mariette, and, if she did not harm Mariette, then whom or what did she harm?

Here is the third celebrated example of a pair of inconsistent, right-seeming claims:

*Sacrifice*
Whenever you are in a position to save the life of a child at a relatively small cost to yourself and no cost to others, you are morally obliged to do so.

*Sackcloth and Ashes*
People living in affluent societies are not morally obliged to give away almost everything they have, for the sake of people in distant, poor societies.

*Sacrifice* sounds right. What kind of a monster would let a child die for the sake of his cufflinks? *Sackcloth and Ashes* sounds right too. Surely we do not have to give away almost everything we have! Cannot we hold onto at least a few small indulgences—a car when we could take the bus, freshly squeezed orange juice when we could get squash?

---

[5] This has been known as an instance of the "Non-Identity Problem" since Parfit (1976; 1983: ch. 16). I will discuss it in detail in Chapter 5.

But the claims are inconsistent. Consider:

Oxfam

The charity Oxfam is soliciting donations for a program that will vaccinate impoverished children against disease. Craftily, the administrators of the program have arranged their finances in such a way that the marginal benefits of further donations are clear: for every $100 you give, around ten more children will be vaccinated. For every ten children vaccinated, around one of them will live through an epidemic of disease that would otherwise have killed him or her.

If *Sacrifice* is right, then it would appear that you are obliged to give your first $100 to the program—by doing so you will save the life of a child at a small cost to yourself. And you are obliged to give your second $100 to the program for the same reason, and your third $100 . . . right down to the point where the marginal cost to you of giving away a further $100 is relatively large. But by that point you will have given away almost everything you have. So, if *Sacrifice* is right, then you are obliged to give away almost everything you have in this case, which contradicts *Sackcloth and Ashes*.[6]

## 0.3. Reflective Equilibrium

The moral to draw from these examples is that not all general normative claims that seem right, at first blush, are right. How, then, are we to decide which to accept? Many normative ethicists would give this advice: "Building a theory of normative ethics is about working towards *reflective equilibrium*. Start by taking all the normative claims that sound right to you, whether they be very general claims about the nature of the good and so forth, or very particular claims about particular cases. Then test them against each other. Look for inconsistencies. If you find inconsistent claims, then discard one or the other. When you make decisions about which claims to discard, do not dogmatically favor the more general over the more specific, or vice versa—consider the strength of your attachment to the respective claims, consider the unity, simplicity, and explanatory

---

[6] The canonic presentation of this problem is in Singer (1972). I will discuss it in detail in Chapters 12 and 13.

power of the emerging theory. If you can find more general claims that will entail and explain disparate, surviving, more specific claims, then adopt them. Repeat this process again and again, until you are left with a simple, consistent theory."[7]

I have never found this advice very helpful. I find it easy enough to identify claims that sound right to me, to test such claims against each other, and to find inconsistencies. But when it comes time to "discard one claim or the other," I often have no idea which way to go. Take the Human Fuel case, for example. *Betterness* and *Violation* both seem right to me. The case shows they are inconsistent. How am I to proceed?

Attending, first, to the unity, simplicity, and explanatory power of the emerging theory, I find that *Betterness* comes out ahead of *Violation*. Precisely explicating the virtues of unity, simplicity, and explanatory power in a theory is a notoriously difficult problem. But any interesting explication of these virtues will cast act consequentialism, the theory that makes *Betterness* its centerpiece, in a flattering light. Act consequentialism can be stated in a sentence:

*Act Consequentialism*
An act is wrong if and only if some alternative to it has a better outcome.

When sharpened up a bit (we need to explain what *alternatives* and *outcomes* are) and combined with an appropriately precise axiology (a theory of what makes one outcome better than another), it nails down the moral status of all acts, performed by anyone, at any time, in any place. *Violation*, on the other hand, is a very local principle. It tells us about the moral status of certain acts that inflict grievous physical harm on unconsenting, innocent people, and nothing else. Some theorists who adopt *Violation* think of it as just one of a patchwork of independent moral principles. These principles together make up a moral theory that is far more complex and disunified than act consequentialism. Others think that *Violation* can be derived from principles that are (at least close to) as simple and unified as act consequentialism—variants of rule consequentialism, contractualism, and Kantian rationalism. But I, for one, find these derivations less than convincing.

---

[7] The name "reflective equilibrium" was coined by John Rawls in Rawls (1971). Rawls traced the idea back to Nelson Goodman's discussion of methods for justifying rules of inductive logic in Goodman (1955).

But unity, simplicity, and explanatory power are not the be-all and end-all of everything in normative ethics. If they were, then moral nihilism (for these purposes: the view that all actions are morally neutral) would be the best theory of all. The method of reflective equilibrium would have me weigh, also, the strength of my attachment to *Betterness* and *Violation*. How strongly am I attached to each?

Well, the first thing I must acknowledge is that, for me, *Violation* has a lot of pull. I expect it has a lot of pull for you too. Imagine ignoring it, and behaving as the act consequentialist would have you behave in the Human Fuel case. Imagine picking Amy up from the first island. Imagine her relief at seeing you. Imagine learning of the second island. Imagine shielding your calculations from Amy (better that she not know about them, really). Imagine creeping up behind her and smashing her head with a heavy spanner. Imagine smashing her head again and again to be sure that she is dead (very important, given what is about to happen). Imagine dragging her body across the deck and cramming it into the boiler. Imagine the temporary loss of power to your boat as the liquids in her body evaporate away. Imagine pungent new smells emanating from the boiler. Imagine the surge of power as her flesh begins to burn. Imagine arriving at the second island. Imagine Brian and Celia's relief at seeing you. Imagine steaming away with that secret smoldering in the middle of your boat ... I expect that, the more carefully you fill in the details of this story in your imagination, the more disgusting you will find it. And I expect that your disgust will have a particular flavor. It will not be the sort of disgust that comes with imagining doing something morally admirable but gross—like diving into a cesspit to save the life of a toddler, or spooning the brains of an injured soldier back into his skull. It will be *moral* disgust. Your imaginary actions will seem to you, in a visceral way, to be wrong.

Fine. Now, what should you and I do with our visceral judgments?

On one way of thinking, we should discard them. All that matters in the Human Fuel case is that, if you do the one thing then two people will be killed, while if you do the other thing then one person will be killed. Our visceral judgments about these sorts of cases are mistaken.

Advocates of this way of thinking owe us a debunking explanation of how we came to be mistaken. And they have many to hand. For example, they can say: "Doubtless the idea of knocking Amy on the head and throwing her in the boiler seems horrific to you, but this is because the immediate consequences of doing so are horrific, and we all have a tendency to focus on the immediate consequences of what we do. This tendency serves us well, most of the time, because most of the time we have far greater control over the immediate consequences of our actions than the distant consequences of our actions. But sometimes it leads us astray. It is leading you astray here. Immediate and distant consequences matter equally much."

On another way of thinking, we should preserve the judgments. Obviously we do not want to demand of our incipient moral theory that it represent all of our visceral judgments about right and wrong as true. We want to leave space for correction. But this visceral judgment is non-negotiable. Its truth is radiant. Any claim with which it is inconsistent should be rejected.

Advocates of this way of thinking, too, owe us a debunking explanation of why we might be inclined to think otherwise, to think that killing Amy is in fact the thing to do. And they, too, have many to hand. For example, they can say: "Look, what matters in this case is that Amy, Brian and Celia each has a right not to be murdered. Philosophers may appreciate that rights matter, and infer that the appropriate thing to do in this case is to ensure that as few people as possible have their rights violated. Malaria is bad, so we should minimize malaria. Violation of rights is bad, so we should minimize violation of rights. But this is a subtle mistake. Rights are not like malaria. The appropriate way to respond to the fact that rights matter is not by *minimizing the violation of rights*, but rather by *not violating rights*."[8]

For each of the two points of view, I think I see it quite clearly, and I can work myself into a frame of mind where it seems like the right one. But which is the right one? I find it very hard to judge. I know, of course, what I would do if I found myself in the Human Fuel case. I would leave Amy alone. I doubt that I would even allow myself to acknowledge that throwing her into the boiler was an option. It would be one of those thoughts that flits around behind the camera of my mind, too shameful and disturbing to be released into view. But would that reflect some deep practical wisdom on my part, or would it reflect moral cowardice? I find it very hard to judge.

[8] See Pettit (1991) for a very clear version of this point.

Is this inability to judge a weakness on my part? Maybe so. Certainly, many of my friends and colleagues have no difficulty with the question. They wholeheartedly embrace one of the views and renounce the other. They think it obvious that we should all do the same. But I take some consolation in the fact that they do not all go the same way. Roughly half of them embrace some form of act consequentialism. Roughly half of them embrace some form of deontology—some view that yields the result that Amy should be allowed to live.

In my experience, feelings run pretty high in this domain. Many act consequentialists tend to think of deontologists as wooly-headed weaklings, as people who would rather obscure the landscape of normative ethics with enigmatic musings about Kant than face up to the fact that, sometimes, contrary to "intuition," they must dirty their hands. Many deontologists tend to think of act consequentialists as accountants-gone-wild, as people who have entirely lost touch with their moral sense, and come to care only about the books. (Nine years ago, when I first arrived at MIT, I taught a graduate seminar on normative ethics. Judy Thomson, whom I *enormously* respect and admire, attended the seminar, and came to suspect that I had an unseemly attraction to act consequentialism. One day, after class, she pressed me on cases like the <u>Human Fuel</u> case. When I confessed to feeling the pull of the act-consequentialist way of thinking about such cases, she threw her hands in the air, gave me a special sort of look, proclaimed my condition "terribly sad,"[9] and walked away. The look made a big impression on me. It was not the fond, indulgent sort of look that you give your wayward young nephew when he tells you that he is thinking of joining the socialist party. It was the sort of look that you give your wayward young nephew when he tells you that he is thinking of joining the Klan.)

It is a curious phenomenon. These are very intelligent people. They are fully aware of the arguments on both sides of the issue. Ask the act consequentialists to make a case for deontology, for pedagogical purposes, and they will say everything the deontologists say, with all the same passion, emphasis, and conviction. Ask the deontologists to make a case for act consequentialism, for pedagogical purposes, and they will say everything the act consequentialists say, with all the same passion,

---

[9] But please do not infer that Judy Thomson's grounds for rejecting act consequentialism come down only to this feeling of terrible sadness. She has a very sophisticated account of where and why act consequentialists go wrong. I will briefly summarize it in Sect. 4.6.

emphasis, and conviction. It does not appear as if the members of either group are *missing something*—as if there is a decisive consideration that has passed beneath their attention. And they all know this. Yet some psychological mechanism causes roughly half of them to break one way and roughly half of them to break the other way.[10]

## 0.4. A Foundational Approach

If you, like me, do not break either way, if you share my ambivalence about these sorts of questions, then you might be interested in a different approach. You might hope to set the "prima facie plausible" normative claims aside and base your theory on firmer foundations. You might hope to fix on some general normative principles that you regard as non-negotiably true. You might hope to take these principles as axioms and derive a normative theory from them. You might hope that the resulting theory would be as solid and pure as an axiomatization of number theory.[11]

---

[10] An untutored outsider might feel that this reflects badly on what normative ethicists are doing. The three problems that I have drawn attention to here are among the most basic problems in normative ethics. They are routinely taught in introductory classes on the subject. The fact that there is no consensus on how to resolve them, and a firm consensus that our present methods of enquiry will not yield a consensus on how to resolve them, might suggest, to the untutored outsider, a weakness in those methods.

Philosophers tend to be wary of indulging such feelings (with some reason—in philosophy, deadlock is everywhere). A good part of our early education consists in stripping them away. David Lewis used to say: "Debates may deadlock. But it does not follow that they are not worth pursuing, or that there is no fact of the matter about who is right."

Back when I was young and impressionable, this struck me as deep wisdom, but now I am not so sure that the moral we were expected to draw from it (that, in philosophy, there is a kind of virtue in sticking to your guns in the face of implacable opposition) is a good one. Often, when philosophical debates deadlock, it seems to me irresponsible to come down firmly on one side or other. Often it seems to me that coming down firmly on one side involves willfully ignoring the powerful considerations that move your opponents.

[11] I should mention that some philosophers might say that this, too, is an application of the reflective equilibrium method, because they characterize the method more broadly than I have done here. Any form of rational inquiry whose goal is a state of reflective equilibrium, a state in which your more general beliefs and more specific beliefs are no longer in conflict (which is to say *pretty much any form of rational inquiry*) counts as an application of the reflective equilibrium method. That is fine by me. But then the advice "pursue reflective equilibrium" is only marginally more helpful than the advice "think harder about the problem."

What sort of "non-negotiable" principles would do the job? A tempting place to start is with principles concerning rationality—principles concerning what it is rational to believe, desire, and do.

This is not an original idea. For almost as long as there have been philosophers, there have been philosophers trying to base ethics on rationality, broadly understood. Plato at least experimented with the thought that morality was about enlightened self-interest. The ancient stoics held as their ideal a life in accordance with reason, free of internal conflict. Kant claimed that moral requirements derived from his categorical imperative, and that his categorical imperative was a requirement of rationality. Generation after generation of neo-Kantians have argued that rationality requires us to be impartial in some way, and this requirement is the source of moral obligation. Most, following the letter of Kant, have argued that the resulting obligations are deontological. Some, like my unrelated namesake R. M. Hare, have argued that the resulting obligations are consequentialist.

Airily sweeping my hand across thousands of years of intellectual history, I say now that none of these projects does the job we want done here. There is a reason why. To derive substantive moral principles from principles of practical rationality you need some very rich principles of practical rationality. But the principles of practical rationality that have the non-negotiable flavor that would make them suitable as foundations for a robust normative theory are relatively impoverished.

When we think of non-negotiable principles of practical rationality, the examples that spring to mind have to do with internal coherence: if you are rational, then your desires are internally coherent (roughly: you do not want one thing and at the same time want another—I will unpack this precisely later) and your behavior is coherent with your desires (roughly: you do not want one thing and do another—again, I will unpack this precisely later). But it is easy to be internally coherent. Internally coherent people may be good people, who want good things and behave in good ways, or evil people, who want evil things and behave in evil ways, or just bizarre people, who want bizarre things and behave in bizarre ways. The history of philosophy is full of examples that illustrate this point. The most famous are due to David Hume. If we take "reason" to place nothing more than coherency constraints upon us,[12] then we must agree with him that

---

[12] Did Hume himself think that reason placed coherency constraints upon us? He did write that someone who fails to choose the proper means to his end makes an "error"—which

'Tis not contrary to reason to prefer the destruction of the world to the scratching of my finger. 'Tis not contrary to reason for me to choose my own total ruin, to prevent the least uneasiness of an Indian or person wholly unknown to me. 'Tis as little contrary to reason to prefer even my own acknowledged lesser good to my greater, and have a more ardent affection for the former than the latter.[13]

It does not follow from my being internally coherent that I will behave in one way or another when placed in a morally portentous situation. I may be an internally coherent saint or an internally coherent psychopath. If we are to derive a substantive, interesting theory of normative ethics from rock-solid axioms, then we will need to supplement principles of internal coherence with something richer.

What might do the trick? One strategy might be to add axioms about the *content* of rational desires—about what it is rational to desire. Some philosophers have claimed that rationality places significant constraints on what we desire. Derek Parfit, for example, has said[14] we have reasons for desiring various things, and that we are more or less rational to the extent that our desires are more or less strongly supported by reasons. Someone whose desires are wildly out of step with reasons (his canonic example is a man who has a healthy desire that he not suffer pain, except on Tuesdays—a man who would rather that he suffer any amount of pain on a Tuesday than any amount of pain on any other day of the week) is, by any standard, irrational. So we might add an axiom that says that, if you are rational, then your desires are not wildly out of step with reasons.

Maybe this claim has the non-negotiable flavor that we want of the axioms of our theory. But, to derive any interesting conclusions about what rational people do in morally portentous situations, we will need to supplement it further, with some specific claims about which kinds of desires are, and which kinds of desires are not, out of step with reasons.

---

might appear to suggest that he thought of the instrumental principle (which says, roughly: *take the known means to your desired ends*—a sort of coherency constraint) as a requirement of rationality. But there are grounds for thinking that the appearance is misleading, that Hume had in mind a person whose error was one of falsely believing something to be a means to his end (see Korsgaard 2008).

[13] From Hume (1740: bk 2, pt 3, sect. 3). The examples are under-described in odd ways. Does the first fellow prefer the destruction of his finger to the scratching of his finger? If not, is his finger not part of the world? But the general moral is clear.

[14] In Parfit (2011a: part one).

(Jane kills one person to prevent two from being killed, because she cares more about *there being less killing* than about *her not killing*. John refuses to kill one person to prevent two from being killed, because he cares more about *his not killing* than about *there being less killing*. If we are to derive any interesting conclusions about their respective actions, we have to say that one of John or Jane has desires out of step with reasons.) These sorts of claims certainly will not have the non-negotiable flavor that we want of the axioms of our theory.

In light of considerations like this, many contemporary philosophers think that the project of deriving a substantial theory of normative ethics from self-obvious axioms is hopeless. Normative ethics is not about cranking out results. It is an altogether subtler business. To do normative ethics well you must do reflective equilibrium well. And to do reflective equilibrium well you must have tact, experience, and sensitivity to the delicate nuances of moral life. This is why pimply adolescents are very good at number theory, but very bad at normative ethics.

I am no longer a pimply adolescent. But I find that the little tact, experience, and sensitivity to the delicate nuances of moral life that I have gained since my pimply adolescence leave me ill-equipped to settle any interesting questions in normative ethics by balancing my intuitions about principles against my intuitions about cases in the subtle ways these philosophers recommend. So, in this book, I want to pursue a more foundational, bottom-up approach further. I think that we can make significant progress in normative ethics by supplementing some very minimal assumptions about rationality with some very minimal assumptions about moral decency.

## 0.5. Moving Forward

In Chapter 1 I spell out my first assumption about moral decency. It amounts to this: if you are decent, then you are at least minimally benevolent towards other people. *When absolutely all other things are equal,* at least, you would rather that other people be better off rather than worse off.

In Chapters 2 and 3 I spell out my first assumption about rationality: if you are practically rational, then, when you do not know what will happen if you do one thing or another, your decisions are guided by the prospects associated with the acts open to you. This is a very intuitive idea, though tricky to put in a precise way, as we will see.

In Chapters 4–6 I put these assumptions to work in normative ethics. Chapter 4 is about saving people from harm. There has been a great (albeit, to outsiders, rather mysterious) controversy in the normative ethics literature over whether and (if so) why, given the choice, we are obliged to save more people, rather than fewer people, from similar harms, and to save a multitude of people from a small harm rather than one person from a large harm. But it follows from the minimal assumptions that, in some circumstances at least (circumstances in which you do not know who you will save by doing one thing or another), if you are decent and rational then you will save more people, rather than fewer, from similar harms, and you will save the multitude from the small harm rather than the one from the large harm.

Chapter 5 is about cases like Not Postponing Conception, cases that raise "the non-identity problem." It follows from our assumptions that, if Mary were decent and rational, then she would not have conceived unhealthy Mariette. It does not follow that she has done something *wrong*. But I will suggest that the two notions *being such that somebody decent and rational would not do it*, and *being wrong*, are closely connected.

Chapter 6 is about cases like Human Fuel, cases that raise the problem of whether it is okay to kill-to-prevent-two-killings. I will argue that, by framing the issue in terms of what a minimally decent and rational person will do in these cases, we add significant force to a traditional objection to the deontologist's treatment of them: the so-called "dirty hands" objection to deontology.

Thus far we have made progress only in cases in which you do not know who you are in a position to harm or benefit by doing one thing or another. In Part II of the book, Chapters 7–11, I will extend the treatment to cover cases in which you do know who you are in position to harm or benefit by doing one thing or another. To do it I will need fancier tools than before.

In Chapter 7 I spell out an assumption about people and their essences. Each of us could have been ever-so-slightly-different along any natural dimension of sameness and difference. You could have been a millimeter taller than you actually are. I could have been conceived a second before I was actually conceived. Barak Obama could have been slightly more irascible than he actually is. Our essences are not perfectly fragile.

In Chapter 8 I spell out a further, quiet assumption about rationality. If you are rational, then your desires are coherent—which means, at least, that your preferences between maximal states of affairs (fully specific ways for everything to be) are transitive.

In Chapters 9–11 I put these new assumptions to work. In Chapter 9 I argue that it follows that, if decency obliges us to prefer, in some circumstances, that some people be better off rather than worse off, then decency and rationality together oblige us to prefer, in some circumstances, that some people be better off rather than other people be better off. I call this the *Morphing Argument.* I explore its consequences for the problems we have looked at so far, problems involving who to save, the non-identity problem, and the problem of whether to kill-to-prevent-killing, in Chapter 10.

Chapter 11 is about the limits of goodwill towards others. One surprising consequence of the morphing argument is that it is impossible to be both rational and minimally benevolent towards *everyone.* Rationality itself places limits on how good-willed we can be.

Which brings us to Part III of the book and the third major problem discussed in this Introduction—our moral obligations towards distant strangers. In Chapters 12 and 13 I argue that the rational requirement that preferences be transitive and the moral requirement that we be at least minimally benevolent towards (some) strangers together place great pressure on us to attend to the plight of needy, distant strangers. It is much harder than we ordinarily think to be both decent and rational. In Chapter 14 I moderate the claim somewhat. Rationality and decency do not demand of us that we be equally devoted to everybody. Being rational involves being committed in a certain way to particular people and their interests.

## 0.6. Two Goals

Part of what I hope to do here is to shed light on some interesting problems in normative ethics. Another part of what I want to do is to show off the benefits of approaching the subject in this way—by thinking about rationality and minimal benevolence. In typical introductory classes in moral philosophy we teach our undergraduates that there are three approaches to normative ethics. There is the consequentialist approach (usually traced back to Jeremy Bentham—with a nod to the ancient

Epicureans), which has it that acting morally is about bringing about the best states of affairs we can. There is the deontological approach (usually traced back to Kant, with a nod to contractualist and rights-based alternatives), which has us focus on the character of the act itself, with an emphasis on whether it is universalizable—on how we would feel about everybody acting this way. And there is the virtue-based approach (usually traced back to Aristotle), which has us focus on how the act reflects on the moral character of the agent—is it the sort of thing that a perfectly virtuous (honest, kind, loving, courageous . . . etc.) person would do? The approach I am exploring here does not fit neatly into any of these traditions. I think this is a good thing, as you will see.

# PART I

# 1

# The Good Will

Here is my first claim: being morally decent involves adopting an attitude of good will toward other people, which involves taking their interests into account, and wishing them well.

This will, I expect, strike you as an obvious truth. Indeed it may strike you as *such* an obvious truth, such an anodyne, saccharine platitude, that you wonder why an author would bother to draw attention to it. In writing it, I am reminded of passages in *It Takes a Village: And Other Lessons Children Teach Us*,[1] in which Hillary Clinton sincerely intones that:

In addition to being read to, children love to be told stories.[2]

and

Brisk walking, hiking and bicycling are all good exercise, and are great ways to spend time together as well.[3]

and

The lessons men and women have learned over thousands of years are available to anyone, in the form of fables, stories, poems, plays, proverbs, and scriptures that have stood the test of time.[4]

She is not wrong. These things are true. But of all the many, many true things that she could have chosen to drawn her reader's attention to, they are among the blandest and least interesting.

But we are doing philosophy now, and philosophers are suspicious people. If Hillary Clinton had published *It Takes a Village* in a philosophy journal, then there would have been objections:

---

[1] Clinton (1996).    [2] Clinton (1996: 94).    [3] Clinton (1996: 108).
[4] Clinton (1996: 137). Credit goes to Martin Amis (1996) for drawing attention to some of these passages in his review of the book.

"So you claim that bicycling is good exercise. What about bicycling downhill, when we would otherwise have to walk? That doesn't sound like very good exercise."

"So you claim that brisk walking is a great way to spend time together. What about when we are briskly walking with someone very unfit, who struggles to keep up, and resents us for it? That doesn't sound like a great way to spend time together."

This would not just be down to temperamental pedantry on the part of the objectors. They have good reason to be suspicious of prima facie obvious truths. In philosophy there is a grand tradition of deriving radical, surprising, wild claims from prima facie obvious truths. So, for example: the philosopher makes a few seemingly harmless claims about material objects. You nod along. Then, Boom! He shows that by nodding along you have committed yourself to denying the existence of composite inanimate objects. There are no tables and chairs.[5] The philosopher makes a few seemingly harmless claims about morality and impartiality. You nod along. Then, Boom! She shows that by nodding along you are committing yourself to the existence of a number, $n$, such that, if the opportunity arises, you ought to kill your mother to cause $n$ rabbits to experience mild, brief pleasure.[6]

The lesson is that, when a philosopher asks you to embrace a prima facie obvious truth, it is worth stepping back a moment and inspecting the object of your embrace. In this case I have said that being moral involves adopting an attitude of good will toward others, which involves taking their interests into account, and wishing them well. It is worth your asking some questions. What exactly do I mean by "taking their interests into account and wishing them well"? What exactly do I mean by "involves"? And who, for that matter, are these "others"? I will address these questions in order.

---

[5]  See Van Inwagen (1990).
[6]  From a philosophy joke (I don't know its origins):
   *Psychopath*: "If you kill your mother then I will cause momentary sexual gratification to sweep through a shed-full of rabbits."
   *Hedonic Utilitarian*: "How big is the shed?"

## 1.1. What is it to Take Another Person's Interests into Account, and Wish him or her Well?

Sometimes I turn my attention to two states of affairs (think of these as *ways for things to be*), and wonder which I would rather came about. So, for example, if you were to float the idea of my submitting myself to a severely calorie-restricted diet, I might think about the consequences of my going either way:

Caloric Restriction
In *Life-Diet*:   I restrict my long-term caloric intake—which gives me a longer, but less vigorous life.
In *No-Diet*:   I eat away—which gives me a shorter, but more vigorous life.

Sometimes I take certain considerations to be reasons to prefer one state of affairs over the other. So, for example, I might take the consideration "in *Life-Diet* I live longer" to be a reason to prefer *Life-Diet*. And I might also take the consideration "in *No-Diet* I have more vigor" to be a reason to prefer *No-Diet*.

My first claim here concerns the considerations that a morally decent person takes to be reasons to prefer states of affairs:

*Minimal Consideration*
Being morally decent involves being *minimally considerate* towards others—I am minimally considerate toward you when, for any states of affairs S, S*, I take the consideration "you are better off in S than in S*" to be a reason to favor S over S*.

My second claim directly concerns a morally decent person's preferences:

*Minimal Benevolence*
Being morally decent involves being minimally benevolent towards others—I am minimally benevolent towards you when, for any states of affairs S, S* such that you are better off in S than in S*, and such that I take myself to have no reason to prefer S*, I prefer S.

These are very weak claims. You probably believe something much stronger. You probably think that being decent not only involves taking other people's interests into account, but also taking other people's interests to be decisive in some cases when there are other things at stake. Consider:

The Fate of the FA Cup

In *Lose*:   Arsenal loses the FA cup.

In *Win*:    Arsenal wins the FA cup after the Manchester United keeper accidentally, acrobatically, hangs himself on the netting of his goal.

I feel for the Manchester United Keeper, so I take the consideration "in *Win* the fellow dies a gruesome, public death" to be a reason to favor *Lose*. But I also support Arsenal, so I take the consideration "in *Lose* Arsenal lose" to be a reason to favor *Win*. You probably think that my being moral involves my taking the former consideration to be decisive. And you probably think that my being moral involves my preferring *Lose* to *Win*.

Well and good, but that is an easy case. There are difficult cases in which serious, well-intentioned people will disagree about whether being decent involves taking other people's interests to be decisive when there are other things at stake. Consider:

Inequality

In *Gold*:      Gardeners working for Mitt Romney discover rich seams of gold beneath the grounds of his New Hampshire property.

In *No-Gold*:   Gardeners working for Mitt Romney do not discover rich seams of gold beneath the grounds of his New Hampshire property.

Some people will say that my being decent involves my preferring *Gold* to *No-Gold*. Mitt is better off in *Gold* than in *No-Gold*, end of story. Others will say that my being decent involves my caring about material inequality. It is at least not indecent of me to take the consideration "in *Gold*, material inequality is yet more egregious" to be decisive. It is at least not indecent of me to prefer *No-Gold*.

Or consider:

Property

In *Smoking*:      Jake consumes too many cigarettes. He is unhealthy and unhappy.

In *No Smoking*:   I steal all of Jake's cigarettes. He is healthier and happier.

Some people will say that my being decent involves my preferring *No Smoking* to *Smoking*. Jake is better off in *No Smoking* than in *Smoking*; that is what matters. Others will say that my being decent involves my caring about property rights. It is at least not indecent of me to take the consideration "in *No Smoking* I violate Jake's property rights" to be decisive. It is at least not indecent of me to prefer *Smoking*.

Or consider:

Murder

In *Injustice*:  Oliver gets away with the murder of a friend-less, relative-less person. Chastened by the experience, he lives a blameless life from then on.

In *Justice*:  Oliver does not get away with the murder. He spends a long time in jail.

Some people will say that my being decent involves my preferring *Injustice* to *Justice*. Oliver is better off in *Injustice* than in *Justice*, end of story. Others will say that my being decent involves my caring about just deserts. It is at least not indecent of me to take the consideration "in *Justice* Oliver gets the punishment he deserves" to be decisive. It is at least not indecent of me to prefer *Justice*.

And there are further difficult cases in which, though most people will agree that my being the embodiment of moral perfection involves my taking other people's interests to be decisive, many serious, well-intentioned people will disagree about whether I stray far from basic moral decency by failing to do so. Recall the Oxfam case from the Introduction:

Oxfam (lightly redescribed)

In *Give*:  I give $1,000 to charity, and some distant children are vaccinated against common diseases.

In *Keep*:  I do not give any money to charity, and the same distant children are not vaccinated against common diseases, and some of them later contract these diseases and die.

Some people will say that I stray far, far from basic moral decency by failing to prefer, all things considered, *Give*. Some distant children are much, much better off in *Give* than in *Keep*. Others will say that I do not stray far from basic moral decency if I take the consideration "I am richer in *Keep*" to be decisive, and prefer *Keep*.

Well and good. I will broach the thorny issue of how to weigh considerations having to do with other people's interests against other considerations later on. But for the moment let us just assume that being moral involves being at least minimally considerate of others and minimally benevolent toward others. Let us see how far we can go with that. For clarity, when we have to make a stronger assumption to make progress, I will FLAG it.

## 1.2. What is it to Say that Being Moral *Involves* Being Good-Willed toward Others?

Some philosophers say that being moral involves exemplifying certain virtues—honesty, integrity, courage, and so forth. Others say that being moral involves bringing about the best available states of affairs. Others say that being moral involves respecting rights. Yet others say that being moral involves giving people what they are owed, under the terms of real or hypothetical contracts.

I do not intend my claim to be in competition with any of these. Maybe being moral does involve respecting rights, giving people what they are owed, bringing about good states of affairs . . . and so forth. My claim is just that it also involves taking other people's interests into account and wishing them well. There is a failing in someone who is honest and courageous, who respects rights, who gives people what they are owed, who brings about good states of affairs, but is indifferent towards the well-being of others, or positively malevolent toward others. And it is a moral failing.

Let me illustrate the idea with a story.

### Bertha and Ben

Bertha and Ben are model citizens in almost every way. They are infallibly courteous towards others. They keep their promises. They do not lie. They respect rights. They run their lives by sophisticated variants of the golden rule: do unto others as you would have them do unto you. They think it is important for them to behave in chivalrous ways, so they help old ladies across the street whenever they can. They think it is important for them to behave in charitable ways, so they give large sums of money to the poor. They are admired by all who know them for being upstanding, tip-top people. But, in spite of all their good deeds, Bertha and Ben are not good-willed. Bertha is indifferent to the plight of others, and Ben positively malevolent toward others. One morning Bertha and Ben read that, in northern India, a small boy has fallen down a deep, narrow well. Rescuers are frantically digging down in an effort to save him. The news leaves Bertha quite cold. She cares no more about whether the boy lives or dies than you care about whether a particular drop of rain falling from the Pacific sky evaporates before it hits sea water. The news does not leave Ben cold. He hopes that the walls of the well will collapse, and that the boy will be trapped in an air pocket, in which he will suffocate slowly, screaming for his mother.

I claim that both Bertha and Ben, though admirable in many respects, are not, morally speaking, all they should be. I have no real *argument* for this claim. But arguments have to stop somewhere. This seems to me as good a place as any.

## 1.3. Who are these "Others" toward whom we must be Good-Willed?

I want to leave this last question open for the moment, largely because I want my claim in this chapter to be planted squarely in the realm of the obvious, and I think it far from obvious just how far our considerateness and benevolence must extend. Take me. I am considerate of, and benevolent toward, my own children, and toward strangers from northern India, but good will has its limits. It does not extend to past strangers, for example. When I learn a little about their lives, and am preparing to learn more, I find that I do not always wish to learn that things went well for them.

So, confronted with this fragment of American history, a letter from Alexander Hamilton, founding father, to his wife, Elizabeth Hamilton, on the subject of their son, Philip Hamilton, then 15 years old:

To Elizabeth Hamilton
Rye 30 Miles from
New York
Tuesday Even [September 12, 1797]
I am arrived here My Dear Eliza in good health but very anxious about my Dear Philip. I pray heaven to restore him and in every event to support you. If his fever should appear likely to be obstinate, urge the Physician to consider well the propriety of trying the cold bath—I expect it will, if it continues assume a nervous

type and in this case I believe the cold bath will be the most efficacious remedy—but still do not attempt it without the approbation of the Physician. Also my Betsey how much do I regret to be separated from you at such a juncture. When will the time come that I shall be exempt from the necessity of leaving my dear family? God bless my beloved and all My Dear Children.
AH[7]

I find that I do not particularly wish that the cold baths did their job and little Philip recovered from his infection. And that is not because I think there is anything else at stake. It is not that I loathe Hamilton and wish ill of his kin. It is not that I think that I think that some kind of sweet justice would have been served if Hamilton were punished for his absentee parenting. It is not that I think his life story would be more poignant if he suffered this loss. No, the whole affair just leaves me cold.

Is this a moral failing on my part? I am inclined to think that it is not. Maybe you disagree.[8] Maybe you think it a failing because you think that being moral involves being at least minimally considerate of, and benevolent towards, *everyone*, *always*. This is a noble view, but it cannot be right. I will argue, in Chapter 11 of this Book, that it is impossible to be both rational and good willed towards everyone, always.

---

[7]  Printed in Alan Hamilton (1910).

[8]  In which case you will be relieved to hear that Philip did recover, though he was killed four years later, in a duel, prefiguring his father's death, also in a duel, two years after that.

# 2

# First Steps: The Morality of Rescue

Morally decent people are at least minimally considerate of, and benevolent toward, other people. This tells us something about what decent people *account for* and *prefer*, but it does not, directly, tell us anything about what decent people *do*. To get some traction on the question of what decent people do, we need some normative principles that link desire to action. The obvious candidates for such principles are principles of practical rationality. Here is one:

*Rational People are Guided by their Preferences*
If you are rational and two actions are open to you, and you have an all-things considered preference for the state of affairs that will come about if you take the one over the state of affairs that will come about if you take the other, then, absent epistemic or physical obstacles (ignorance, paralysis, etc.), you will not take the other.

It is a simple principle, and it allows us to draw conclusions about how people who are both decent and rational will behave in some simple cases. For example:

Small Differences
While idly steaming through the South Seas, I receive a distress call. Amanda has recently been stranded on a nearby island. Mine is the only boat in the area. If I do not get over there with my provisions, then she will die of thirst in a day or two. There are two routes to her island, one to the west, the other to the east. At first I see nothing to be said for taking one route rather than the other. The routes are equally safe. The routes are equally temperate. Both will take about three hours . . . I check my map carefully . . . no, the western route will take three

hours, the eastern route two and a half hours. Amanda is in no danger of dying in the next three hours, but the more quickly I get to her the happier she will be. So which way am I to go, east or west?

See Fig. 2.1.

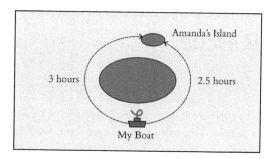

**Figure 2.1**

In this case, supposing that I see nothing to be said for my taking the western route, we can conclude that, if I am decent and rational, then I will head east, not west.

So, if we are decent and rational, our behavior will not display malevolence toward others, or perfect indifference to their interests. Well and good, but this does not take us very far into the jungle of moral theory. In any interesting decision problem there is at least something to be said on either side, some kind of conflict. Our principles tell us nothing about how decent and rational people resolve conflicts. So, for example, our principles tell us nothing about how a decent and rational person will behave in a case like this:

The Sunset

As before, but this time, if I go west, I will get a better view of the setting sun.

See Fig. 2.2.

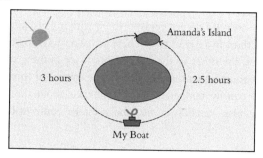

**Figure 2.2**

*Minimal Consideration* tells us that, if I am decent, then I will take the consideration "going east will be better for Amanda" to be a reason to go east, but it does not tell us that I will prefer to go east, because it does not tell us anything about how I will weigh that consideration against one that I take to be a reason to go west: "by going west I will place myself at a more pleasing angle to the sun."

Nor do the principles tell us how I will proceed when other people's interests conflict—how I will behave in cases where doing one thing is better for one person, doing another thing is better for another person. For normative ethicists, this is when rescue cases get interesting. Three sorts of cases have been the main focus of discussion and controversy: cases in which I have a choice between benefiting *many people a lot* or *few people a lot*, cases in which I have a choice between benefiting one person *slightly more* or another person *slightly less*, and cases in which I have a choice between benefiting *many people a little* or benefiting *few people a lot*.

## 2.1. A First Look at Three Controversial Rescue Cases

In this section I will just describe the three kinds of case and try to give a sense of why they are controversial, putting off a careful discussion of them until later.

Here is an example of a rescue case in which I have a choice between benefiting *many people a lot* or *few people a lot*.

### 1 or 2? Inter-Personal Conflict
This time the radio tells me that Astrid has recently been stranded on an island three hours to my west, while Beth and Chris have recently been stranded on an island three hours to my east. Sadly, I have very limited supplies of fuel. I can save Astrid. I can save Beth and Chris. I cannot save Astrid, Beth, and Chris. I know that they are roughly the same age, and that none of them has any compelling claim to being

more important than the others. I have no special relationship with any of them. So which way am I to go, east or west?

See Fig. 2.3.

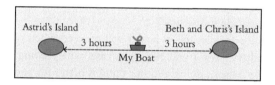

**Figure 2.3**

   This sort of case was made famous by a 1977 paper by John Taurek.[1] Taurek argued, provocatively, that it is not true that I ought to head directly east, on the grounds that Astrid is one and Beth and Chris are two. What I ought to do is toss a coin, and be guided by the outcome of the toss.

   Taurek was moved by two ideas. His first idea was that the act-consequentialist treatment of the case—I ought to head east without further ado because it will be better, overall, if I head east—is mistaken. He attributed the mistake to a failure to recognize that "persons are separate." He was here picking up on a tradition in normative ethics whereby philosophers argue that there is a deep difference between cases in which a decision impacts on one person, harming him or her in some ways and benefiting him or her in other ways, and cases in which a decision impacts on different people, harming some of them and benefiting others. The latter kind of decision may, on balance, make the world better *for some people*, worse *for other people*, but there is no morally relevant sense in which it makes the world better or worse *simpliciter*. (I will discuss this idea further in Section 4.6.)

   Taurek's second idea had to do with fairness. What I ought to do in these sorts of cases is be fair to all parties. It would be unfair to Astrid to head east on the grounds that she is one and Beth and Chris are two. To be fair to Astrid, Beth, and Chris, I must give them an equal chance of survival. Giving them an equal chance of survival involves tossing a coin or spinning a bottle, or something like that.

---

[1] See Taurek (1977).

Few contemporary writers accept Taurek's conclusion. Most think that indeed I ought to head directly east, to save the two rather than the one.[2] But many contemporary writers are sympathetic to Taurek's first idea, the idea that the consequentialist treatment of the case is mistaken. For these philosophers, the challenge is to explain why I ought to head east. It is not because the world will be better if I head east, and I have a standing obligation to make the world better. So why is it?[3]

Let us postpone answering such questions for the moment, and move onto an example of the second kind of controversial rescue case—a case in which I have a choice between benefiting one person *ever-so-slightly less* or another person *ever-so-slightly more*:

## Small Differences, Inter-Personal Conflict

This time I discover that Andy has been stranded on an island to my west, Ben on an island to my east. Again, I have very limited supplies of fuel. I can save one or the other but not both. Both islands are three hours away . . . I check my map . . . no, the western island is three hours away, the eastern island two and a half hours away. Neither Andy nor Ben is in danger of dying in the next three hours, but for each of them, the quicker I get to him, the happier he will be. So which way am I to go, east or west?

See Fig. 2.4.

**Figure 2.4**

In this case Taurek would again say that I ought to toss a coin. There is no morally significant sense in which the world will be better *simpliciter* if I head east. To be fair to Andy and Ben, I must give them an equal chance

---

[2] Most, but not all. Tyler Doggett stands with Taurek. (See Doggett 2009, forthcoming.) Also, the idea that these sorts of decisions ought to be made by weighted lottery (in this case giving Ben and Chris a 2/3 chance, Andy a 1/3 chance), discussed by John Broome in Broome (1984, 1998), has gained some supporters (see Timmerman 2004).

[3] There is a big literature on efforts to give non-consequentialist explanations of why I should save the many. I will not summarize it in detail here. Much of it focuses on, or

of survival. But even some philosophers who reject Taurek's view of fairness, and his proposal that I ought to spin a coin in <u>1 or 2? Inter-Personal Conflict</u>, resist the proposal that I ought to head directly east in this new case. For example, Frances Kamm appeals to what she calls the "Principle of Irrelevant Utilities."[4] In a context like this, when lives are at stake, small considerations, like "there will be a half hour less waiting if I head east," are *morally irrelevant.*[5] And, says Kamm, it would be wrong to head directly east on the basis of a morally irrelevant consideration. By heading directly east on the basis of a morally irrelevant consideration I would be disrespecting Andy in a morally culpable way. Kamm has a variety of quite complex explanations of and justifications for the principle, but the central idea is intuitive enough: my decision is portentous and grave. It is inappropriate to make so portentous and grave a decision on such trivial grounds.

The third sort of controversial rescue cases are ones in which I have a choice between conferring small benefits on many people or big benefits on few people. Some philosophers say that in these cases it is a mistake to take the small benefits to the many to outweigh the big benefits to the few. They find inspiration in a classic example of Tim Scanlon's:

> Suppose that Jones has suffered an accident in the transmitter room of a television station. Electrical equipment has fallen on his arm, and we cannot recue him without turning off the transmitter for fifteen minutes. A World Cup match is in progress, watched by many people, and it will not be over for an hour. Jones' injury will not get any worse if we wait, but his hand has been mashed and he is receiving extremely painful electric shocks. Should we rescue him now or wait until the match is over? Does the right thing to do depend on how many people are watching—whether it is one million or five million or a hundred million? It seems to me that we should not wait, no matter how many viewers there are . . . [6]

---

branches from, Tim Scanlon's contractualist explanation in Scanlon (1999: sect. 5.9), and from twenty-five years of work by Frances Kamm (see Kamm 1984, 2005, for a sense of how that work has evolved).

[4] See Kamm (1993: ch. 8).

[5] Kamm uses "I will save a flower by going in this direction" and "I will cure a sore throat by going in this direction" as examples of considerations that are morally irrelevant when lives are at stake. I am taking it that she would say the same for "there will be a half hour less waiting if I head in this direction."

[6] Scanlon (1999: 235).

Looking at this evocative example as a piece of philosophical machinery, serving the purpose of showing us that in rescue cases we should not take small suffering on the part of the many to outweigh big suffering on the part of a few, I find it less helpful than it might have been. First, the case is polluted by the proximity of this fellow Jones. By implication we are close to him, and vividly aware of the suffering he will endure if we leave things alone. But we are not close to all of the many football fans, not vividly aware of all of the suffering they will endure if we intervene. This may be morally significant. Second, the case is polluted by an action/inaction asymmetry. We prevent Jones from suffering big time by doing something. We "prevent" the many from suffering small time by doing nothing. This, too, may be morally significant.

Looking at the example as cultural artifact, I find it amusing that Scanlon chose *soccer*. Why not American football or basketball or baseball . . . ? (Hundreds of millions of people watch the NBA finals. Hundreds of millions of people watch the Superbowl.[7]) The answer, I guess, is that these examples are all about eliciting clear and forthright intuitions, and soccer brings out the intuition in the clearest and most forthright way . . . for Americans. People from the desolate reaches of Not-America, in my experience, find the intuition harder to access: "It's the World Cup!" they say, "The *WORLD CUP!* Sure, Jones is in pain, but sometimes you have to take one for the team."[8]

I will work with a different example here:

---

[7] Indeed, from a nakedly utilitarian perspective it is not at all clear that the World Cup is a good thing in the first place. There are 204 teams competing, of which 203 get knocked out, often in the most tantalizing and unjust of circumstances—causing global anguish, pain, and mourning. Much better to block the signal, trapped worker or no trapped worker.

[8] There is a film called *The Dish*, loosely based on history, about people operating a satellite dish relaying television signals from the Apollo 11 moon landing. As Armstrong takes his small step away from the lunar module, high winds are streaming around the dish, winds that threaten to destroy it and them (their office is beneath it) if they keep it focused on the moon. Heroically, they disregard the threat. The dish survives. The signal is relayed. And then we pan away from the claustrophobic confines of their workspace, to joy and awe in the faces of people all over the world. *It was worth it*—the film wants us to think—*They are so many.* And we do think this. Of course, a cynic might say that we are predisposed to think that hundreds of millions of people watching the planting of an American flag on the Moon is very different, very much more worthy of sacrifice, from hundreds of millions of people watching the planting of an Argentinian hand on the World Cup. But let us not indulge cynics.

Save One from Five Hours of Waiting or Six from One Hour of Waiting?

This time Alex is an hour to my west, Brian, Charles, Dave, Edward, Frederick, and George an hour to my east. And this time there are other boats in the area. There is a boat steaming toward the west island. It will get there in six hours. There is a boat steaming toward the east island. It will get there in two hours. I have nothing better to do than hurry up the rescue. But which way should I go? I can save six people from an hour of suffering by heading east, and one person from five hours of suffering by heading west.

See Fig. 2.5.

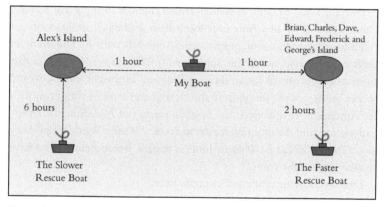

Figure 2.5

On one way of thinking, the way of thinking associated with the *utilitarian* tradition in normative ethics (which says, roughly, that behaving morally is about maximizing aggregate pleasure, minimizing aggregate suffering), the key feature of this example is that there will be a total of twelve hours of painful waiting if I head east, a total of thirteen hours of painful waiting if I head west. Thirteen hours of painful waiting is, other things being equal, worse than twelve hours of painful waiting. So, supposing that the hours of painful waiting would be roughly comparable in morally relevant respects (none more intensely painful than any other), it will be better if I head east. I ought to head east.

On another way of thinking, the way of thinking that Scanlon is, broadly speaking recommending, we should attend to the fact that, if

I head west, then painful waiting will be more-or-less evenly distributed across people (two hours each for six of them, one hour for one of them), while if I head east the distribution will be uneven (one hour each for six of them, six for one of them.) This matters. I ought to protect against that one person suffering so much. I ought to head west.

## 2.2. Opaque Variants of the Controversial Cases

Now, the principles that we have seen so far, *Minimal Consideration, Minimal Benevolence,* and *Rational People are Guided by their Preferences,* tell us nothing about how I will behave in these cases, if I am decent and rational. *Minimal Consideration* tells us that, if I am decent, then I will take myself to have a reason to head east (arising from my good will toward the person/people on the east island), and I will take myself to have a reason to head west (arising from my good will toward the person on the west island). But it does not tell us what my all-things-considered preference will be.

Fair enough. These sorts of cases are very difficult. I will postpone discussing them further until the second part of this book. For now, over the next two and a half chapters, I will address some easier variants of them—cases in which I do not know who is where. Here are the variants of the first two cases:

1 or 2? Opaque Inter-Personal Conflict
Again the radio tells me that Astrid, Beth, and Chris have been stranded in my vicinity, one of them on an island three hours to my west, the other two on an island three hours to my east. But this time I do not know who is where. I regard all possible arrangements of people-on-islands as equally likely. So which way am I to go, east or west?

See Fig. 2.6.

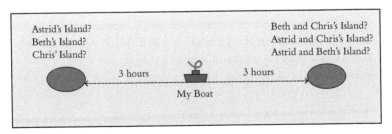

Figure 2.6

### Small Differences, Opaque Inter-Personal Conflict

Again the radio tells me that Andy and Ben have been stranded in my near vicinity, one on an island three hours to my west, the other on an island two and a half hours to my east. But this time I do not know who is where. I regard it as equally likely that Ben is to my west, Andy to my east, and that Andy is to my west, Ben is to my east. So which way am I to go, east or west?

See Fig. 2.7.

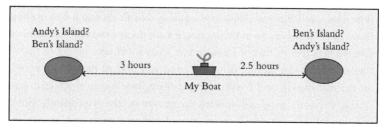

**Figure 2.7**

I will argue that, in these cases, if I am decent and rational, then I will head east. The argument will take some time to develop. I will begin with one not entirely satisfactory argument, and then improve upon it in Chapters 3 and 4.

## 2.3. Appealing to Expected Utility

Let us step back and look at the central question that we are asking here. The question is this: supposing that I am minimally considerate of, and benevolent toward, the people on the islands, what, rationally, ought I to do in these cases in which I do not know who is where? Philosophers and economists have designed a sophisticated theory, *expected utility theory*, to answer questions of this general kind—questions about what people who do not know precisely what will happen if they do one thing or another ought, rationally, to do, given their preferences between states of affairs.[9]

---

[9] I should mention that there is some disagreement about whether expected utility theory tells us what we rationally ought to do (take the option with highest expected utility) or just what we rationally ought to desire or prefer (we ought to prefer that propositions with higher

So a promising first step is to think about what the expected utility theorist would say.

Here is the basic idea behind expected utility theory. To find out what I ought, rationally, to do, first we identify the relevantly different options available to me. Next we identify the relevantly different states of affairs that, so far as I know, might come about if I take one option or another. Next we associate a *utility function*, a function from states of affairs to numbers, with my preferences between the states of affairs. This is a function that, intuitively, represents how much I desire the states of affairs—the higher the number it assigns to a state of affairs, the more I desire it. Next we associate *expected utilities* with the options available to me, where the expected utility of an option is determined, roughly, by how likely I think it is that various states of affairs will come about if I take the option, weighted by how desirable I take those states of affairs to be. Finally we say that it is rationally permissible to take an option if and only if no alternative to it has higher expected utility.

This may seem complicated. To get a sense of how it works, let us apply it to the <u>Small Differences, Opaque Inter-Personal Conflict</u> case. In this case the relevantly different options open to me are:

Heading west.
Heading east.

The relevantly different states of affairs that I might bring about are:

A:   In which I head west and save Andy in 3 hours.
B:   In which I head west and save Ben in 3 hours.
A+:   In which I head east and save Andy in 2.5 hours.
B+:   In which I head east and save Ben in 2.5 hours.

What about utility functions that represent my preferences? Well, the assumption that I am minimally benevolent does not tell us enough about my preferences to determine precisely which utility functions represent my preferences in this case. We know that I prefer A+ to A, B+ to B, but we do not know, for example, whether I prefer A+ to B, so we do not know whether I regard A+ as more or less desirable than B. Indeed, we do not know whether *any* utility functions represent my preferences.

---

expected utility be true). For present purposes I see no harm in interpreting it in the stronger way—as a theory of what we rationally ought to do.

My preferences can be represented by a utility function only if my preferences have certain formal features: only if they are *irreflexive* (there is no state of affairs that I prefer to itself), *transitive* (for any states of affairs *x*, *y*,*z*, if I prefer *x* to *y*, *y* to *z*, then I prefer *x* to *z*), and *negatively transitive* (for any states of affairs *x*,*y*,*z*, if I have no preference between *x* and *y*, *y* and *z*, then I have no preference between *x* and *z*). But we do not know whether my preferences have these features. Maybe I prefer A+ to itself. Maybe I prefer A+ to A, A to B, but I do not prefer A+ to B. Maybe I have no preference between A+ and B, B and A, though I prefer A+ to A. All we know is this: if there is a utility function that represents my preferences, then it assigns higher value to A+ than to A, higher value to B+ than to B.

This tells us something about the expected utilities associated with the options open to me. If there is a utility function that represents my preferences, $U$, then

The expected utility of my heading west is: $0.5U(A) + 0.5U(B)$.
The expected utility of my heading east is: $0.5U(A+) + 0.5U(B+)$.

Since $U(A+) > U(A)$ and $U(B+) > U(B)$, the expected utility of my heading east must be greater than the expected utility of my heading west. So, just so long as my preferences can be represented by a utility function, I will maximize expected utility by heading east.

The same goes for the 1 or 2? Opaque Inter-Personal Conflict case. In this case the relevantly different options available to me are again:

Heading west
Heading east

And the relevantly different states of affairs that I might bring about are:

A:   in which I head west and save Andy.
B:   in which I head west and save Ben.
C:   in which I head west and save Chris.
AB:  in which I head east and save Andy and Ben.
AC:  in which I head east and save Andy and Chris.
BC:  in which I head east and save Ben and Chris.

And, if we succeed in representing my preferences with a utility function, $U$, then the expected utilities associated with the options will be:

The expected utility of my heading west: $1/3U(A) + 1/3U(B) + 1/3U(C)$. The expected utility of my heading east: $1/3U(AB) + 1/3U(AC) + 1/3U(BC)$.

Since I prefer AB to A, AC to C, BC to B, it must be that $U(AB) > U(A)$, $U(AC) > U(C)$ and $U(BC) > U(B)$, so the expected utility of my heading east must be greater than the expected utility of my heading west. So, just so long as my preferences can be represented by a utility function, I will maximize expected utility by heading east.

This looks like progress. We now have an argument that, if you are decent and rational and your preferences have a certain structure (your preferences can be represented with a utility function), then you will head east in these opaque cases: if you are decent then you will be minimally benevolent. If you are minimally benevolent and your preferences can be represented with a utility function, then you will maximize expected utility by heading east in these cases. If you are rational, then you will maximize expected utility when you can.

## 2.4. Worries

But this argument is, as I said, less than entirely satisfactory.

For one thing, it assumes, with the decision theorists, that acting rationally is about maximizing expected utility. And, while the "utility" that decision theorists talk about is very different from the "utility" that utilitarian moral philosophers talk about (the former is fixed by our preferences, the latter by facts about what is valuable for its own sake), the idea that acting rationally is about *maximizing* something does sound suspiciously utilitarian. The broad goal here is to see how far we can get toward resolving deadlocks in normative ethics by making uncontroversial assumptions about decency and rationality. We certainly are not going to make progress toward this goal by building utilitarian assumptions into our conception of rationality.

For another thing, the conclusion says something about how I will behave only if I am benevolent, and I am rational, and my preferences between maximal states of affairs have certain properties (for example, *irreflexivity, transitivity, negative transitivity*) in virtue of which they can be represented by a utility function. What if my preferences do not have all these properties?

Here is a way of giving this second worry some force. It often happens that there are items A, A+, B, B+, such that we prefer A+ to A, B+ to B, but we do not prefer A or A+ to B or B+. One example:

### The Fire

Firefighters are retrieving possessions from my burning house. Should I direct them towards the Fabergé egg in my drawing room or the wedding album in my bedroom? The Fabergé egg was commissioned by Czar Alexander III of Russia, as an Easter surprise for the Empress Consort. It has survived revolution, war, and upheaval on a grand scale, and is now regarded as the finest relic of the gaudy, opulent Romanov dynasty. The wedding album, on the other hand, is an irreplaceable reminder of happy times when my wife and I were young and carefree. As I think, in turn, of losing the one or the other, my emotions and inclinations vacillate wildly, never settling down to the point where it would be fair to describe me as having an all-things-considered preference between:

A: The firefighters saving the Fabergé egg.

and B: The firefighters saving the wedding album.

Force me to choose and I will choose. But my choice will have an arbitrary flavor. And learning that there is a $100 bill lying beside the egg or the album will not rid it of this flavor. When I compare B to:

A+: The firefighters saving the Fabergé egg, plus $100.

and A to:

B+: The firefighters saving the wedding album, plus $100.

I remain just as ambivalent as before. I have no all-things-considered preference between A+ and B, B+ and A, though I do prefer A+ to A, B+ to B.

In this example my attitude is unstable, one of turbulent confusion. But the attitude may be altogether calmer. Another example:

### The Dinner

It is dinner-time. Should we go the Indian restaurant or the Chinese restaurant? We have visited both many times. We know their pluses and minuses. The Indian restaurant is less far to walk. It serves up a sublime mango lassi. The Chinese restaurant is cheaper. Its raucous atmosphere is more child-friendly. All in all it is a wash for me. I have no all-things-considered preference between:

A: Our going to the Indian restaurant.

and B: Our going to the Chinese restaurant.

And, learning that it is dollar-off day at either restaurant will not give me an all-things-considered preference. When I compare B to:

A+: Our going to the Indian restaurant and saving $1.

and A to:

B+: Our going to the Chinese restaurant and saving $1.

it remains a wash for me. I have no all-things-considered preference between A+ and B, B+ and A, though I do prefer A+ to A, B+ to B.

In all such cases our preferences are negatively intransitive—we do not prefer A+ to B, we do not prefer B to A, but we do prefer A+ to A.

The worry is that the rescue cases we have been looking at are precisely the sort of cases in which it might be natural to have patterns of preference like this. I say "might be," because the cases are in yet further respects underdescribed. How much do I know about Andy and Ben? Suppose that it is like this:

Small Differences, Fully Transparent Inter-Personal Conflict

I know a great deal about Andy and Ben. Andy is a math professor at a state university in northern New England. By afternoon he researches fiendishly difficult and obscure problems in number theory, by morning he drags hordes of unwilling undergraduates through their required calculus courses. He has a bright-eyed, glass-half-full outlook, and an anarchic sense of humor that has settled just beneath the sedate surface of his life. He is beloved and needed by his wife and 11-year-old son. Ben works part-time for UNESCO's Education of Children in Need Program, part-time as a novelist. He grew up in France, England, and Italy. The resulting sense of displacement survives in his novels, which have a beautiful, sad, lyrical quality. Even now he has not fully settled down. He shuttles his young family back and forth between London and the Loire Valley, in central France. He is affectionate and kind.

Andy and Ben are real people, whom I know very well. I will not add more detail to their descriptions, in part because I do not want to embarrass them further, in part because the example will work best if you substitute real people, whom you know very well, in their place.

I am sure that, if I were in a position to save Andy or Ben, and I turned my attention to the states of affairs I might be in a position to bring about:

A:    My saving Andy in three hours, and leaving Ben to die.
B:    My saving Ben in three hours, and leaving Andy to die.
A+:   My saving Andy in two and a half hours, and leaving Ben to die.
B+:   My saving Ben in two and a half hours, and leaving Andy to die.

I would prefer A+ to A, B+ to B, but have no settled preferences between A or A+ and B or B+. I see many ways in which Andy's death would be terrible, many quite different ways in which Ben's death would be terrible. In this context, half an hour here or there would not tip any balances for me. And it is not that learning more about A, B, A+, and B+ would give me a settled preference for A+ over B, or for B+ over A. It is not as if I really care about the number of instances of pleasure, or the number of satisfied desires, had by Andy, Ben, and their families, and learning more about A, B, A+, and B+ would tell me that there are more in A+ than in B, or that there are more in B+ than in A. Nor (contra a certain sort of utilitarian) do I think that learning more about the states of affairs should give me settled preferences. Indeed, when I really think about Andy, Ben, and their families, the suggestion that I should gain a preference between saving one and saving the other by counting up instances of pleasure or counting up satisfied desires seems to me ridiculous.

So, if we are to draw any interesting conclusions about how decent and rational people will behave in these contexts, then we need to take a view about how decent, rational people with negatively intransitive preferences will behave in these contexts. And, for present purposes, we need to support it by appealing to something other than a maximizing conception of rationality.

This is a tricky matter. These contexts raise a problem that standard theories of rationality do not help us solve. In the next chapter I will describe the problem, and suggest a way to solve it.

# 3

# Rational Responses to Sweetening Insensitive Preferences

It often happens that there are items A, A+, B, B+ such that we prefer A+ to A, B+ to B, but we do not prefer A or A+ to B or B+. In the previous chapter I drew attention to three cases in which I might have patterns of preference like this: The Fire, The Dinner, and Small Differences, Fully Transparent Inter-Personal Conflict.

What is it rational for me to do in such cases? Classical expected utility theory will not help us answer this question. To apply classical expected utility theory we must associate a utility function, $U$, with my preferences such that, for all outcomes $x,y$, $U(x) > U(y)$ iff I prefer $x$ to $y$. Such a function exists only if my preferences between outcomes are negatively transitive (which means, recall, that for any states of affairs $x,y,z$, if I have no preference between $x$ and $y$, and no preference between $y$ and $z$, then I have no preference between $x$ and $z$). My preferences are negatively intransitive (I have no preference, recall, between A and B, and no preference between B and A+, but I prefer A+ to A).

"So much the worse for the question," a classical expected utility theorist might say. "There is no sense in asking what it is rational for you to do while your preferences are negatively intransitive. If you want guidance from the theory of practical rationality, reflect a bit, render your preferences negatively transitive, and then come back to us."

This is an unhelpful response. I looked to the theory of practical rationality for guidance. It gave me none. It will guide me if I render my preferences negatively transitive, but I have no inclination to do that. And, even if I did have an inclination to do it, doing it would involve acquiring or dropping preferences. It is not so easy to acquire or drop preferences at will.

A more constructive response is to extend the standard theory of rational decision under conditions of uncertainty to cover situations in which we have negatively intransitive preferences. But there is a curious problem that comes up as soon as we try to do this. I will describe this problem, and two solutions to it, in this chapter.

## 3.1. Opaque Sweetening

Let us consider a case that is less emotionally charged, a case that does not involve desperate people starving or thirsting to death on desolate islands. Let us suppose that you have two items I want. Call them "A" and "B." Let us suppose, also, that I would rather have A-and-a-dollar than just A, and rather have B-and-a-dollar than just B, but that I have no preference between having A and having B, between having A and having B-and-a-dollar, between having A-and-a-dollar and having B, or between having A-and-a-dollar and having B-and-a-dollar. And let us suppose that we play a sort of game:

Two Opaque Boxes
You show me items A and B, a dollar, a coin, and two opaque boxes. You toss the coin and, governed by the toss (heads—left, tails—right), place item A in one box and item B in the other. I do not see which item went where. You toss the coin again and, governed by the toss, place the dollar inside the right box. I see that, which leaves me with credence 0.5 that things are like so:

| Left Box | A | | Right Box | B+$1 |

and credence 0.5 that things are like so:

| Left Box | B | | Right Box | A+$1 |

Then you invite me to walk away with one of the boxes.

## 3.2. Why you might Think I should Take the Sweetened Option

Given what I know and prefer, what is it rationally permissible for me to do in this case? Here are two seemingly powerful arguments to the conclusion that it is rationally impermissible for me to take the left, unsweetened box:

*Argument 1. I Have No Reason to Take the Left, Rather than the Right, Box*

Imagine I take out a sheet of paper and try to list the pros and cons of taking the left and right boxes. What can I write in the Pro-Right-Rather-than-Left column? Here is one thing I can write:

Pro-Right:  If I take the right box, then I will get that extra dollar, but if I take the left box, then I will not.

What can I write in the Pro-Left-Rather-than-Right column? Nothing. This will not do:

Pro-Left:  If I take the left box, then I will get something I want.

If I take the right box then I will get something I want too. Nor will this do:

Pro-Left:  If I take the left box, then there is a 0.5 chance I will get A.

If I take the right box, then there is a 0.5 chance I will get A too. There is no consideration that I can produce in favor of taking the left box rather than the right box. In philosophy-speak: I have a reason to take the right box rather than the left box, no reason to take the left box rather than the right box.

Now here is a claim about practical rationality and reasons:

*Rational Permissibility Tracks Reasons*

If you are rational and two options are open to you, and you have a reason to take the one-rather-than-the-other, and no reason to take the other-rather-than-the-one, then it is rationally impermissible to take the other.

Being rational involves being guided by your reasons. When you have a reason to do one thing, and no reason to do anything else, then your reasons are guiding you in only one direction.

It follows that it is rationally impermissible for me to take the left box.

*Argument 2. I Will Improve my Prospects by Taking the Right Box*

Let the *prospect* associated with an option be, roughly, a representation of how likely I think it that one thing or another will happen if I take the option. To be precise, let it be the set of pairs $<c,o>$ such that $o$ is an outcome that might, for all I know, come about if I take the option, and $c$ is my credence that the outcome will come about if I take the option.[1] Here is a claim about prospects and rational permissibility:

*Prospects Determine Permissibility*
Facts about what it is rationally permissible for me to do are determined by facts about the prospects associated with the options available to me.

What it is rationally permissible for me to do depends only on the things I think might happen if I take the options open to me, and how likely I think them to happen.

Now consider another game:

One Opaque Box
You show me items A and B, a dollar, a coin, and one opaque box. You toss the coin and, governed by the toss, place item A or item B in the box. I do not see which. Then you invite me to walk away with the box and the dollar, or just the box.

Obviously I have to accept the dollar in this case. But the prospects associated with the options available to me in this case are the same as the prospects associated with the options available to me in the Two Opaque Boxes case. In this case, the prospect associated with my taking the box alone is $\{<0.5, A>, <0.5, B>\}$ (which is to say that I think it 0.5 likely that I will end up with A, 0.5 likely that I will end up with B, if I take the box alone), and the prospect associated with my taking the box and the dollar is $\{<0.5, A+>, <0.5, B+>\}$. In the Two Opaque Boxes case the prospect associated with my taking the left box is $\{<0.5, A>, <0.5, B>\}$,

---

[1] If we wish to avoid committing ourselves to the denial of causal decision theory, then we should understand my "credence that the outcome will come about if I take the option" in a particular way. It is not just my credence in the outcome, conditional on my taking the option. Rather, my credence in outcome o, relative to option a, is $\sum_d(P(d).P(o/ad))$, where d is a variable ranging over dependency hypotheses, "P(d)" refers to my credence in dependency hypothesis d, and "P(o/ad)" refers to my credence in outcome o, conditional on my taking option a and dependency hypothesis d being true. But this will not make a difference in any of the cases I discuss here.

and the prospect associated with my taking the right box is {<0.5, A+>, <0.5, B+>}.[2] So, by *Prospects Determine Permissibility*, in the <u>Two Opaque Boxes</u> case it is rationally impermissible to take the left box.

## 3.3. Why you might Think it is not the Case That I Should Take the Sweetened Option

Is that the end of the matter—I have to take the right box? Maybe not. Here are two seemingly powerful arguments to the conclusion that it is rationally permissible for me to take the left, unsweetened box.

*Argument 3.  I Know I have no Preference for the Contents of the Right Box*

Being rational involves, at least in part, acting on preferences between outcomes. So, surely:

*Recognition*
Whenever I have two options, and I know that I have no preference between the outcome of the one and the outcome of the other, it is rationally permissible for me to take either.

In this case, I know that I have no preference between the outcome of my taking the left box and the outcome of my taking the right box. Either there is A in the left box, B + $1 in the right box—in which case I have no preference between the outcome of my taking the left box and the outcome of my taking the right box. Or there is B in the left box, A + $1 in the right box—in which case I have no preference between the outcome of my taking the left box and the outcome of my taking the right box. So it is rationally permissible for me to take the left box.

---

[2] "But they are not exactly the same," you might say. "In the first case, the prospect associated with my taking the left box is {<0.5, I get A and could have gotten B +>, <0.5, I get B and could have gotten A +>}. In the second case the prospect associated with my taking the box alone is {<0.5, I get A and could have gotten B+>, <0.5, I get B and could have gotten A+>}. Different prospects." True, and if, in addition to caring about what I get, I care about whether what I get is preferable to what I leave on the table, then I have reason to treat this difference as significant. But if I do not care about whether what I get is preferable to what I leave on the table, then I have no reason to treat this difference as significant.

*Argument 4: It is Okay to Defer to my Better-Informed Self*

Roughly: I know for sure that, if I were to see inside the boxes, I would have no preference for taking the right box. And it is rationally permissible for me to defer to my better-informed self.

More carefully: thinking of a *state of affairs* as a way for things to be, and thinking of a *maximal state of affairs* as a precise way for everything to be, here are two very plausible principles concerning rational permissibility:

*Deference*
If I know that any fully informed, rational person, with all and only my preferences between maximal states of affairs, would have a certain array of preferences between sub-maximal states of affairs on my behalf, then it is rationally permissible for me to have that array of preferences between sub-maximal states of affairs.

*Permissibility of Action Follows Permissibility of Preference*
If I have just two options, and it is rationally permissible for me to have no preference for my taking the one, and no preference for my taking the other, then it is rationally permissible for me to take the one and rationally permissible for me to take the other.

In this case I know that any fully informed, rational person, with all and only my preferences between maximal states of affairs, would have no preference for my walking away with the right box. So, by *Deference*, it is rationally permissible for me to have no preference for walking away with the right box. So, by *Permissibility of Action Follows Permissibility of Preference*, it is rationally permissible for me to walk away with the left box.

## 3.4. Take the Sweetened Option

We have two ways of thinking about rationality. Call the first (take the right box!) way of thinking *prospectism* and the second (take either box!) way of thinking *deferentialism*. Which of them is right? I think this is a difficult, open problem. I feel the pull of both. But, on balance, I lean toward prospectism. It is not that I have a dazzling, decisive argument that goes significantly beyond what I have said already. It is rather that I accept the idea that being rational involves being sensitive to reasons, and I think that, by appealing to this idea, we can explain why the deferentialist arguments are both attractive and wrong.

The deferentialist arguments are attractive because sometimes, when I learn that any fully informed, rational person with all and only my preferences between maximal states of affairs (henceforth, for brevity: *my better informed self*) would lack an all-things-considered preference for my taking the right box, it does indeed cease to be true that I have a reason to take the right box and no reason to take the left box.

Suppose I learn that my better-informed self would prefer that I take the left box. Now there remains something to be said for my taking the right box:

Pro-Right:   If I take the right box, then I will get that extra dollar.

And there is something new to be said for my taking the left box:

Pro-Left:   My better-informed self would prefer that I take the left box.

So the prospectist reasoning does not kick in. I am under no rational obligation to take the right box.

Or suppose I learn that my better-informed self would be all-things-considered indifferent in a sweetening *sensitive* way between my taking the left and right boxes (lightly sweeten either box and he would prefer it, lightly sour either box and he would dis-prefer it). Again there remains something to be said for my taking the right box:

Pro-Right:   If I take the right box, then I will get that extra dollar.

And there is something new to be said for my taking the left box:

Pro-Left:   Call the collection of things in the left box that I do not know to be in the left box (which is to say everything in the left box) the *unknown contents of the left box*. Call the collection of things in the right box that I do not know to be in the right box (which is to say everything in the right box minus that dollar) the *unknown contents of the right box*. My better-informed self would prefer to have the unknown contents of the left box to the unknown contents of the right box.

So, again, the prospectist reasoning does not kick in. I am under no rational obligation to take the right box.

The arguments are wrong because, in the special case where I learn that my better-informed self would lack-all-considered preferences between my taking the left and right boxes in a sweetening *insensitive* way (lightly sweeten or sour either box and he would still lack a preference), the prospectist reasoning does kick in. In that case the something to be said for my taking the right box remains:

Pro-Right:    If I take the right box, then I will get that extra dollar.

But there is nothing new to be said for my taking the left box. I cannot say that my better-informed self would prefer the contents of the left box to the contents of the right box. I cannot say that he would prefer the invisible contents of the left box to the invisible contents of the left box. I have no reason to take the left box. So, in this special case, I have most reason to take the right box.

## 3.5.  An Aside: Formal Prospectist Decision Theory

My goal in this chapter was just to make a case for the prospectist way of thinking about cases like Two Opaque Boxes. I am done with that. But in the previous chapter I mentioned that classical expected utility theory is silent with respect to these questions, because classical expected utility theory does not tell us what it is rationally permissible to do when preferences are negatively intransitive. You may be wondering, then, how we might extend classical expected utility theory so that it gives broadly prospectist answers about what it is rationally permissible to do when preferences are negatively intransitive (if you were not wondering this, and you have no patience for technical material, then please skip ahead to Chapter 4.)

This is fairly straightforward. Here is a rough statement of a decision theory I will call *formal prospectism*: we say that it is rationally permissible for me to take an action if and only if, for some way of rendering my preferences negatively transitive by keeping the preferences I have and adding new ones, the standard theory says that no alternative has higher expected utility.

Here is a more accurate, formal statement of the theory. First some terminology: where $U$ is a function that assigns numbers to outcomes, say that *U represents a coherent completion of my preferences* when, for all outcomes $o_1, o_2$, if I prefer $o_1$ to $o_2$, then $U(o_1) > U(o_2)$, and for all prospects $p_1, p_2$, if I prefer $p_1$ to $p_2$ then $\sum_o(Pp_1(o).U(o)) > \sum_o(Pp_2(o).U(o))$, where o is a variable ranging over outcomes and "Pp(o)" refers to the probability assigned to outcome o by prospect p.

Now for the central claim:

> *Formal Prospectism*
> It is permissible for me to choose an option iff, for some utility function that represents a coherent completion of my preferences, U, no alternative has greater expected U-utility.[3]

In the <u>Two Opaque Boxes</u> case, formal prospectism says that it is rationally impermissible for me to take the left, unsweetened box. Why? Well, I prefer A+ to A, and B+ to B, so for any function, $U$, that represents a coherent completion of my preferences, $U(A +) > U(A)$, and $U(B +) > U(B)$. So for any function, $U$, that represents a coherent completion of my preferences, the expected $U$-utility of my taking the right box $(0.5U(B+) + 0.5U(A+))$ is greater than the expected $U$-utility of my taking the left box $(0.5U(A) + 0.5U(B))$.

## 3.6. A Yet Further Aside: Formal Deferentialist Decision Theory

You may also be wondering about how we might extend classical expected utility theory so that it gives broadly deferentialist answers about what it is rationally permissible to do when preferences are negatively intransitive (again, if you are not wondering this, and you have no patience for technical material, please skip ahead to Chapter 4).

---

[3] What is the "expected U-utility" of an act? You can interpret this in different ways, depending on how you feel about Newcomb problems, causal and evidential decision theory. If you wish to be a causalist prospectist, then interpret it in a standard causalist way: the expected $u$-utility of act a is $\sum_d(P(d).u(ad))$, where d is a variable ranging over dependency hypotheses, propositions concerning how things beyond my control are, and "P(d)" refers to my credence that hypothesis d is true, and "ad" refers to the outcome of my taking act a, if hypothesis d is true. If you wish to be an evidentialist prospectist, then interpret it in a standard evidentialist way: $\sum_d(P(d/a).u(ad))$. This will not make a difference in any of the cases I discuss here.

The extension is much less straightforward. A natural first move is to partition logical space into a set of *dependency hypotheses*—thinking of a dependency hypothesis as a maximally specific proposition concerning how things that matter to me causally depend on my present actions.[4] As a notational matter, let "P(d)" refer to my credence that dependency hypothesis d is true, and let "od" refer to the outcome of my taking option o, if dependency hypothesis d is true. We can then restate the "Recognition" principle from the previous section in a more precise way:

*Recognition*
It is rationally permissible for me to choose option o if, for all alternatives open to me a, and all dependency hypotheses in which I have positive credence d, I do not prefer ad to od.

This is fine, so far as it goes, but it is not a general theory of decision, a theory that gives us full necessary and sufficient conditions for rational permissibility. It gives us one sufficient condition for rational permissibility, but it tells us nothing about cases in which the condition does not apply. For example:

*Two More Opaque Boxes*
You show me items A and B, a coin, and two opaque boxes. Then you toss the coin and, governed by the toss, place item A in one box and item B in the other. I do not see which item went where. Then, with some determinate probability, you either do or do not switch the item in the right box with item C—*where C is an item that I prefer to both A and B*. I do not see whether you made the switch.

In this case I do not know that I have no preference for the outcome of my taking the right box. I do know that I have no preference for the outcome of my taking the *left box*. But maybe the right box contains item C. If it does, then I have a preference for the outcome of my taking the right box. The Recognition principle is silent.

What do we want our general theory to say about this sort of case? I suggest that we want it to say the following:

---

[4] This term was introduced by David Lewis in Lewis (1981). Other philosophers, and many decision theorists, talk of "states" and "states of nature."

*Mild Chancy Sweetening*
When I do not have a strong preference for C over A and B, and my credence that you made the switch is small, it is rationally permissible to take the left box. (The right box has been mildly sweetened—not by a certain dollar, as in the original case, but by a small chance that it contains something that I regard as a little bit better than either A or B.)

Why? Well, we do not want the theory to say that it is permissible to ignore a certain-dollar-sweetening, but impermissible to ignore (for example) a one-in-a-million-chance-of-a-hundred-dollars-sweetening. I far prefer a certain dollar to a one in a million chance of a hundred dollars.

*Powerful Chancy Sweetening*
When I have a strong preference for C over A and B, and my credence that you made the switch is large, it is rationally impermissible to take the left box. (The right box has been *powerfully sweetened*—by a large chance that it contains something that I regard as much better than A or B.)

Why? Well, obviously, if I am almost certain that the right box contains C, and C is a billion dollars, then I ought to take it.

Is there a moderately natural, general theory of decision that says all these things? I think so. Here is a rough statement of the theory I will call *formal deferentialism*: to find out if an action is permissible, I go to each relevant dependency hypothesis in turn. I take the coherent completion of my preferences that is most flattering to the action, supposing that the dependency hypothesis is true. I assign utilities to each of the actions open to me accordingly. I multiply these utilities by my credence that the dependency hypothesis is true . . . and move on to the next dependency hypothesis. I sum up. If there is some way of doing this on which the action comes out ahead of (or at least *not behind*) its competitors, then the action is permissible.

Here is a more accurate, formal statement of the theory. First some terminology. Let C be the set of utility functions that represent coherent completions of my preferences. Let a *regimentation* of C be a subset, R, of C such that for some outcomes A, B, for any function $g$, $g \in R$ iff $g \in C$ and $g(A) = 1$ and $g(B) = 0$. (Note that it follows from the fact that utility functions are unique under positive affine transformation[5] that, if R is a regimentation of C, then, for each coherent completion of my preferences, R has one[6] and only one[7] representative of it as a member.)

Some more terminology: for any regimentation R, let the *dependency-expansion* of R be the set of functions $f$ such that for any dependency hypotheses d, for some function $r$ in R, for all actions open to me, a, $f$(ad) = $r$(ad). (Each function in the dependency-expansion of R, for each dependency hypothesis, agrees with some function in R on the utilities of the states of affairs that will come about if I act one way or another and the dependency hypothesis is true.)

Now for the central claim:

*Formal Deferentialism*
It is permissible for me to choose an option iff, for some regimentation, R, of the set of utility functions that represent my preferences, for some function r in the dependency-expansion of R, no alternative has higher expected r-utility.[8]

In our original *Two Opaque Boxes* case, deferentialism says that it is rationally permissible to take the left, unsweetened box. In that case there are two relevant dependency hypotheses. According to the first, the left box contains A, the right B+. According to the second, the left box contains B, the right A+. For any regimentation, R, of the utility functions that represent coherent completions of my preferences, some functions in R assign A utility greater than or equal to B+, others assign B utility greater than or equal to A+. Choose one of the former, call it $U_1$, and one of the

---

[5] Function $v$ represents the same complete, coherent preferences as function $u$ iff for some number i>0, for some number j, for all x, $v(x) = iu(x) + j$.

[6] Proof: take any coherent completion of my preferences, and a function that represents it, $g$. Now let $h$ be the function such that for all x $h(x) = (1/(g(A)-g(B))).g(x) - (g(B)/(g(A)-g(B)))$. By construction, $h(A) = 1$, $h(B) = 0$. And $h$ represents the same coherent completion of my preferences as $g$, because for some number i>0, for some number j, for all outcomes x, $g(x) = ih(x) + j$.

[7] Proof: suppose that $g$ and $h$ are functions in R that represent the same coherent completion of my preferences. Because $g$ and $h$ are functions in R, $g(A) = h(A) = 1$, and $g(B) = h(B) = 0$. Because $g$ and $h$ represent the same coherent completion of my preferences, for some number i>0, for some number j, for all outcomes x, $g(x) = ih(x) + j$. Solving for i and j, i = 1 and j = 0. Function $g$ is function $h$.

[8] Again, please feel free to interpret "expected r-utility" in the causalist or evidentialist way, depending on your feelings about Newcomb problems.

latter, call it $U_2$. Notice that $(0.5(U_1(A)) + 0.5(U_2(B))) \geq (0.5(U_1(B +)) + 0.5(U_2(A +)))$, so for some function $f$ in the dependency-expansion of R, $(0.5(f(A)) + 0.5(f(B))) \geq (0.5(f(B +)) + 0.5(f(A +)))$, so for some function $f$ in the dependency-expansion of R, the expected $f$-utility of taking the left box is greater than or equal to the expected $f$-utility of taking the right box.

And, more generally, deferentialism entails the principles I have called *Recognition*,[9] *Mild Chancy Sweetening*, and *Strong Chancy Sweetening*.

[9] To be accurate: if we plug the causalist expected-utility formula into Deferentialism, then it entails the Recognition principle simpliciter. If we plug the evidentialist expected-utility formula into Deferentialism, then it entails the Recognition principle except in Newcomb cases—cases where I care about how things out of my control are, and my conditional credence in things out of my control being one way or another, varies with actions available to me.

# 4

# Efficiency and the Greater Good

Back to the point. We have two theories of rational decision under conditions of uncertainty: prospectism and deferentialism. I favor prospectism. What does this tell us about the poor people abandoned by pirates back in Chapter 2?

## 4.1. Opaque Small Differences Redux

Recall the predicaments Andy, Ben, and I were in:

Small Differences, Opaque Inter-Personal Conflict
One of Andy and Ben is three hours to my west, the other two and a half hours to my east. I do not know who is where.

See Fig. 4.1.

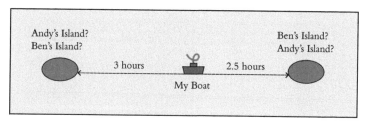

Figure 4.1

In this case, supposing that prospectism is true, it follows that, if my options are *directly heading east*, and *directly heading west*, and I am minimally considerate, minimally benevolent, and rational, then I will head east. This conclusion is supported both by the informal arguments for prospectism that we saw in the previous chapter, and by formal prospectist decision theory.

The informal "most reasons" argument: imagine that I try to list the pros and cons of heading east and west. What can I write in the Pro-West column? Nothing. What can I write in the Pro-East column? I can write: "Will have somebody in my boat in two and a half hours." I have a reason to head east, no reason to head west. So I have most reason to head east. So, if I am rational, I will head east. Rational people do what they have most reason to do.

The informal "better prospects" argument: the prospects associated with the options that are open to me in this case are just the same as the prospects associated with the options open to me in another case:

### Small Differences, Opaque No-Conflict
I know that one of Andy and Ben is stranded on a nearby island, while the other is stranded on a distant island, far beyond the range of my boat. I do not know who is where. There are two safe routes to the nearby island, a western route and an eastern route. As before, the western route will take three hours, the eastern route two and a half hours.

See Fig. 4.2.

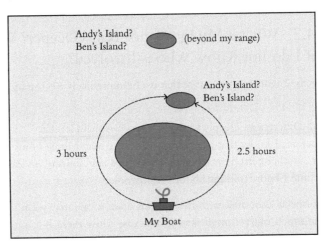

Figure 4.2

In both cases there are four relevantly different outcomes that might come about:

A:    in which I head west and pick up Andy in 3 hours, and Ben dies of thirst.

B:    in which I head west and pick up Ben in 3 hours, and Andy dies of thirst.

A+:   in which I head east and pick up Andy in 2.5 hours, and Ben dies of thirst.

B+:   in which I head east and pick up Ben in 2.5 hours, and Andy dies of thirst.

In both cases the prospect associated with heading west is ½ each of A and B, while the prospect associated with heading east is ½ each of A+ and B+. But clearly, if I am minimally benevolent and rational, then I will head east in the second case. So, by *Prospects Determine Rational Permissibility*, if I am both minimally benevolent and rational, then I will head east in the first case.[1]

The argument from formal prospectist decision theory: if I am minimally benevolent, then I will prefer A+ to A, B+ to B. It follows that, for any completion of preferences, the heading east option will have higher expected utility than the heading west option. So, if I am minimally benevolent, then it is rationally impermissible for me to head west.

## 4.2. What if My Ignorance Runs Deeper? What if I do not Know who is Involved?

Similar arguments apply to a case that is a bit more likely to crop up in real life:

Small Differences, Deeply Opaque Inter-Personal Conflict
As before, I know that one person is on the island three hours to my west, another person on the island two and a half hours to my east. But this time I know nothing about these people.

The prospects associated with the options open to me may seem to have become much more complicated in this case (now there is a minuscule

---

[1] Note that the notion of "utility" did not figure in either of the previous two arguments. This should answer the person for whom this talk of a rational requirement to "maximize utility" was evidence that we are somehow smuggling utilitarian assumptions into our picture of rationality.

chance that, by heading east, I will be saving Barak Obama, and a minuscule chance that, by heading east, I will be saving Shania Twain, and a minuscule chance that, by heading east, I will be saving my next-door neighbor...). But, by the same reasoning, if I am decent and rational, then I will head east. The quick way to see this is to note that the prospects associated with the options open to me are relevantly the same as the prospects associated with the options open to me in:

### Small Differences, Deeply Opaque No-Conflict
Again, I know that one person is stranded on a nearby island, while another is stranded on a distant island, far beyond the range of my boat. As before, I can get to the nearby island in three hours by heading west, two and a half hours by heading east. But this time I know nothing about these people.

And obviously I will head east in this case, if I am minimally benevolent and rational.

## 4.3. Objection: What about Fairness?

"But wait," you may be bursting to say. "These arguments fail to engage with the points made by Taurek and Kamm. They pointed out that in all realistic cases like this there are chancy further options, like *flipping a coin and being governed by the outcome of the flip*, or *spinning a bottle and being governed by the outcome of the spin* . . . and the like. Taurek argued that, when such options exist, you must take one, because proceeding directly east or west will be unfair to the person you leave to die. Kamm argued that (in the <u>Small Differences</u> case at least) you must take one because by proceeding directly east you would be inappropriately sensitive to irrelevant utilities."

Fair enough. To put this point within the framework we have been developing here, there are really three relevantly different options available to me:

Directly heading west.
Directly heading east.
Flipping a coin and going with the outcome of the flip.

The first option has two possible outcomes:

A:    In which I head west and save Andy in 3 hours.
B:    In which I head west and save Ben in 3 hours.

The second option has two possible outcomes:

A+:    In which I head east and save Andy in 2.5 hours.
B+:    In which I head east and save Ben in 2.5 hours.

The third option has four possible outcomes:

$Flip_{A+}$:    In which I flip, then head east and save Andy in 2.5 hours.
$Flip_A$:    In which I flip, then head west and save Andy in 3 hours.
$Flip_{B+}$:    In which I flip, then head east and save Ben in 2.5 hours.
$Flip_B$:    In which I flip, then head west and save Ben in 3 hours.

I might have an all-things-considered preference for all of the flip out-comes over all of the non-flip outcomes. I might be able to explain why (maybe, following Taurek, I take the view that, in all of the flip outcomes I treat Andy and Ben fairly, while in all of the non-flip outcomes I treat at least one of them unfairly; maybe, following Kamm, I take the view that in all of the non-flip outcomes I am unduly sensitive to "irrelevant utilities"). This would not make me less than minimally benevolent (in the compari-son between, for example, A+ and $Flip_A$, all other things would not be equal. $Flip_A$ would satisfy a desire of mine: for example, the desire that I be fair, or the desire that I not be sensitive to "irrelevant utilities"). And, in light of my preferences, it would not, then, be rational for me to head east directly. It would be rational for me to flip a coin.

This is quite true. The conclusion (if I am minimally considerate, benevolent, and rational then I will directly head east) follows only if I take there to be no reason to do anything other than head directly east. If, for me, heading west has a romance that heading east cannot match, or if I love the thrill that comes with flipping a coin and submitting myself to the Fates, or if I think it fairer to flip a coin, the conclusion does not follow.

You may even have a stronger point in mind. You may think that I ought to take these considerations of fairness or "irrelevant utility" to be decisive—I ought to prefer the flip outcomes to the non-flip outcomes on the grounds that, in the non-flip outcomes, I treat someone unfairly or pay undue heed to irrelevant utilities. So, if I am decent (I have all the preferences I ought to have) and rational, then I will flip.

Now, to be entirely true to the spirit of my project here, I should really just note that this is all fine and move on. My project is to see how far we can venture into the jungle of normative ethics armed only with minimal consideration, minimal benevolence, and rationality. Minimal consideration, minimal benevolence, and rationality tell us nothing about fairness or about the significance of these so-called irrelevant utilities.

But I will mention, in passing (it is time for my first FLAG), that I find these views about fairness and the significance of "irrelevant utilities," when applied to opaque cases, hard to swallow.

Let us start with fairness. I can certainly see ways of filling in the details of the story that would make it seem as if I do treat the fellow on the west island unfairly by steaming directly east:

### Prejudice

I know that the pirates have a prejudice against the race and religion of one of Andy or Ben. I know that they placed that person on the west island, further away from natural shipping routes, to minimize the chances that he would be saved.

If I head directly east, then I am indulging the pirates' prejudice against the person on the west island. That is unfair.

But suppose it is not like that:

### Dumb Luck

I have no reason to think that the pirates anticipated my arrival. Nor do I read anything significant into the fact that I happen to be closer to one island than another. That just came down to the vicissitudes of wind, wave, and current.

Now I find it hard to persuade myself that I behave unfairly to the fellow on the west island by steaming directly east. I am steaming directly east because the east island happened to be closer to me. That seems to me no more unfair than steaming east because a coin happened to land heads.

Why might one think otherwise? Well, Taurek never explicitly addressed cases like this, cases in which I do not know who is where,[2] but remember his turn of phrase: to be fair to both parties I must "give them an

---

[2] Taurek merely stipulated that, in the cases he was considering, I know that there are "no morally relevant differences" between the people I am in a position to save. As the Andy and Ben case illustrates, there is a significant question about just what it would take for there to be

equal chance of survival." People have argued to me[3] that in this case by heading directly east I do not give the person on the west island, whoever he may be, "an equal chance of survival," in the sense of the term that is relevant to whether I treat him fairly. Yes, I act in such a way as to make it the case that I regard it as equally likely that Andy will survive and that Ben will survive. But, to be fair, I must "give them an equal chance" in a more robustly objective sense of the term.

Something more must be said here. Just how "robustly objective" do the chances have to be? Here are some decision procedures:

*Proximity*: I head toward the closer island.

*Bible*: I open my ship's bible and count up the number of words on the first page of Genesis—if it is odd then I will head east, if it is even then I will head west.

*Algorithm*: I turn on my ship's computer and run the "random number" generator (which outputs a number between 0 and 1, following an algorithm that is entirely unknown to me). If it gives me a number >0.5 then I will head east, if it gives me a number <0.5 then I will head west.

*Coin*: I spin a coin—heads and I will head east, tails and I will head west.

*Photons*: I fire a small batch of photons southwards through a narrow slit—if more deflect east then I will head east, if more deflect west then I will head west.

Which of them is good enough?

A natural way to develop the idea that just equalizing my own credences that Andy and Ben will live is not good enough is by appeal to the attitudes of an informed observer.[4] Suppose that I use *Proximity* as a tie-breaker. Suppose that Andy is, in fact, stranded on the further, western island. Someone who knows this will not regard it as equally likely that Andy and Ben will survive, if I head east. Such a person will say: "From my point of view, by heading directly east you give Andy no chance of survival." And we should take this point of view to be the one that matters.

---

no morally relevant differences between distinct individuals. Maybe Taurek was thinking of childless twin accountants, or something like that.

[3] Thanks to Judy Thomson.

[4] Thanks again to Judy Thomson for pressing this line of thought to me.

This is why, by using *Proximity* as a tie-breaker, I treat Andy unfairly. By using *Proximity* as a tie-breaker, I fail, in the relevant sense, to give Andy and Ben equal chances of surviving.

But note that the same is true of somebody who knows the number of words on the first page of Genesis in the ship's bible. From this person's point of view, *Bible* gives one of Andy or Ben no chance of survival. And the same is true of somebody who knows the algorithm that governs the ship's "random number" generator, and of somebody who knows (by way of knowing the temporary state of the universe and the laws that govern its evolution) the side on which the coin will fall, and of somebody who knows (by way of an oracle whose insight into the future defies physical explanation) the angles at which particular electrons will deflect when fired through slits. From these people's points of view, the other decision methods leave one of Andy or Ben with no chance of survival. Why not take their points of view to be the ones that matter?

Perhaps because these people's states of knowledge are *abnormal*. I should give Andy and Ben an equal chance of survival relative to a normal state of knowledge about their situation. But what is a normal state of knowledge? Why is it normal to know the precise sailing times for the boat to the respective islands, but abnormal to know the number of words on the first page of Genesis in the ship's bible? And why does this matter?

Perhaps because these people know more than Andy and Ben themselves do. I should give Andy and Ben an equal chance of survival relative to what they themselves know about their situation. But again, why does this matter? Suppose that I leave Ben to die because he is on the further island. Why should the question of whether I treated him fairly turn on whether, at the time I made my decision, he knew the precise location of my boat?

Maybe there is some other, principled, explanation of why *Proximity* is an unfair decision procedure, *Photons* a fair decision procedure. But I do not yet see how it would go.

What about the "irrelevant utilities" worry? I do feel the force of a worry in this vicinity quite strongly in *transparent* cases, cases in which I know precisely who is where. When I know that Andy, with all of his wonderful qualities (the irreverent sense of humor...etc.) is in one direction, and Ben, with all of his quite different, wonderful qualities (the nuanced sense of poetic displacement...etc.) is in the other, then it does seem to be a sort of mistake to say "Andy is a half hour closer, so I will save him." The mistake comes in thinking that my reasons to save Andy and Ben are perfectly balanced against each other, so that any further reason to save Andy will tip the balance in his favor. And it is not a benign mistake. My reasons to save Andy and Ben are not perfectly balanced against each other, because their lives are valuable in very different, incommensurable ways. By failing to acknowledge this, I am failing to acknowledge them as individuals.

And I feel the force of another worry in this vicinity in opaque cases in which the interests of an otherwise-uninvolved third party play the role of sweetener. Consider:

Cassandra's Wallet
I know that one of Andy or Ben is on an island three hours to my west, the other on an island three hours to my east. I do not know who is where. But I do know that Cassandra's wallet is on the east island.

If I head east on the grounds that I can thereby pick up Cassandra's wallet for her, then I am implicating her in the decision in a certain way. I am making it the case that her interest in retrieving her wallet determined that the person on the eastern island be saved, the person on the western island be left to die. It seems to me at least consistent with my being morally decent that I prefer to avoid implicating her in the decision in this way. (I certainly would not tell her about it if I did it. And is that not some evidence that it is an undesirable thing?)

But these worries do not apply to the opaque case we have been focusing upon. In this case the consideration that the island to my east is a half hour closer is the only reason I have to go one way or the other, so I am not making any kind of mistake or in any way failing to acknowledge Andy and Ben as individuals by taking this reason to tip the balance in favor of my going east. Nor am I implicating any otherwise-uninvolved third parties in the decision.

## 4.4. Many or Few Redux

Now let us get back to the main thrust of the argument, and look at the second sort of opaque rescue cases, the ones in which I must choose between rescuing many people or few people. Remember the predicament Astrid, Beth, and Chris were in:

### 1 or 2? Opaque Inter-Personal Conflict

I know that one of Astrid, Beth, and Chris is on an island three hours to my west, the other two on an island three hours to my east. I do not know who is where.

See Fig. 4.3.

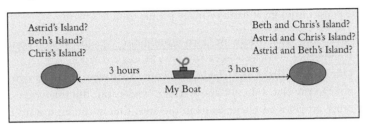

Astrid's Island?
Beth's Island?
Chris's Island?

Beth and Chris's Island?
Astrid and Chris's Island?
Astrid and Beth's Island?

3 hours

3 hours

My Boat

**Figure 4.3**

Once again, supposing that prospectism is true, it follows that, if my options are *directly heading east* and *directly heading west*, and I am minimally considerate, minimally benevolent, and rational, then I will head east. Again, this conclusion is supported both by the informal arguments for prospectism that we saw in the previous chapter, and by formal prospectist decision theory. There are six things that might end up happening:

O1: I head west, save Astrid, and leave Beth and Chris to die.
O2: I head west, save Beth, and leave Astrid and Chris to die.
O3: I head west, save Chris, and leave Astrid and Beth to die.
O4: I head east, save Beth and Chris, and leave Andy to die.
O5: I head east, save Astrid and Chris, and leave Beth to die.
O6: I head east, save Astrid and Beth, and leave Chris to die.

The prospect associated with my heading west is 1/3 each of O1 to O3, and the prospect associated with my heading east is 1/3 each of O4 to O6. Since minimal benevolence requires of me that I prefer O4 to O3, O5 to O1, and O6 to O2, it must turn out that, for every completion of my preferences, heading east has higher expected utility than heading west. I am rationally required to head east.

## 4.5. Generalizing the Argument

Just how far does this reasoning go? Does it follow that, if we are minimally considerate, minimally benevolent, and rational, then we will act like utilitarians in all these sorts of cases? Does it follow that, whenever we are doling out benefits to unknown recipients, we will always do so in what we believe to be the most efficient way—where efficiency is about minimizing total suffering?

No it does not. Consider an opaque variant of the third sort of case we looked at in Chapter 2, a case in which I have to choose between saving one person from great harm or many people from less harm:

### Save One from More or Two from Less? Opaque Inter-Personal Conflict

One of Alex, Brian, and Charles is an hour to my west, the other two an hour to my east. I do not know who is where. But this time there are other provisioned rescue boats in the area. One steaming toward the west island will get there in two and a half hours. One steaming towards the east island will get there in two hours. I can save two people from an hour of suffering by heading east, and one person from an hour and a half of suffering by heading west.

See Fig. 4.4.

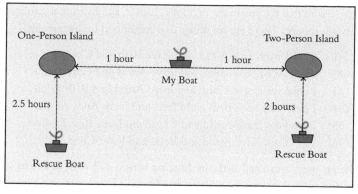

**Figure 4.4**

Utilitarians would (on the supposition that all the suffering would be comparable) recommend that I head east. Better to prevent two hours of suffering than one and a half hours of suffering—no matter that the two would be distributed across two people's lives, while the one and half would be concentrated in one person's life.

But we are not in a position to get that result. In this situation the six things that might happen are:

O1: I head west, Alex suffers one hour, Brian and Charles two hours.
O2: I head west, Brian suffers one hour, Alex and Charles two hours.
O3: I head west, Charles suffers one hour, Alex and Brian two hours.
O4: I head east, Brian and Charles suffer one hour, Alex two and a half hours.
O5: I head east, Alex and Charles suffer one hour, Brian two and a half hours.
O6: I head east, Alex and Brian suffer one hour, Charles two and a half hours.

The prospect associated with my heading west is 1/3 each of O1 to O3 and the prospect associated with my heading east is 1/3 each of O4 to O6. If minimal benevolence required of me that I prefer O4 to O3, O5 to O1, and O6 to O2, then minimal benevolence and rationality together would require of me that I head east. But minimal benevolence does not require these things of me. Alex is worse off in O4 than O3, Brian worse off in O5 than O1, Charles worse off in O6 than O2.

Someone moved by Scanlon's concerns about aggregation might applaud this result. But things are less clear-cut than they seem. The line of reasoning we have been pursuing here does entail that, in some situations, if we are decent and rational, then we will choose to save many people from a small amount of further suffering rather than choose to save a few people from a large amount of further suffering. Consider:

## Save One from More or Two from Less? Opaque Inter-Personal Conflict II

There is an island an hour to my west, an island an hour to my east, and an island to my north-east, a further hour from the island to my east. Alex, Brian, and Charles are stranded on these islands, one per island, but I do not know who is where. As before, there are other boats in the area. There is a boat steaming towards the west island. It will get there in two and a half hours. There's a boat steaming towards the east island. It will get there in two hours. It will take a further hour to get to the north-east island. As before, I have nothing better to do than hurry up the rescue. But which way should I go? I can save two people from an hour of suffering each by heading east-and-then-north-east, and one person from an hour and a half of suffering by heading west.

See Fig. 4.5 (with one person, I do not know who, on each island).

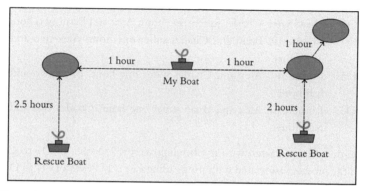

**Figure 4.5**

In this situation the twelve things that might happen are:

O1:   I head west, Alex suffers one hour, Brian two hours, Charles three hours.

O2:   I head west, Alex suffers one hour, Charles two hours, Brian three hours

O3:   I head west, Brian suffers one hour, Alex two hours, Charles three hours.

O4:   I head west, Brian suffers one hour, Charles two hours, Alex three hours.

O5:   I head west, Charles suffers one hour, Alex two hours, Brian three hours.

O6:   I head west, Charles suffers one hour, Brian two hours, Alex three hours.

O7:   I head east, Alex suffers 2.5 hours, Brian one hour, Charles two hours.

O8:   I head east, Alex suffers 2.5 hours, Charles one hour, Brian two hours.

O9:   I head east, Brian suffers 2.5 hours, Alex one hour, Charles two hours.

O10:   I head east, Brian suffers 2.5 hours, Charles one hour, Alex two hours.

O11: I head east, Charles suffers 2.5 hours, Alex one hour, Brian two hours.

O12: I head east, Charles suffers 2.5 hours, Brian one hour, Alex two hours.

The prospect associated with my heading west is 1/6 each of O1–O6. The prospect associated with my heading east is 1/6 each of O7–O12. Minimal benevolence requires of me that I prefer O7 to O4, O8 to O6, O9 to O2, O10 to O5, O11 to O1, and O12 to O3, so minimal benevolence and rationality together require of me that I head east, that I save the two people to my east from suffering an extra hour each, rather than save the one person to my west from suffering an extra one and a half hours.

We can make this effect very extreme. Suppose that in Fig. 4.6 (which is even more egregiously out of scale than usual) one person is on each of the islands.

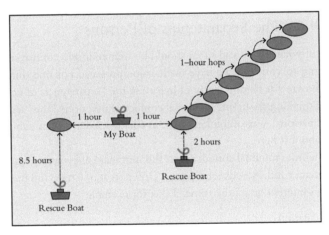

Figure 4.6

In this case minimal benevolence and rationality compel me to head east, to save the eight people in that direction from suffering an extra hour each, rather than save the one person to my west from suffering an extra seven and a half hours.

So, generally speaking, when does the reasoning apply, and when does it not apply? Well, to put it technically, it will apply whenever four conditions hold:

(i)  There is a group of people that I must, on pain of indecency, be minimally considerate of and benevolent toward.

(ii)  There is a person in that group, $p$, way for her to be, $w$, such that my credence that $p$ will be way $w$ if I perform the one action exceeds my credence that $p$ will be at least as well off as that if I perform the other action.

(iii)  The converse is not true. There is no person in that group, $p$, way that he or she might be, $w$, such that my credence that $p$ will be way $w$ if I perform the other action exceeds my credence that $p$ will be at least as well off as that if I perform the one action.

(iv)  Nothing else that I care about is at stake.

Under these conditions, the reasoning tells us that, if I am decent and rational, I will perform the one action.

## 4.6.  The Separateness of Persons

None of what I have said so far should be tremendously controversial or surprising to you. But we have made some progress. For one thing, we have shown that there is a way of bypassing the "separateness of persons" way of thinking about inter-personal conflicts. I mentioned the "separateness of persons" way of thinking back in Chapter 2. Let me say something more about it here.

Sometimes minimal consideration and minimal benevolence require us to arbitrate conflicts between a person's interests at one time and that same person's interests at another time. Take, for example:

Vaccination

My toddler does not like being at the business end of a needle. Should I drag her, screaming, to her scheduled vaccinations?

In this case there are two salient states of affairs.

| In *Intra-Personal Sacrifice*: | She gets her scheduled vaccinations today, and does not contract a vicious case of polio later. |
|---|---|
| In *Intra-Personal No-Sacrifice*: | She does not get her scheduled vaccinations today, and contracts a vicious case of polio later. |

I recognize that things are worse for her today in *Intra-Personal Sacrifice*—she is forced to witness a needle piercing her flesh, she acquires yet another reason to distrust adults who speak to her in soothing tones. I recognize that things are worse for her later in *Intra-Personal No-Sacrifice*—she is sick for a long time, and suffers residual paralysis for the rest of her life. But, being decent, I prefer *Intra-Personal Sacrifice* to *Intra-Personal No Sacrifice*, because I take the view that the costs to her are not evenly balanced. The costs to her in *Intra-Personal No-Sacrifice* far outweigh the costs to her in *Intra-Personal Sacrifice*. She has a better life, overall, in *Intra-Personal Sacrifice*.

But minimal consideration and minimal benevolence alone do not require us to arbitrate conflicts between the interests of different people. Take, for example:

Fanconi Anemia
My son has fanconi anemia. A bone marrow donation from my toddler daughter will brighten his prospects considerably. Should I drag her, screaming, into the operating theater?

In this case there are two salient states of affairs:

In *Inter-personal Sacrifice*: My daughter suffers today, my son does not suffer a great deal later.

In *Inter-personal No-Sacrifice*: My daughter does not suffer today, my son suffers a great deal later.

I recognize that things are worse for my daughter in *Inter-Personal Sacrifice*. I recognize that things are worse for my son in *Inter-Personal No-Sacrifice*. I could prefer *Inter-Personal Sacrifice* to *Inter-Personal No-Sacrifice*, taking the view that the costs to my son and daughter are not evenly balanced. The costs to my son in *Inter-Personal No-Sacrifice* far outweigh the costs to my daughter in *Inter-Personal Sacrifice*. But minimal consideration and minimal benevolence do not require this of me. The principles are silent.

Some very influential philosophers would welcome this silence. John Rawls, Robert Nozick, and Judy Thomson, among others, have argued that, if I weigh up costs and benefits across lives in the way that I weigh up costs and benefits within lives, under the impression that something morally important hangs on the result, then I am making a mistake. *Inter-Personal Sacrifice* is better than *Inter-Personal No-Sacrifice* for my son, *Inter-Personal No-Sacrifice* better than *Inter-Personal Sacrifice* for my daughter. There is no morally important sense in which *Inter-Personal Sacrifice* is simply better, or overall preferable, or to-be-favored, just because his suffering in *Inter-Personal No-Sacrifice* outweighs hers in *Inter-Personal Sacrifice*.

Indeed, the way these influential philosophers tell the story, this mistake has played a pivotal role in the history of normative ethics. From Jeremy Bentham and John Stuart Mill on, legions of philosophers have been drawn to utilitarianism, and the allure of utilitarianism derives from the allure of the mistake. As Rawls puts it:

The most natural way, then, of arriving at utilitarianism (although not, of course, the only way of doing so) is to adopt for society as a whole the principle of rational choice for one man. Once this is recognized, the place of the impartial spectator and the emphasis on sympathy in the history of utilitarian thought is readily understood. For it is by the conception of the impartial spectator and the use of sympathetic identification in guiding our imagination that the principle for one man is applied to society. It is this spectator who is conceived as carrying out the required organization of the desires of all persons into one coherent system of desire; it is by this construction that many persons are fused into one.[5]

Traditional utilitarians take an approach to cases like the Vaccination case that is fitting and good, and then try to extend it to cases like the Franconi Anemia case. Just as, in the Vaccination case, I can and should say that the short-term costs to my daughter are outweighed by the long-term benefits to her, so in the Fanconi Anemia case I can and should say that the short-term costs to my daughter are outweighed by the long-term benefits to my son. What matters is maximizing aggregate well-being. How well-being is distributed across people matters not at all.

Rawls, Nozick, and Thomson offer different accounts of exactly why this is a mistake. Rawls's account is open to interpretation. He says that we thereby "do not take seriously the distinction between persons." But he does not fully explain what the "distinction between persons" is, and why we should be taking it seriously.

Nozick's view is clearer. For Nozick the mistake consists in failing to acknowledge the fact that nothing with morally significant interests has different people as proper parts. Nozick writes:

Individually, we each sometimes choose to undergo some pain or sacrifice for a greater benefit or to avoid a greater harm: we go to the dentist to avoid worse suffering later; we do some unpleasant work for its results; some persons diet to improve their health or looks; some save money to support themselves when they are older. In each case, some cost is borne for the sake of the greater overall good.

[5] Rawls (1971: sect. 1.5).

Why not, *similarly*, hold that some persons have to bear some costs that benefit other persons more, for the sake of the overall social good? But there is no *social entity* with a good that undergoes some sacrifice for its own good. There are only individual people, different individual people, with their own individual lives. Using one of these people for the benefit of others, uses him and benefits the others. Nothing more. What happens is that something is done to him for the sake of the others. Talk of an overall social good covers this up. (Intentionally?) To use a person in this way does not sufficiently respect and take account of the fact that he is a separate person, that his is the only life he has.[6]

If my son and daughter were parts of a social creature that suffered a little, *in its daughter-ish part*, in *Inter-Personal Sacrifice*, and suffered a great deal, *in its son-ish part*, in *Inter-Personal No-Sacrifice*, then we might say that *Inter-Personal Sacrifice* was, overall, better for the creature—the suffering in its son-ish part in *Inter-Personal Sacrifice* outweighs the suffering in its daughter-ish part in *Inter-Personal No-Sacrifice*. And, if the interests of the creature mattered, maybe this would give us reason to favor *Inter-Personal Sacrifice*. By attributing significance to the "overall good," we are tacitly supposing that such a creature exists. But no such creature exists.

For Thomson the mistake emerges from our being lulled by the surface syntax of phrases in which "good" and "better" figure into thinking that states of affairs can be better or worse. But this is not so. It can be that this is a better car than that. It can be that this is a better knife than that. It cannot be that this is a better state of affairs than that. In her terms: "state-of-affairs is not a goodness fixing kind." The most we can say when comparing states of affairs is that one or other is better in a way. *Inter-Personal Sacrifice* is better in a way—it is better for my son. *Inter-Personal No-Sacrifice* is better in a way—it is better for my daughter. Neither is just better.[7]

But, whatever the source of the mistake, Rawls, Nozick, Thomson, and many others agree that it is a mistake to think that we should, as a matter of course, arbitrate conflicts between different people by weighing costs and benefits to the one against costs and benefits to the other.

What we have seen in the previous three chapters is that, even if this way of thinking is correct, even if I am not obliged to think it *better simpliciter* that one person suffer less rather than another suffer more, I must sometimes, on pain of being irrational or indecent, weigh different

---

[6] Nozick (1974: 32–3).

[7] See Thomson (1993) for an early statement of her view. See Thomson (2008) for the most recent version.

people's interests against each other. Just so long as I am minimally considerate, minimally benevolent, and rational, then sometimes, when I do not know very much about the people whose lives I am in a position to affect, I must behave as if their interests were perfectly balanced on a scale—a scale that will be decisively tipped by the tiniest grain of reason on either side.

For another thing, we have already said enough to draw some conclusions about two of the vexing problems from the Introduction: the "non-identity problem" and the problem of whether to kill-to-prevent-killings.

# 5

# The Same-Number Non-Identity Problem

## 5.1. A Canonic Presentation of the Problem

Remember Mary, the mother we talked about in the Introduction:

Not Postponing Conception

Mary is recovering from German measles. Her doctor recommends that she postpone her efforts to conceive a child for a couple of months. If she conceives a child in the next couple of months, then the child will, most likely, have significant health problems. Mary has no strong reasons to conceive a child immediately, but she does have a mild preference for *getting on with it*. She gets on with it. Nine and a half months later baby Mariette is born, with significant health problems. This is not a disaster— Mary is a woman of means, so Mariette's health problems do not impose a burden on wider society, and, on balance, Mariette has a rewarding life. But it is not great either—Mariette's health problems are a chronic source of anxiety, pain, and frustration to her.

Most people, when they think about Mary's behavior, have a more or less inchoate sense that something has gone awry, morally speaking. To put it in more precise terms than may be warranted by the inchoate sense: Mary does something wrong. She ought to have followed her doctor's advice, and waited a couple of months.

Why does Mary do something wrong? As I said earlier, normative ethicists, following Derek Parfit, would call this an instance of the "non-identity problem," more specifically the "same-number non-identity problem" (to distinguish it from the problem of what to say about cases in which our choices influence not just which people will exist, but also how many people will exist). They think it deserves the name "problem," rather than "question" or "query," because many of the obvious answers turn out to be unsatisfactory. I will briefly survey these answers here, and some reasons why normative ethicists have taken them to be unsatisfactory.

> *First Answer:*   Mary does wrong by making things worse for Mariette. It would have been better for Mariette if Mary had waited.

The problem with this answer is that, as we saw in the Introduction, it seems plausible to think that Mariette would not have been better off if Mary had waited, because Mariette would not have existed if Mary had waited. More carefully, the following all seem true:

*Reshuffling the Genetic Deck*
Most probably, if Mary had waited two months to conceive a baby, then she would have conceived a baby as genetically different from the actual Mariette as typical non-twin siblings are different.

*Genetic Essentialism*
If Mary had conceived a baby as genetically different from the actual Mariette as typical non-twin siblings are different, then Mariette would never have existed.

*Existence does not Harm Mariette*[1]
It would not have been better for Mariette if she had never existed.

It follows that, most probably, Mary has not made Mariette worse off. Most probably, it would not have been better for Mariette if Mary had waited.

> *Second Answer:*   Mary does wrong by making things worse. It would have been better (not *better for Mariette*, just *better*) if Mary had waited.

This was Parfit's solution to his problem. He appealed to a principle he called "The Same Number Quality Claim, or Q":

> If, in either of two possible outcomes the same number of people would ever live, it would be worse if those who live are worse off, or have a lower quality of life, than those who have ever lived.[2]

---

[1] I should mention that at least one philosopher denies this. See Benetar (1997), an essay aptly titled: "Why it is Better Never to Come Into Existence." This is an almost comically bleak view.
[2] Parfit (1983: 360).

If Mary had waited, then she would have conceived a child who would have been better off than Mariette actually is. So, by Q, things would have been better if Mary had waited. So she did wrong by failing to wait.

There are at least two reasons why many philosophers find Parfit's answer prima facie unsatisfactory. The first is that it is far from obvious that Mary has brought about a worse outcome by failing to wait. Obviously those philosophers who were moved by the "separateness of persons" objection to utilitarianism will not accept this. They will say that when we have two outcomes, one better for one person, the other better for another person, there is no interesting sense in which one can be just better than another. But the objectors need not be so radical. A quieter, and I think more sensible, objection is that Mary does not bring about a worse outcome in virtue of incommensurability in the values that determine who is better off than whom. Consider three outcomes:

M−: (the actual outcome) in which Mary conceives Mariette and Mariette has an on-balance-good-life, mildly blighted by health problems.

M: in which Mary conceives Mariette and Mariette has a life just like her actual life, but without the health problems.

J: in which Mary conceives John, a child very different from Mary, with different passions, habits, and patterns of thinking, and John goes on to live a healthy life.

It may be that Mariette in M is better off than Mariette in M−. It may also be that Mariette in M is no better or worse off than John in J. But it does not follow that John in J is better off than Mariette in M−. Just as there is incommensurability in the values that determine which of two restaurants is better, so there is incommensurability in the values that determine which of two people is better off.

Most probably, if Mary had waited to conceive a child, then she would have brought about an outcome like J. So, most probably, she would have brought about an outcome no better or worse than the actual outcome.

The second reason to find Parfit's answer prima facie unsatisfactory is that it is far from obvious that, when we make decisions about procreation, we have a standing obligation to make the world a better place. My wife and I did not conceive a child last year. Suppose that the world would have been better if we had conceived a child, not in virtue of the benefits that the child would have bestowed on actual people, but in virtue of the fact that the child would have been happy and healthy and fun-loving and so forth. Suppose that we were in a position to know that. Does it follow that we did something wrong? I say it does not! This is a sparklingly clear example of a case in which traditional act consequentialism seems too demanding. We are under no obligation to make the world better by creating happy children if we do not feel like doing so. So why does Mary have an obligation to make the world better by creating happ*ier* children if she does not feel like doing so?[3]

Moved by worries like this, several philosophers have returned to the idea that Mary's wrong is somehow personal. It is not about how she stands in relation to the world. It is about how she stands in relation to Mariette.

*Third Answer:*    Mary does wrong by somehow wronging Mariette, though she does not make Mariette worse off.

There are many ways to develop this answer. One is to say that Mary has wronged Mariette by violating Mariette's rights—you can violate somebody's rights without making them on balance worse off.[4] Another is to say that Mary has harmed Mariette in an illegitimate way—you can harm someone in an illegitimate way without making them worse off.[5]

One concern about these proposals is that they seem to invoke non-standard notions of "right" and "harm." What right of Mariette's does Mary violate? A right-not-to-be-born-with-health-problems-when-the-alternative-is-never-being-born-at-all?[6] Do we really have such rights? And can we really harm someone when they are predictably much better

---

[3] I should note that Parfit is agnostic about whether we make the world better by creating happy children. He showed, in the last part of Parfit (1983), that some formidable obstacles stand in the way of a full theory of when worlds containing different numbers of people are better or worse than one another. But that does not block the point being made here. The point is conditional: suppose I would have made the world better by conceiving a child last year. It does not follow that I did wrong by holding back.

[4] This broad approach was taken by James Woodward in Woodward (1986), and, more recently, by David Velleman in Velleman (1986).

[5] Variants of this approach are taken by Seana Schiffrin (see Schiffrin 1999), by B. Steinbock and R. McClamrock (see Steinbock and McClamrock 1994), and by Elizabeth Harman (see Harman 2004).

[6] David Velleman talks of a "right to be born into good enough circumstances" (Velleman 2008: 275). He also says: "A child to whom we give a lesser initial provision will have been wronged by our lack of due concern for human life in creating him—our lack of concern for human life itself, albeit in his case" (2008: 276). I do not think it necessary to show that Mary has violated any right of Mariette's, but, as you will see in the next section, I agree that it is helpful to focus on the attitudes of the parents.

off as a result of what we do? Can this, the fact that we "harmed" them in this odd way, really explain why we do wrong?

Another concern is that the proposals struggle to distinguish between cases that really should be distinguished. Contrast Not Postponing Conception with this case:

Going Ahead
Mary is trying to conceive a child. Her doctor tells her that if she succeeds then her child will have moderate health problems—"You can't avoid that. It's genetics." Mary does not let this cramp her style. Nine and a half months later baby Mariette is born, with just the health problems that Mary's doctor foresaw. This is not a disaster—on balance, Mariette has a rewarding life. But Mariette's health problems are a chronic source of anxiety, pain, and frustration to her.

If Mary harms Mariette, or violates her rights, in Not Postponing Conception, then it would seem that she does the same in Going Ahead. After all, the only difference between the cases is that in Not Postponing Conception there is a salient counterfactual alternative in which Mary conceives a different, healthy child—and that difference does not seem to bear on whether Mary harms Mariette or violates her rights. But we do not want to say that she does wrong or wrongs Mariette in Going Ahead.[7]

Will no straight answer work? Some philosophers have come to think so. They say that, after thirty years of failing to answer the question, we should conclude that it contains a false presupposition.

Fourth Answer: In fact Mary does no wrong. Once again, careful reflection shows us that a powerful moral intuition is misguided.[8]

This is a conclusion-of-the-last-resort. Let us see if we can avoid it.

---

[7] Parfit made a version of this point in response to Woodward in Parfit (1986). Schiffrin and Harman are both aware of it. Schiffrin appears to embrace the conclusion that Mary does wrong in the second case, and run with it—the harms that we bring upon our progeny by creating them are not, in general, balanced by the benefits of existence. Harman argues that, to explain why Mary does wrong in the first case but not in the second, we need to focus not just on the harm she did, but also on her reasons for action. In the first case she has weak reasons not to wait. In the second case she has strong reasons to go ahead (she wants a baby, we may assume, and this is the only way to have one). As you will see in the next section, I do not think it necessary to show that Mary has harmed Mariette in these cases, but I agree that it is helpful to focus on Mary's reasons for action.

[8] This view is taken by Melinda Roberts in Roberts (1998), and by David Boonin in Boonin (2008). Both philosophers work hard to persuade us that our intuitions about cases like Mary's are distorted by nearby cases, cases in which Mary does make somebody worse off.

## 5.2. Solving the Same-Number Non-Identity Problem

Happily, the assumptions we have made about benevolence and rationality give us an easy solution to the same-number non-identity problem. As a warm-up, consider a simpler, very unrealistic version of Mary's case.

Not Postponing Conception (Simplified)
As before, but this time Mary takes herself to be capable of conceiving only two children—Mariette and Jimmy. Mary regards it as equally likely that she will conceive either, whether or not she goes ahead or waits.

In this case, supposing that decency requires of Mary that she be minimally benevolent toward her future children and rationality requires of her that she follow the recommendations of prospectism, if Mary is decent and rational then she will wait.

The laborious way to see this is to observe that Mary has two relevantly different options:

Going full-steam ahead
Waiting

And there are four relevantly different things that might end up happening:

M−: in which Mary conceives Mariette, and she is unhealthy.
J−: in which Mary conceives Jimmy, and he is unhealthy.
M: in which Mary conceives Mariette, and she is healthy.
J: in which Mary conceives Jimmy, and he is healthy.

The prospect associated with going full-steam ahead is ½ each of M− and J−, while the prospect associated with waiting is ½ each of M and J. Supposing Mary is minimally benevolent toward the children she is in a position to have, she must prefer M to M−, J to J−. So, for any completion of her preferences, waiting must have higher expected utility than going full-steam ahead. So, by prospectism, it is rationally impermissible for her to go ahead.

The quick way to see it is to note that the prospects associated with the options open to her in this case are just the same as the prospects associated with the options open to her in:

Not Taking the Pills (Simplified)

Mary is pregnant, and recovering from German measles. Her doctor recommends that she take some pills. If she does not, then her child will, most likely, have significant health problems. If she does, then her child will, most likely, be healthy. She takes herself to have been capable of conceiving only two children—Mariette and Jimmy. She regards it as equally likely that either child is in her belly, whether or not she takes the pills.

And obviously Mary will take the pills in this case, if she is minimally benevolent toward her children and rational.

Now, in the realistic case the prospects associated with Mary's options are much more complicated (she has little idea what child she will conceive if she goes full-steam ahead, little idea what child she will conceive if she waits). But, just so long as the following as true:

Invariance   For any given child she might have, she regards it as no more or less likely that she will have that child if she waits than if she goes full-steam ahead.

then she will wait, if she is minimally benevolent and rational. The quick way to see why this is so is to note that, if Invariance is true, the prospects associated with the options available to her are relevantly just the same as the prospects associated with the options available to her in another case:

Not Taking the Pills

Again she is pregnant, and recovering from German measles. Again her doctor recommends that she take some pills. If she does not, then her child will, most likely, have significant health problems. If she does, then her child will, most likely, be healthy. But this time (as with real pregnancies) she does not have restricted ideas about whom she might have conceived.

And obviously she will take the pills in this case, if she is both minimally benevolent toward her children and rational.

## 5.3. Mariette's Complaint

So that is the solution to the same-number non-identity problem: if Mary were decent and rational, then she would have waited. Given the way she behaved, there must have been something defective about her—she was either rationally defective or morally defective.

Does it imply that Mary has somehow wronged *Mariette*? Well, a nice feature of the solution is its explanation of why Mariette, of all the people in the world, has a special complaint against Mary. Mariette cannot say: "You made me worse off." But she can say this: "Supposing that you acted rationally, you must not have been minimally benevolent toward all the children you were in a position to conceive. In particular (supposing you were not positively ill-willed toward any of the children you were in a position to conceive), you must not have been minimally benevolent toward *me*. You must not have preferred state of affairs M, in which I am healthy and conceived three months later, to state of affairs M−, in which I am unhealthy and conceived three months earlier. That is not just bad parenting. It is an improper indifference to *me*, an attitude that I am uniquely qualified to resent and complain about."

## 5.4. Objection: Again, what about Fairness?

"But wait," you might say. "What about Taurek and fairness? Does not fairness demand that we flip a coin when lives are at stake? Indeed, whether or not Taurek is right about saving one or many, is it not manifestly unfair to let *mild health issues* be a tie-breaker when lives are at stake? Consider one more rescue case:

Disease-Based Small Differences, Opaque Inter-Personal Conflict
As before, I know that one person is on an island to my west, another person on an island to my east, and I know almost nothing about these people. But this time both islands are three hours away. The only asymmetry I am aware of is this: the person on the western island has had health problems since birth.

Suppose I head east, on the grounds that the person on the eastern island will most probably be healthier, if I save him or her, than the person on the western island will be, if I save him or her. Then the western person might complain: 'This is desperately unfair! First I had to live with health problems. Then you used this very fact as grounds for saving eastern-person and leaving me to die. It is unfair to use my misfortune as grounds for further disadvantaging me.'"

Has the western person got a point? Maybe so. But, even if we concede the point, there is an important difference between this case and the Not Taking the Pills case. In the Not Taking the Pills case, if Mary waits to conceive her child, there is nobody unfairly discriminated against on grounds of his or her health, because the child Mary would have conceived if she had gone full-steam ahead never exists. These issues of fairness just do not arise when we think about procreation.

## 5.5. Objection: Contrary Desires

"But wait," you might say. "The argument applies only when Mary takes herself to have *no* reason to go full-steam ahead. Just so long as there is something else at stake for her, no matter how fickle (Scorpio-babies are just *so hip* right now!), it does not follow from what we have said that, if she is benevolent and rational, then she will heed her doctor's advice."

True, if we are to show that decency and rationality commit her to waiting in this new case, then we will need to assume that, to be decent, you must be more than just minimally considerate of, and minimally benevolent toward, the children you are in a position to have. You must also take considerations to do with the interests of the children you are in a position to save to have significant weight when they conflict with other considerations.

This is a further assumption, so it deserves another FLAG. But it is a safe assumption. Consider:

Not Taking the Mildly Unpleasant Pills
Again Mary is pregnant, and recovering from German measles. Her doctor recommends that she take some pills. If she does not, then her as-yet-unborn child will, most likely, have significant health problems. If she does, then her child will, most likely, be healthy. But this time the taking of the pills is very mildly unpleasant to her. They will not make her sick, but they are large, and swallowing them is a bit of a chore.

We all think that, in this case, if Mary is decent, then she will take the consideration "taking the pills will be good for my as-yet-unborn child" to be decisive. Her all-things-considered preference will be for chore-somely taking the pills and giving birth to a healthy child.

If this assumption is correct, if decency requires of you that you take considerations to do with the interests toward your children to have significant weight, then, by the same arguments as before, decency and rationality together require of Mary that she heed her doctor's advice when doing so will frustrate her mild desire to have a Scorpio-baby.

Just how far does this go? Just how considerate and benevolent must we be? Do decency and rationality together require of Mary that she heed her doctor's advice in these cases?

### Not Postponing Conception for a Long Time
Once again Mary's doctor recommends that she postpone her efforts to conceive a child, otherwise her child will most likely have significant health problems. But this time it is a two-year postponement, and she is at the tail end of her fertility curve. If she waits, then she may never have a child at all.

### Not Taking the Sickening Pills
Once again Mary is pregnant, and her taking some pills will, most likely, save her child from significant health problems. But this time there is a significant chance that the pills will damage Mary's liver.

I do not know. We have reached a point where platitudes about benevolence and practical rationality will not help us.

## 5.6. Objection: Desires about People Need People

"But wait," someone might say. "We have assumed that decency requires of Mary that, prior to conception, she be benevolent toward her future children, that she prefer, for example, that Jimmy live a better life than a worse life. But Jimmy does not, and will never, exist! You cannot have desires about things that never exist."

Maybe this is right. If so, then it is not right to say that decency requires of Mary that she have desires *about Jimmy*. But we can still say that it requires of her that she have some desires in the close vicinity. Consider my son Inigo. He is, touch wood, quite healthy. It might not have been like this. He might have come down with polio last year. Contrast a richly detailed description of the life he would have led if he had caught polio last year with a richly detailed description of his actual life. Suppose these descriptions had been presented to me before Inigo existed. "Here are two ways things might go. First, you conceive a child on this date . . . genetically like so . . . and you name him 'Inigo' . . . and he comes down with polio, suffering terribly . . . Second, you conceive a child on the same date . . . genetically just the same . . . and you name him 'Inigo' . . . and he does not come down with polio . . ." I think that, though I may have been incapable of forming desires about Inigo, in particular, I would and should, on pain of indecency, have desired that things go the second way. And that is all we need.

## 5.7. Objection: Essentialism about Origins

"But wait," someone might say. "If Mary understands what makes people who they are, then *Invariance* will not be true of her in the non-identity case. That principle says:

> *Invariance*   For any given child Mary might have, she regards it as no more or less likely that she will have that child if she waits than if she plunges full-steam ahead.

But people are essentially around the times at which they are conceived—they could not have been conceived at other times. Take Elizabeth II, for example. She was conceived in July 1925. If her parents had conceived a baby six months earlier, then, even if the baby had been genetically just the way she actually is, even if the baby had gone on to have a life just like her actual life (the crown, the solid pastel overcoats, the dour expression, and so forth), Elizabeth would never have existed. If Mary understands this deep fact about our essences, then she will not regard it as no more or less likely, for any given child she might have, that she will conceive that child if she waits than if she goes full-steam ahead. She will think, rather, like this. "Look, there's a range of different children I might conceive if I go full-steam ahead. Choose one of them, call him John, with a particular genetic profile, call it G-John. There is a very small chance that I will conceive John if I go full-steam ahead, but there is absolutely no chance that I will conceive John if I wait, because John can be conceived only this month. True, if I wait, then there is a very small, equal chance that I will have a child with the genetic profile G-John, but this child would not be John. He would be a qualitatively similar, numerically distinct child."

This is a funny view about essence and possible children. I think that, if my parents had conceived a child in January 1971, genetically just like me, and that child had gone on to live a life just like mine, up to the point where he wrote a book just like this one, then I would have been conceived six months before I was actually conceived. Of course, it is very unlikely that this would have happened, if they had conceived a child in January 1971. But, if they had somehow managed it, then the baby would have been *me*.

No matter. I will show, in the second part of this book, that, even if Mary adopts the highly unobvious view about essence and possible children, if she is decent and rational then she will heed her doctor's advice in the non-identity case. This is because, if she is decent and rational, then she will prefer that she conceive a particular healthy child at a certain time, rather than conceive a genetically identical, numerically distinct, unhealthy child some time earlier.

My argument will also allow us to cut yet further into the jungle of normative ethics, to address cases in which I know precisely who I am in a position to benefit by doing what.

# 6

# Killing-to-Prevent-Killings

## 6.1. Dirty Hands

Recall, from the Introduction:

Human Fuel

While piloting a steel, steam-engined boat across the bleak South Seas, you receive a distress call from Amy, who has been left to die of thirst on a nearby, bare island by cruel pirates. Knowing that you are the only boat in the area, you pick her up, and then receive another distress call from Brian and Celia, left to die of thirst on a not-so-nearby, bare island by more cruel pirates. You do not have enough coal to get to them, and no part of your steel boat will serve as fuel . . . but Amy is both large and dehydrated . . . Knock her on the head, shove her in the furnace and you will make it over there. And nobody but you will ever know.

As I said, this is a very important sort of case in normative ethics. It divides *act consequentialists* from their opponents, *deontologists* (the more unwieldy, but more accurate, term is *agent-relative constraints theorists*). Act consequentialists tend to say[1] that it is permissible or obligatory to shove Amy in the furnace. Acting rightly is all about doing the best you can, and it will be better if one person dies than if two people die. Deontologists tend to say[2] that it is not. Acting rightly is all about respecting rights (or not-violating hypothetical contracts, or abiding by excellent rules), and you will be

---

[1] Of course, one might be an act consequentialist and hold that the state of affairs in which you kill Amy and thereby prevent Brian and Celia from being killed is worse than the state of affairs in which you do not, and Brian and Celia are killed. This is an interesting but unpopular view.

[2] And one might be a deontologist and say that, though we have inviolable rights, we do not have an inviolable right not to be killed to prevent others from being killed. This is another interesting but unpopular view.

egregiously violating Amy's rights by killing her. And, as I mentioned, much has been written on this dispute, with much back and forth between the two sides. In this chapter I will focus on one strain of the dispute: the "dirty hands" objection to deontology.

Here is a charge that consequentialists level at deontologists:

"Put in this situation in which you can kill one person to prevent two people from being killed, you refrain from killing, and you do so willfully. You willfully favor a state of affairs in which two people are killed by someone else, call it *Refrain*, over a scenario in which one person is killed by you, call it *Kill*. Now, the only morally relevant differences between the states of affairs are that in Refrain an extra person dies, and in Refrain *you* are not doing any killing. If you favor Refrain it must be because you care about the second difference (surely you don't want an extra person to die!). But that's just selfishness on your part. You don't want to get your hands dirty. And you would rather that an extra person die than that your hands be dirty. Maybe, with great effort, you can persuade me that morality allows us to be selfish in this way, but you will never persuade me that morality requires us to be selfish in this way."

Deontologists standardly say two, quite different things in reply. The first:

"Yes, I willfully favor the state of affairs Refrain over the state of affairs Kill. Yes, in Refrain I do no killing. But it is a mistake to say that this, and the fact that 'an extra person dies' in Refrain, are the only morally relevant differences between Refrain and Kill. Amy lives in Refrain, but dies in Kill! That is a big difference between the states of affairs. Why did you not note it as a morally relevant difference? I guess because you think that Amy's death in Kill is *cancelled out* by Brian's death in Refrain. You think this because you are in the grip of an utterly wrong-headed utilitarian moral theory, where you think of things that happen to people as morally relevant to the extent that they add value to the world or subtract value from the world, and where you regard people as interchangeable bearers of value, like coins. The loss of one quarter is cancelled out by the acquisition of another. The death of one person is cancelled out by the saving of another. But I entirely reject that theory."

The second:[3]

"Yes, I bring about Refrain. Yes, there is a sense in which I do so 'willfully'—there is nothing interfering with me, I act from my own free will. But you are mis-characterizing my motivational structure by saying that I 'want' Refrain to come about or that I 'prefer' that Refrain come about. I whole-heartedly prefer, want, wish, desire in every interesting sense of the term, that Kill come about. It is just that my desires do not move me to act in this case. In this case I act, not out of inclination, but out of *duty*."

I will argue, in this chapter, that the line of reasoning we have been pursuing so far shows that the first reply does not do the work that deontologists need it to do. This alone is progress, I think, in debates about killing. I will then look at what more we need to assume in order to reject the second reply.

## 6.2. Ignorant Killing

Notice that the reasoning we have been pursuing so far sheds no direct light on Human Fuel. In Human Fuel I know full well that it is Amy whom I am considering throwing in the boiler. But it does some shed light on some cases in the vicinity, cases in which I do not know exactly whom I am in a position to kill.

Fuel in a Gorilla Suit
As before, you discover that Amy, Brian, and Celia have been left to die of thirst on nearby islands by cruel pirates, one on an island nearer to you, the other two on an island farther from you. But this time you do not know who is where. As before you head to the near island. But this time you find that the cruel pirates have taped the person on the near island into a gorilla suit. You grab him or her by the copious body hair, and heave him or her into your boat. What to do now? You lack coal to get to the other two. But this person in a gorilla suit is fat and dehydrated . . .

In this case there are six things that might end up happening:

O1:  You run out of fuel, and Brian and Celia die of thirst.
O2:  You run out of fuel, and Amy and Celia die of thirst.
O3:  You run out of fuel, and Amy and Brian die of thirst.

---

[3] Thanks to David Sussman for first putting this to me.

O4: You shove Amy in the boiler, and rescue Brian and Celia.
O5: You shove Brian in the boiler, and rescue Amy and Celia.
O6: You shove Celia in the boiler, and rescue Amy and Brian.

The prospect associated with shoving the person in the gorilla suit in the boiler is 1/3 each of O4–O6. The prospect associated with not shoving the person in the gorilla suit in the boiler is 1/3 each of O1–O3. So, if you are rational, then, just so long as you prefer O5 to O1, O6 to O2, and O4 to O1, you will shove. A deontologist who does not shove in this case must, supposing that she is rational, either not prefer O5 to O1, or not prefer O6 to O2, or not prefer O4 to O1.[4]

Now suppose we accuse the deontologist of selfishness, as before. Can she defend her attitude? Well, notice that this time she cannot say: "True, I don't prefer [for example] O5 to O1, but there are many morally relevant differences between O5 and O1, beyond the fact that I kill in O5 and I refrain from killing in O1—*different people die in O5 and O1*." She cannot say this because it is not true—Brian and Celia die in O1, only Brian dies in O5. This time the only relevant differences between the two states of affairs are that in O1 Celia dies, and in O1 you do no killing.[5]

So, in this case, the deontologist's first defense against the "Dirty Hands" objection does her no good. She must appeal to her second defense.

## 6.3. Acting against your Preferences

Is the deontologist's second defense any good? First, we need to get a sense of how, exactly, that defense is supposed to go. What does the

---

[4] Will deontologists refrain from shoving? A sociological observation: though there are differences between Human Fuel and Fuel in a Gorilla Suit, I do not know of a deontologist who thinks the differences morally significant. I do not know of a deontologist who thinks it impermissible to shove Amy in the boiler in Human Fuel, permissible to shove the person in the gorilla suit in the boiler in Fuel in a Gorilla Suit. This is not an accident. All of the arguments in favor of not killing in Human Fuel that we reviewed back in the Introduction tell in favor of not killing in Fuel in a Gorilla Suit.

[5] Of course there are some other differences. In O1 Brian dies of thirst, in O5 he dies in a ship's boiler. In O5 his death plays a causal role in the saving of others, in O1 he is killed, but his death plays no such role. If we think these differences are relevant, then we should consider, at the cost of some realism, a case in which the potential killings are all of the same type (by killing one person in a certain way as a means to saving others, I can prevent two people from being killed in the same way as a means to saving others . . . etc.). I will not try your patience by spelling this out.

deontologist mean by saying that she acts against her preferences when she refrains from shoving the gorilla-suited person in the boiler?

The deontologist has certain mental attitudes. For example, she believes some things, she desires other things, and she takes certain considerations to be reasons to desire, believe, and do yet other things. One thing she might mean is that her action is not guided by these mental attitudes. She refrains from shoving the gorilla-suited person in the boiler in spite of all her beliefs, desires, and taking-considerations-to-be-reasons.

This does not seem psychologically realistic. It certainly does look as if the deontologist takes some considerations to be decisive reasons to refrain from shoving the gorilla-suited person in the boiler: *that would be killing the person!* ... *it would be a gross violation of the person's rights!* ... etc. And it certainly does look as if these considerations move her to refrain from shoving the gorilla-suited person in the boiler.

Nor, even if it were true, would it amount to much of a defense. If the deontologist's actions were entirely irresponsive to her reasoning, then she could fairly be described as irrational.

Another thing the deontologist might mean is that there are two kinds of thing she has practical attitudes toward: *states of affairs* and *actions*. These are different. States of affairs are ways for collections of entities to be. Actions are things you do. And, while her actions are of course guided by her attitudes, they are not guided by her attitudes toward states of affairs. She wholly prefers, for example, O5, the state in which she kills Brian, and Amy and Celia survive, to O1, in which the pirates kill Brian and Celia, and Amy survives. But it is her attitude toward the actions of leaving-the-person-in-the-gorilla-suit alone and shoving-the-person-in-the-gorilla-suit-in-the-boiler that guides her. She prefers the former.

I find this a bit mysterious. Actions and states of affairs are intimately connected. The deontologist knows that, if she performs the action of shoving-the-person-in-the-gorilla-suit-in-the-boiler, then she will bring about a state of affairs in which she shoves a person in a gorilla suit in a boiler. She decisively disfavors the action on the grounds that it involves grossly violating someone's rights. Why, then, does she not decisively disfavor the state of affairs on the grounds that it involves her grossly violating someone's rights? And is it really true that she does not decisively disfavor the state of affairs? After all, she willfully, knowingly, brings it about when she has the chance.

A less mysterious, to me, way of developing much the same idea appeals to two different senses of the words "prefer," "desire," "want," and "favor." To prefer, or want, or desire, or favor in the *narrow* sense is to have an attitude that guides your affective responses to things happening. So, if you desire$_{narrow}$ something, then, typically, absent complications, you will take pleasure in it happening, or take pleasure in the prospect of it happening, or take pleasure in the news that it has happened. To prefer, or want, or desire, or favor in the *wide* sense is to have an attitude that guides your actions. So, if you desire$_{wide}$ something, then typically, absent complications, you will try to bring it about.

These two sorts of wanting may come apart. In masochistic moments you may truly say:

"It's precisely because I don't want$_{narrow}$ to do it, that I want$_{wide}$ to do it."

In generous moments you may truly say:

"I don't want$_{wide}$ to do what I want$_{narrow}$ to do, I want$_{wide}$ to do what you want$_{narrow}$ to do."

And, when you are preparing to satisfy some onerous duty, and I ask you whether you really want to do it, you may truly say:

"Yes, I want$_{wide}$ to do it. But no, I do not want$_{narrow}$ to do it."

On this way of thinking, this is exactly what is going on with the deontologist in Fuel in a Gorilla Suit. She prefers$_{narrow}$ outcome O5, in which she kills Brian, to outcome O1, in which the pirates kill Brian and Celia. If she were unsure about whether she had killed Brian or the pirates had killed Brian and Celia, the news that she had killed Brian would please her. But she prefers$_{wide}$ outcome O1 to outcome O5. That is why she refrains from killing.

And, on this way of thinking, in assessing the deontologist for rationality, we must attend to whether her actions are guided by her wide preferences—which indeed they are. But in assessing her for moral decency we must attend to whether her narrow preferences are selfless and pure—which indeed they are.

Is this a good defense? We have arrived at another obstacle that platitudes about practical rationality and decency will not help us surmount. Some further assumptions are needed. Time for another FLAG.

We do tend to think that sometimes being a decent person involves acting willfully but *grudgingly*—doing something while taking no pleasure in doing it. Back when I was in prep school it was part of the job of a headmaster to administer beatings. My own headmaster did this with a theatrical display of anguish and pain. It really did hurt him as much as it hurt us—or so we were led to think. My cousin's headmaster maintained no such posture. Offenses committed on a Sunday (when the boys had most freedom to offend) were punished the next Saturday, to draw out expectation. When the dread day arrived, the headmaster would summon boys individually to his desk, on which he would have placed the beating-slipper, to focus attention, and treat them to a sermon on earthly iniquity, always culminating with the line "So, ——, you've had your fun, now I'll have mine!"

History has not been kind to my cousin's headmaster. People tend to think ill of him (though, curiously, my cousin does not—which says something about the effects of English boarding school on a developing psyche). But history has been kinder to my headmaster. He wanted the best for us, and suppressed his pacifistic instincts.

Maybe history has judged wisely concerning the two headmasters. But my headmaster's attitudes were importantly unlike the deontologist's attitudes in the <u>Fuel in a Gorilla Suit</u> case. For the deontologist, the telling consideration is this:

Pro-O1: In O1, *I* do no killing.

The deontologist concedes that it would reflect badly on her character if she took this consideration to be a decisive reason to prefer_narrow O1 (in which someone else kills Brian and Celia) to O5 (in which she kills Brian). But she does take this consideration to be a decisive reason to prefer_wide O1 to O5 (it is the only thing that O1 has going for it, in relation to O5) and she claims that this does not reflect badly on her character.

What made my cousin's headmaster a morally suspect fellow was his taking pleasure in his boys' pain—or, to put it in the clunky but accurate terminology we have been using, that he took the consideration

Pro-Beating: It will cause the boys pain.

to be a decisive reason to prefer_narrow that he punish them. But, just as this reflected badly on his character, so it would have reflected badly on his character if he had taken Pro-Beating to be a decisive reason to prefer_wide that he punish them. My headmaster, on the other hand, took a different consideration:

Pro-Beating*: This will benefit the boys, in the long run.

to be a decisive reason to prefer$_{wide}$ that he punish his boys. And it would not have been unseemly (though psychologically unrealistic) to have taken this to be a decisive reason to prefer$_{narrow}$ that he punish them.

So the challenge for the deontologist is to explain how there can be *one* consideration such that it would be unseemly for her narrow, affect-guiding attitudes to be sensitive to it, but seemly for her wide, action-guiding attitudes to be sensitive to it.

I am not optimistic that a convincing explanation can be given. In this case it seems to me that, if the deontologist would evince unseemly self-preoccupation (not *selfishness*, exactly, because it is not her interests she is caring about, but her status as one who does not violate rights) by taking pleasure from a state of affairs O1 coming about, rather than a state of affairs like O5, then she would evince the same unseemly self-preoccupation by moving to bring about a state of affairs like O1, rather than a state of affairs like O5.

The general principle that would give us this result is

*Dominance*:
If you are decent and the only relevant-to-you differences between state of affairs S and state of affairs S* are:
   (i) S significantly pareto-dominates S*. All the same people exist in S and S*. Everybody (including yourself, remember) is at least as well off in S as in S*. Somebody is significantly better off in S than in S*.
   (ii) You stand in different causal relations to the good and bad things that happen to people in S and S*.
then you prefer S to S*.

Roughly, if you are decent, then you care more about good things happening to people (including yourself) than you care about whether you make good or bad things happen to people.

This is a powerful principle, with far-ranging implications. I will explore them further in Part III.

# PART II

# Introduction to Part II

The reasoning from the past six chapters gives out at the point where we come to know about precisely whom we are in a position to benefit by doing what. It tells us nothing about what I will do if I am decent and rational and I come to know that Andy is on the closer eastern island, Ben on the farther, western island. It tells us nothing about what Mary will do if she is decent and rational and comes to know (by some extraordinary means—by consulting an oracle or what-not) precisely whom she will conceive if she goes full-steam ahead and precisely whom she will conceive if she waits. To tackle these sorts of cases we need some more powerful tools to work with. I will develop such tools in the next five chapters.

# 7

# Robust Essences

My feet are currently resting on a table. The table could have been an inch to the right of where it actually is. The table could not have been a luminous ball of plasma $7 \times 10^8$ meters in diameter, protected from gravitational implosion by fusion in its core. In philosophy speak: the table is *contingently* where it actually is, *essentially* not-a-star. All such facts, facts about how the table could and could not have been, are facts about the *essence* of the table.

This chapter is about the essences of people. In the first section I will make one small claim about the essences of people. Then I will defend it against objections.

Before we get to that, I should mention that there has been a good deal of sophisticated philosophical work on essence, mostly conducted under the guise of "theories of the semantics of de re modal sentences" (theories about what makes sentences about how particular things could or could not have been true or false). I will discuss these theories in Chapter 9, but largely ignore them in this chapter. There is a point to this. The small claim around which this chapter is centered is compatible with all mainstream general theories of de re modality. If it were incompatible with a general theory of de re modality, then that would be a serious problem for the theory.

## 7.1. Imperfect Fragility

How different could people have been? On one view there are no limits to how different they could have been. Barack Obama could have been an early twentieth-century European dictator. Hillary Clinton could have been a pterodactyl's left kidney. Gary Kasparov could have been a chess-board. You could have been a cloud of sulfur in the atmosphere of Venus.

Most people reject this view. They think that, for some dimensions of qualitative sameness and difference, there are limits to how different people could have been along these dimensions. They make claims like this:

*Parental Essentialism*
All people have their parents essentially. No person could have had different parents than he or she actually had.

*Psychological Essentialism*
All people have some component of their psychology essentially. No person could have been very different, psychologically speaking, than he or she actually is.

*Genetic Essentialism*
All people have some component of their genome essentially. No person could have been very different, genetically speaking, than he or she actually is.

What would render such claims false? The existence of people whose essences are more robust along the relevant dimensions. People like:

Peter: whose Essence is Highly Robust with Respect to *Parenthood*
Peter's father is Patrick. He could have had a different father. If Peter's mother had had a secret, brief tryst with Mike the milkman and (by a strange fluke) the result had been a child exactly like the actual Peter in all interesting non-parental respects (genetically just like the actual Peter, born at the same time as the actual Peter . . . and so on), then Peter would still have existed. He would have been Mike's son.

Phil: whose Essence is Highly Robust with Respect to *Psychology*
Phil is a kind old fellow. But he could have had a very different psychology. Phil is the only child of Phyllis. If scientists had kidnapped Phyllis's only child immediately after his birth and subjected him to Orwellian reconditioning in a successful effort to create a monster, utterly different from the actual Phil in all interesting psychological respects, but just like the actual Phil in all interesting non-psychological respects, then Phil would still have existed. He would have been mean.

Gawain: whose Essence is Highly Robust with Respect to *Genetics*
Gawain is tall, male, dark-haired, and brown-eyed—all the result of his genes. But he could have had very different genes. If, at just the time

Gawain was actually conceived, his parents had conceived a small, female, blonde-haired, and blue-eyed child, then Gawain would still have existed. He would have been small, female, blonde-haired, and blue-eyed.

Maybe you find it obvious that the claims are true, that there are no people like Peter, Phil, and Gawain. Maybe you find it obvious that they are false, that there are such people. Maybe you do not know what to think.

No matter. My argument in this part of the book will rest on a very weak claim about essence, a claim that I expect you to agree with. Here is the first component of the claim:

*Personal Essence is not Perfectly Fragile*
All people could have been ever-so-slightly different along any natural dimension of qualitative sameness and difference.

What would render this false? The existence of people whose essences are perfectly fragile along some natural dimension of qualitative sameness and difference, people like:

Psamantha: whose Essence is Perfectly Fragile with Respect to *Psychology*
Psamantha could not have been in any way different, psychologically speaking, from the way she actually is. So, for example, Psamantha has always had a mild aversion to peas. If her parents had raised a child lacking an aversion to peas, but in all other respects just like the actual Psamantha, then Psamantha would never have existed.

Gene: whose Essence is Perfectly Fragile with Respect to *Genetics*
Gene could not have been in any way different, genetically speaking, from the way he actually is. Focus, for example, on a tiny fragment of Gene's noncoding (so-called 'junk' or 'inert') DNA. If the meiotic process that actually gave rise to Gene had gone ever so slightly differently, and that tiny fragment had been ever-so-slightly different, then Gene would never have existed, though there would have existed a child just like the actual Gene in all non-genetic respects.

Bertha: whose Essence is Perfectly Fragile with Respect to *Time-of-Birth*
Bertha was born on February 8, 2006 at 23:17:45. She could not have been born a second later. Bertha's mother, Jane, squeezed her out with one long, final push. If Jane had paused to collect her breath, then Bertha would never have existed.

Cosmo: whose Essence is Perfectly Fragile with Respect to *Time-of-Conception*

Cosmo was conceived on July 28, 2002 at 20:43:21, when a particular sperm (call him Sam) met a particular egg (call her Eve). Cosmo could not have been born a second later. If Sam-the-sperm had waggled his tail one less time, and met Eve-the-egg a second later, and the result had been a baby exactly like the actual Cosmo in all interesting non-time-of-conception respects, who went on to live a life exactly like Cosmo's in all interesting non-time-of-conception respects, then Cosmo would never have existed.

But I say that there are no such people. We are all more robust than this. Here is the second component of my claim:

*Knowledge of Robustness*

Our knowledge that actual people do not have perfectly fragile essences is not based on knowledge of precisely how they are, qualitatively speaking.

What does this mean? It means that we may know that people do not have perfectly fragile essences, though we know almost nothing about their particular features. I know that you, dear reader, could have been an inch taller than you actually are. But I have no idea of exactly how tall you are. If I were preparing to meet you and measure you for the first time, then it would be right (though, I admit, a tad *strange*) for me to think:

If my dear reader turns out to be five feet tall, then it will turn out that he or she could have been five feet and one inch tall. If my dear reader turns out to be six feet tall, then it will turn out that he or she could have been six feet and one inch tall. Whatever height my dear reader turns out to be, it will turn out that he or she could have been an inch taller than that.

And if I were preparing to enquire about your date of birth, then it would be right for me to think:

If it turns out that my dear reader was born on April 3, 1971, then it will turn out that he or she could have been born on April 2, 1971. If it turns out that my dear reader was born on August 29, 1946, then it will turn out that he or she could have been born on August 28, 1946. Whatever the day on which my dear reader turns out to have been born, it will turn out that he or she could have been born a day earlier.

And if I were preparing to discover (don't ask how) the moment at which you were conceived, then it would be right for me to think:

"If it turns out that my dear reader was conceived on March 16, 1964 at 9:16:37 pm, then it will turn out that he or she could have been conceived on March 16, 1964 at 9:16:36 pm. Whatever the second at which my dear reader turns out to have been conceived, it will turn out that he or she could have been conceived a second earlier."

I take this to be obvious. But, once again, a great deal of weight is going to rest on this claim, so let me anticipate some objections.

## 7.2. Objection: Does this not Mean we are *not at all* Fragile—that there are no Limits to How Different we could have Been?

"But wait!" you might say. "If there's anything at all that the history of Western Philosophy definitively, unequivocally teaches us, it is that we should be suspicious of claims about small-differences-not-making-big-differences. Take the key premise of the famous Sorites argument:

*Small Differences*
For any number $n$, if $n$ grains of sand, placed on top of one another and allowed to settle under the influence of gravity, do not make a heap of sand, then $n+1$ grains of sand, placed on top of one another and allowed to settle under the influence of gravity, do not make a heap of sand.

It looks highly "obvious" to the uninitiated. But the initiated know that it must be false, because it entails, absurdly, the falsity of:

*Heap and No Heap*
Two grains of sand, placed on top of one another and allowed to settle under the influence of gravity, do not make a heap of sand. But a billion grains of sand, placed on top of one another and allowed to settle under the influence of gravity, do make a heap of sand.

Does not Knowledge of Robustness have similarly absurd implications? You have said that it would be right for you to think:

"If my reader is 5 feet tall, then he or she could have been 5 feet and
1 inch tall."
"If my reader is 5 feet and 1 inch tall, then he or she could have been
5 feet and 2 inches tall."

. . .

"If my reader is 6 feet, 11 inches tall, then he or she could have been
7 feet tall."
Does it not follow that it would be right for you to think:
"If my reader is 5 feet tall, then he or she could have been 7 feet tall."

And, by repeated application of this reasoning, does it not follow, absurdly,
that it would be right for you to think:

"If my reader is a mousey old lady from Dorset, then she could have
been a violent young weight-lifter from Australia."

Does it not follow, absurdly, that our essences are not at all fragile?

No, it does not follow. You cannot make inferences of this type from
sentences of this type—sentences that contain subjunctive conditionals
nested inside indicative conditionals. Here is a simple example that should
illustrate why: I am due a birthday present from you, and I know you have
five options:

a dirt cheap gesture-at-a-present—costing $5
a forgettable little present—costing $20
a cautious, solid present—costing $50
a pick-of-the-bunch present—costing $100
a disturbingly over-the-top present—costing $500

My spies tell me that you have selected a present, and that it is less than you
can afford, but I do not know which you have selected or what you can
afford. In these circumstances, it is right for me to think:

"If my dear reader bought me the dirt cheap gesture-at-a-present, then
he or she could have bought me the forgettable little present."
"If he or she bought me the forgettable little present then he or she
could have bought me the cautious, solid present."

. . .

"If he or she bought me the pick of the bunch present then he or she
could have bought me the disturbingly over-the-top present."

But it does not follow that it is right for me to think:

> "If my dear reader bought me the dirt cheap gesture-at-a-present, then he or she could have bought me the disturbingly over-the-top present."

Maybe, if you bought me the dirt cheap gesture-at-a-present, the forgettable little present is all you could have afforded.

And here is a more careful, formal analysis of the mistake the objector is making. By *Knowledge of Robustness* there is some sequence of exclusive (it cannot be that more than one of them is true) propositions $P_0, \ldots, P_k$, such that:

(i) Each proposition in the sequence describes, in great qualitative detail, a way for the world to be.

(ii) The propositions in the sequence differ only with respect to the life they attribute to the reader of my book.

(iii) For each $P_i$, it is right for me to think "If $P_i$ is true, then it will turn out to be true of the reader of my book that, if $P_{i+1}$ had instead been true, he or she would still have existed."

(iv) $P_0$ describes my reader as a mousey old lady from Dorset.

(v) $P_k$ describes my reader as a young weight-lifter from Australia.

The worry is that this entails that it would be right for me to think:

> "If $P_0$ is true, then it will turn out to be true of the reader of my book that if $P_k$ had instead been true then she would still have existed."

Why accept this entailment? Maybe the objector thinks it falls out of the logic of conditional propositions. Let "$Rx$" stand for "x is my reader," Let "$\rightarrow$" stand for the indicative conditional and let "$\square\rightarrow$" stand for the counterfactual conditional. I have said that it is appropriate for me to accept all of:

(0)$P_0 \rightarrow \exists x(Rx \wedge P_1 \square\rightarrow Rx)$
(1)$P_1 \rightarrow \exists x(Rx \wedge P_2 \square\rightarrow Rx)$
...

(k)$P_{k-1} \rightarrow \exists x(Rx \wedge P_k \square\rightarrow Rx)$

And maybe this might seem like a good inference-schema:

$$\frac{A \rightarrow (B \square\rightarrow C)}{B \rightarrow (C \square\rightarrow D)}$$
$$\overline{A \rightarrow (B \square\rightarrow (C \square\rightarrow D))}$$

So it might seem that (0) and (1) entail:

(I)$P_0 \rightarrow \exists x(Rx \wedge P_1 \square \rightarrow (Rx \wedge P_2 \square \rightarrow Rx))$

And maybe this might seem like a good inference-schema:

$$\frac{A \rightarrow (B \square \rightarrow (C \square \rightarrow D))}{A \rightarrow (C \square \rightarrow D)}$$

So it might seem like I entails:

(I\*)$P_0 \rightarrow \exists x(Rx \wedge P_2 \square \rightarrow Rx)$

And by repeated application of this reasoning, we get:

(C)$P_0 \rightarrow \exists x(Rx \wedge P_k \square \rightarrow Rx)$

But both inference-schemas are bad. To see why the first is bad, we need look no further than the birthday-present case. Let A be the proposition that you give me the $5 gift, B the proposition that you give me the $20 gift, C the proposition that you can afford the $20 gift, D the proposition that you can afford the $50 gift. Now the antecedents hold but the consequent does not.

## 7.3. Objection: Might we not be at the Limit of our Essence?

"But wait!" you might say. "Can we really know, without knowing exactly how actual people are, qualitatively speaking, that their essences are not perfectly fragile along some dimension? How do we know that someone has not reached the limit of his or her essence? How do we know, for example, that there is not someone in India who is exactly 6 feet tall, and essentially between 5 and 6 feet tall?"

I am not entirely sure what to make of this worry. Perhaps the best I can do is to sketch out a general theory of essence that would give it some force, and then say why I think it is false.

Suppose that essence worked like this. For each person who may or may not exist down here on Earth, there exists, in some noumenal realm, a *paradigm* of that person, with certain precise qualities. So, for example, there is a paradigm Barack Obama. Whether Barack Obama exists down here on Earth is determined by whether, down here on Earth, there is a person sufficiently qualitatively similar to the paradigm-Barak Obama (see Fig. 7.1).

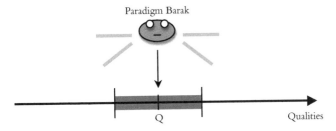

**Figure 7.1**

The paradigm-Barack Obama has qualities Q. If someone with sufficiently similar qualities (represented by points in the shaded region) exists down here on Earth, then Barack Obama exists down here on Earth. Otherwise he does not.

If essence worked like this, then we should reject *Knowledge of Robustness*. Concerning my dear reader, I should think:

> "Maybe my dear reader is taller than his or her paradigm. Indeed, maybe my dear reader is as much taller than his or her paradigm as it is possible for him or her to be. Maybe my dear reader has reached the *limit of his or her essence*. If so, then he or she could not have been a quarter inch taller than he or she is."

But essence does not work like this. There is no external paradigm-you. *You* are the paradigm-you, the very best exemplar of yourself.

## 7.4. Objection: Could People have Failed to be People?

"But wait!" you might say. "Maybe it is possible to reach the limit of your essence. All people are essentially people. No person could have been a cat, or a dog, or a stone. No person could have failed to be a person. Now take a person who is, along some natural dimension of qualitative sameness and difference, *right on the edge* of being a person—nothing that is further along the dimension than she actually is counts as a person. This person could not have been any further along the dimension than she actually is— if she could have been ever-so-slightly further along the dimension then she could have failed to be a person, but she could not have failed to be a person."

This worry raises some very interesting and complex issues concerning the shape and precision of the boundaries between people and non-people. But we need not get into these issues here. For present purposes we only need our principle to apply to *central* people—people who are nowhere near the boundaries between people and non-people. For present purposes the following, restricted principles will do fine:

*Personal Essence is not Perfectly Fragile (Restricted)*
All central people could have been ever-so-slightly different along any natural dimension of qualitative sameness and difference.

*Knowledge of Robustness (Restricted)*
Our knowledge that actual, central people do not have perfectly fragile essences is not based on knowledge of precisely how they are, qualitatively speaking.

## 7.5. Objection: Are there really *Context-Independent Facts* about Essence?

"But wait!" you might, finally, say. "We have been doing some very old-fashioned metaphysics here. We have been proceeding as if it makes sense to ask, in a vacuum, about which doctrines about essence are correct. Maybe this is not right. Maybe the truth or falsity of claims about essence is a context-dependent matter. Sometimes, in some contexts, it is appropriate to think of essences as more fragile. At other times, in other contexts, it is appropriate to think of essences as more robust."

I am sympathetic to the view that the truth or falsity of claims about essence is a context-dependent matter, so let me say something about the context in which we are operating here. It is one in which we are interested in assessing just what the requirement of decency, Minimal Benevolence, amounts to. A decent person is minimally benevolent toward other people. This sometimes involves wishing that things had gone differently from the way they actually went. When? Well, at a minimum it involves wishing that things had gone otherwise in a situation like this:

### Bertha's Better Birth

Bertha was born on February 8, 2006 at 23:17:45. I learn that, if Bertha's mother, Jane, had paused to collect her breath for just one instance late in labor, then she would have given birth to a baby just like the actual Bertha in every respect but these: the baby would have been born a second later than Bertha actually was, and the baby would have been slightly better off than Bertha actually is (fill in the details as to why in whatever way you like).

If I am decent, then I will have a wish (albeit very mild) that Jane had paused to collect her breath during labor. That would have been better for Bertha. I will not fail to have such a wish on the grounds that Bertha was essentially born at the moment she was born, that if Jane had paused Bertha would never have existed.

And so it is for all natural dimensions of sameness and difference—height, weight, genetic constitution, time of conception . . . etc. That is my claim. In Chapter 9 I will put it to work. But first I need to say something more about coherence and rationality.

# 8

# Rational Constraints on Desire-Like Attitudes

So much for essence. Now I will make some claims about rationality. Again, I think that they fall squarely within the realm of the obvious. But, again, I will try to state them in exquisitely painful detail. If you have little patience for this sort of thing, then I recommend that you skip ahead to the next chapter. The basic message of this chapter is that, if you are rational, then you will be coherent in what you desire (where being coherent involves, at least, having *transitive* preferences—preferring one thing to another whenever you prefer the one to a third thing, and that third thing to the other), and you will act on your coherent preferences.

Now for the detail. The claims I will be making concern propositional attitudes of a certain kind—*conative attitudes*. First I need to explain carefully what these things are.

What are propositional attitudes? Let us start with that question, and let us start with a paradigmatic propositional attitude: belief. On a standard way of thinking, my believing involves my taking a certain attitude, the *belief attitude*, toward a proposition—where the proposition is what it is that I believe. And there are many other attitudes that I can take toward the same proposition: just as I can believe that $p$, so I can wonder whether it is the case that $p$, fear that $p$, expect that $p$, . . . and so on. These are different kinds of propositional attitude.

In the spirit of Hume, philosophers tend to attribute great significance to the distinction between propositional attitudes that seem relevantly like beliefs, and propositional attitudes those that seem relevantly like desires. Belief-like attitudes (known to philosophers as *cognitive* attitudes) include:

believing that . . .
suspecting that . . .

thinking it unlikely that . . .
supposing that . . .

Desire-like attitudes (known as *conative* attitudes) include:

desiring that . . .
hoping that . . .
wishing that . . .
dreading that . . .

Although it is difficult to draw a precise line between the cognitive and conative attitudes (should *being shocked to hear that* . . . count as cognitive or as conative or as some sort of hybrid or as something else entirely?), most attitudes seem to fall squarely into one class or the other.

Some claims about rationality concern cognitive attitudes. For example, we might say that, if you are rational, then for all propositions, $p$, $q$:

*Non Contradiction*
If you believe that $p$ then you do not believe that not-$p$.

and

*Closure*
If you believe that $p$ and you believe that if $p$ then $q$, and it is a matter of some significance to you whether $q$, then you believe that $q$.

These claims concern what philosophers call "epistemic rationality." The claims about rationality that I will be making here concern conative attitudes. They concern what philosophers call "practical rationality."

## 8.1. Rational Constraints on the Structure of your Conative Attitudes

The first seven claims concern the *structure* of your conative attitudes. I will just state them in this section, and discuss why we should believe them in the next.

We begin with a principle concerning the structure of your all-things-considered preferences between maximal states of affairs. A state of affairs is a way for things to be. A maximal state of affairs is a fully precise way for everything to be—if things are this way, then there are no further things, and no further ways they might or might not be. A preference between maximal states of affairs, *a*, *b*, is a conative attitude that has as its objects the proposition that state of affairs *a* is actual and the proposition that state of affairs *b* is actual.

The principle says that, if you are rational, then for any maximal states of affairs *a,b*:

(R1) *Uniqueness of Preference*
Either          (i) you have no preference between *a* and *b*.
exclusive-or    (ii) you prefer *a* to *b*
exclusive-or    (iii) you prefer *b* to *a*

The *exhaustiveness* of the list of possibilities guarantees that there is some conative attitude that you take toward *a* and *b*—even if it is the attitude of not having a preference between them. The *exclusiveness* of the possibilities guarantees that you do not both have and fail to have a preference between *a* and *b*, and that any preferences you have are asymmetric—you do not both prefer *a* to *b*, and *b* to *a*.

Fair enough. Next we have a similar principle concerning the structure of a *higher level* all-things-considered conative attitude. Let me explain what this means. When you desire that *x* (or hope that *x*, or fear that *x* . . . etc.), say that you have a *level one conative attitude*, an attitude that is directed at a single proposition, *x*. When, of *x* and *y*, you would prefer that *x*, say that you have a *level two conative attitude*, an attitude that is directed at a pair of propositions. When, of *x*, *y*, and *z*, you would prefer that *x*, or of *i, j*, and *k*, you would prefer that *j or k*, say that you have a *level three conative attitude*, an attitude that is directed towards a triple of propositions . . . And so on.

The principle concerns your level three preferences. If you are rational then for any maximal states of affairs *a,b,c*:

(R2) *Uniqueness of Level Three Preference*
Either (i) you do not have a level three preference
exclusive-or    (ii) you have a level three preference for *a*
exclusive-or    (iii) you have a level three preference for *b*
exclusive-or    (iv) you have a level three preference for *c*
exclusive-or    (v) you have a level three preference for *a or b*
exclusive-or    (vi) you have a level three preference for *a or c*
exclusive-or    (vii) you have a level three preference for *b or c*

The *exhaustiveness* of the list of possibilities guarantees that there is some level three attitude that you take towards *a,b,c*—even if it is the attitude of having no level three preference. The *exclusiveness* of the possibilities guarantees asymmetric weighting—a level three preference for *a* cannot be accompanied by a level three preference for *b*, for example.

Next we have some principles that establish consistency between your all-things-considered level two and three attitudes. If you are rational, then for any maximal states of affairs *a,b,c*:

(R3) *One Place Level Three Preferences Carry Downwards*
You have a level three preference for *a*, from *a,b,c*
iff
you prefer *a* to *b*, and *a* to *c*.

(R4) *Two Place Level Three Preferences Carry Downwards*
You have a level three preference for *a* or *b*, from *a,b,c*
iff
you prefer *a* to *c*, and *b* to *c*, and you have no preference between *a* and *b*.

(R5) *Level Three Indifference Carries Downwards*
You have no level three preference, from *a,b,c*
iff
you have no preference between *a* and *b*, *a* and *c*, or *b* and *c*.

These principles entail some principles that figure prominently in the philosophical literature on rational choice theory. If you are rational then for any maximal states of affairs *a,b,c*:

(R6) *Expansion Consistency*
If you prefer *a* to *b*, then
either you have a level three preference for *a*, from *a,b,c*
or you have a level three preference for *a* or *c*, from *a,b,c*
or you have a level three preference for *c*, from *a,b,c*.[1]

---

[1] A proof that R6 follows from R1–R5: suppose that you prefer *a* to *b*. What third-order attitude do you have toward *a,b,c*? By R2, from *a,b,c*

| | |
|---|---|
| either | (i) you have no third-order preference |
| or | (ii) you have a third-order preference for *a* |
| or | (iii) you have a third-order preference for *b* |
| or | (iv) you have a third-order preference for *c* |
| or | (v) you have a third-order preference for *a or b* |
| or | (vi) you have a third-order preference for *a or c* |
| or | (vii) you have a third-order preference for *b or c* |

Roughly speaking: your positive second-order preferences are reflected in your third-order preferences.

(R7) *Contraction Consistency*
> If, from *a,b,c*, you have a level three preference for *a*, or for *a* or *b*, then you prefer *a* to *c*.[2]

Roughly speaking: your positive third-order preferences are reflected in your second-order preferences.

(R8) *Transitivity*
> If you prefer *a* to *b*, and you prefer *b* to *c*, then you prefer *a* to *c*.[3]

## 8.2. Why Accept These Constraints?

Should we believe R1–R5, and all that they entail?

Well, I think that R1 and R2 come for free. The rational among us satisfy these principles because we all satisfy these principles. Take R1. It says that the rational among us do not have symmetric preferences. But none of us has symmetric preferences. There is just no way for a brain to be wired that would be make it appropriate to say of its owner that, for some maximal states of affairs *a*, *b*, he or she has an all-things-considered preference for *a* over *b*, and an all-things-considered preference for *b*

---

For reductio, suppose (i). Then, by R5, you have no preference between *a* and *b*, and you prefer *a* to *b*—a contradiction. For reductio, suppose (iii). Then, by R3, you prefer *b* to *a*, and you prefer *a* to *b*—which contradicts R1. For reductio suppose (v). Then, by R4, you have no preference between *a* and *b*, and you prefer *a* to *b*—a contradiction. For reductio, suppose (vii). Then, by R4, you prefer *b* to *a*, and you prefer *a* to *b*—which contradicts R1. That just leaves (ii), (iv), and (vi) as open possibilities.

[2] A proof that R7 Contraction Consistency follows from R2–R5: this is immediate. Suppose that you have a level-three preference for *a*, from *a,b,c*. Then, by R3, you prefer *a* to *b*. Suppose that you have a level-three preference for *a* or *b*, from *a,b,c*. Then, by R4, you prefer *a* to *b*.

[3] A proof that R8 Transitivity follows from R1–R5: suppose that you prefer *a* to *b*, and *b* to *c*. Since you prefer *a* to *b*, by Expansion Consistency (which we know follows from R1–R5), from *a,b,c*

> either    (i) you have a third-order preference for *a*
> or    (ii) you have a third-order preference for *a* or *c*
> or    (iii) you have a third-order preference for *c*

For reductio, suppose that (ii). Then, by R5, you prefer *c* to *b*, and you prefer *b* to *c*—which contradicts R1. For reductio, suppose that (iii). Then, by R4, you prefer *c* to *b*, and you prefer *b* to *c*—which contradicts R1. So it must be that (i). So, by R3, you prefer *a* to *c*.

over $a$. Our concept of all-things-considered preference leaves no space for this possibility.

One might think that R3, R4, and R5 also come for free. Take R3, for example. One might think that there is just no way for a brain to be wired that would make it appropriate to say of its owner that, for some maximal states of affairs $a,b,c$, he or she prefers $a$ to $b$, and $a$ to $c$, but has no level-three preference for $a$. Our concepts of level two and three preference leave no space for this possibility.

This does not seem right. Philosophers have provided numerous examples of situations in which stable, clear-headed people end up with intransitive preferences because of the principled methods they use to go about making comparisons between alternatives. Indeed, some serious philosophers have claimed that they themselves would compare things in this way. Perhaps these philosophers are wrong; perhaps they really have transitive preferences. But the charitable thing to do is to take them at their word.

Here is an example of a case in which a principled method of comparison yields intransitive preferences.

### The Blue Carpet

You want to buy a carpet. An artisan offers you two, of the same dimensions, made from the same material. One is grey, on sale for $400. The other has been treated with a rare and expensive dye distilled from the irises of Himalayan markhors. It is stunning, palatinate blue, on sale for $500. You would rather buy the $500 carpet. After all, if you are going to be paying all that money, why not pay that little bit extra for something really superb? But then he mentions that he can offer you another carpet, treated with slightly less of the expensive dye, for $495. It is pairwise-indistinguishable-to-the-naked-eye from the $500 carpet (put them down next to one another, in ordinary light, and you will not be able to tell them apart—of course, if you had an electron microscope you might be able to tell them apart, but you do not have an electron microscope). You would rather buy that than the $500 carpet. Why pay extra when you cannot tell the two carpets apart? But then he mentions that he can offer you yet another carpet, treated with yet slightly less of the expensive dye, for $490. It is pairwise-indistinguishable-to-the-naked eye from the $495 carpet . . . and so on and so forth . . . until he mentions that he can offer you another, grey carpet, treated with none of the expensive dye, for $400. It is pairwise-indistinguishable-to-the-naked eye from the $405 carpet he just showed you.

Your preferences between states of affairs are intransitive. Consider the states of affairs:

S0:   In which you pay $400 for the grey carpet.

S1:   In which you pay $405 for a carpet treated with a very little bit of blue dye.

S19:   In which you pay $495 for a carpet treated with a very little bit less dye than the $500 carpet.

S20:   In which you pay $500 for the stunning, palatinate blue carpet.

You prefer S0 to S1, S1 to S2, . . . S19 to S20. But you prefer S20 to S0.

In this case you are not whimsical or confused. Something about your principled method of comparing states of affairs yields intransitive preferences (roughly: it is that you take differences in the amount of blue dye infused into the carpets to matter, except when these differences fall below the threshold of pairwise-distinguishability-to-the-naked-eye.)[4] But, principled or no, R8 says you are irrational.

That was just one example of a principled method of comparison yielding intransitive preferences. There are many, many other examples in the literature. Before we get to some more, it may be helpful to have a general way of representing the circumstances in which such examples arise.

Suppose that your preferences between entities of a certain kind are determined by how these entities are along certain dimensions $D_1$, $D_2, \ldots D_n$. So, in the Blue Carpet case, your preferences between carpets are determined by how they are along two dimensions—how expensive they are, and how much blue dye is infused into their fabrics.

When your preferences between entities of kind k are determined by how they are along $n$ dimensions, say that $n$-tuple $<a,b,\ldots,c>$ *beats* $n$-tuple $<x,y,\ldots,z>$ when you prefer a kind k entity with $D_1, D_2, \ldots,$ $D_n$ values $a,b,\ldots,c$, to a kind k entity with $D_1, D_2, \ldots, D_n$ values $x,y,\ldots,$ $z$. And say that $n$-tuple $<a,b,\ldots,c>$ *ties with* $n$-tuple $<x,y,\ldots,z>$ when

---

[4] The first example of this sort of case that I know of is in Quinn (1990). In Quinn's example the trade-off is between money and levels of electricity pulsing through your body. When differences in electricity level fall below the threshold of pairwise-distinguishability (flip back and forth between the levels and you will be unable to distinguish them), your preferences are sensitive only to money.

you have no preference between a kind k entity with $D_1, D_2, \ldots, D_n$ values a,b,...,c, and a kind k entity with $D_1, D_2, \ldots, D_n$ values x,y,...,z.

Now suppose that your preferences are such that for any n-tuple P, the collection of $n$-tuples that beat it forms a bounded region of $n$-space. Call the boundary of this region the *Beats-P Boundary*. Fig. 8.1 is an example (for $n = 2$).

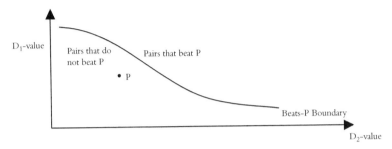

**Figure 8.1**

We now have a nice way of representing the sorts of situations in which intransitivity arises. Your preferences are intransitive when there are $n$-tuples P, Q such that Q beats P and the Beats-Q Boundary crosses the Beats-P Boundary. Fig. 8.2 is an example (for $n = 2$).

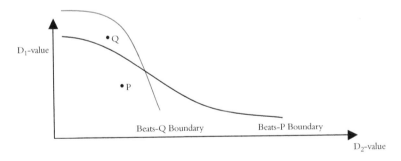

**Figure 8.2**

To see why this means that your preferences are intransitive, look at $n$-tuple R (see Fig. 8.3). R beats Q and Q beats P, but R does not beat P. So you prefer entities with $D_1$- and $D_2$-values represented by R to entities with $D_1$- and $D_2$-values represented by Q, and you prefer entities with $D_1$- and $D_2$-values represented by Q to entities with $D_1$- and $D_2$-values represented by P, but you do not prefer entities with $D_1$- and

$D_2$-values represented by R to entities with $D_1$- and $D_2$-values represented by P.

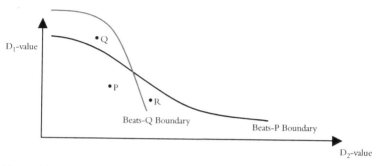

**Figure 8.3**

Say that a beats-P boundary is *exhaustive* when all points on the boundary tie with P, all points to one side beat P, and all points to the other side are beaten by P. It follows from the above that, if all points in the space have exhaustive beats-boundaries, your preferences are intransitive if and only if there are points P, Q such that the beats-boundary for Q crosses the beats-boundary for P.

So, supposing that all points in the space have exhaustive beats boundaries, your preferences are transitive if and only if beats-boundaries never intersect—as, for example, shown in Fig. 8.4.

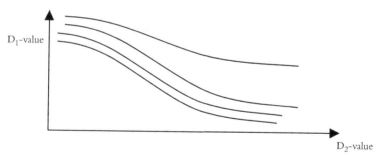

**Figure 8.4**

Under these circumstances all beats-boundaries for points in the space will be what economists call *indifference curves*—any point on the boundary ties with any other point on the boundary, any point to the one side beats any point to the other side.

We can now represent what is going on in cases like the <u>Blue Carpet</u> case, in which the thought that, "when it is my comfort/pleasure at stake, pairwise-indistinguishable differences along the dimension that determines my comfort/pleasure do not matter" is doing the work. In this case your preferences between states of affairs S1 and S10 are determined by their values along two dimensions—how much money you have left in your pocket when you leave the shop, and how much of the gorgeous blue dye is infused into the carpet. For any dye level, $x$, there is a *zone of phenomenal indistinguishability* such that carpets represented by points in this zone are pairwise-indistinguishable-to-the-naked eye from carpets with dye level $x$ (see Fig. 8.5).

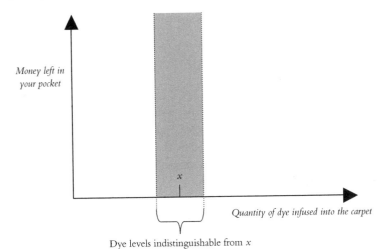

Figure 8.5

And, within this zone, the Beats-Boundary of any point representing a carpet with dye level $x$ is flat. Why? Because you reason that pairwise-indistinguishable-to-the-naked eye differences in dye level do not matter at all: what makes the blue dye good is the way it looks, so why care about differences that your eyes cannot detect? So, when you compare carpets with pairwise-indistinguishable-to-the-naked eye dye levels, you care only about the price.

So, for a given amount of money left in your pocket, $y$, the Beats-Boundary for $<x,y>$ will have the basic shape shown in Fig. 8.6. Points to the north-east of the boundary beat $<x,y>$. Points to the south-west of the boundary do not beat $<x,y>$.

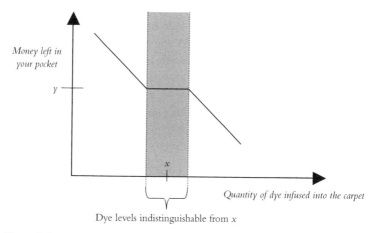

**Figure 8.6**

And, if we concentrate on a north-west to south-east diagonal (decreasing money, increasing dye levels) (see Fig. 8.7) the beats-boundaries of points along this diagonal form a thin *braid* (see Fig. 8.8). Because the beats-boundaries are exhaustive, and they cross, you have intransitive preferences.

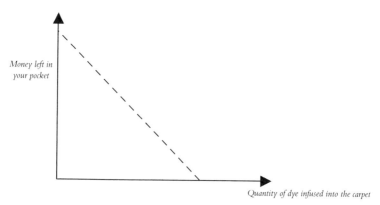

**Figure 8.7**

Not all the cases in which, supposedly, it makes sense to have intransitive preferences involve sensory indistinguishability. There are other kinds

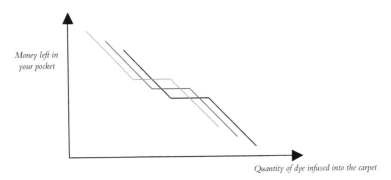

**Figure 8.8**

of cases in which some people take it that, when differences along one dimension become very large, then differences along another dimension cease to matter. Here are two:

### Intensity vs Duration

Grade pain by level. For level 0 pain think of a hangnail, for level 1 pain think of walking on a blister, for level 2 pain think of multiple blisters, . . . for level 10 pain think of the worst pain you have experienced, and be assured that it is *much worse than that.* Consider, now, these states of affairs:

> S0:  In which you endure level 10 pain for a day.
> S1:  In which you endure level 9 pain for 2 days.
> S2:  In which you endure level 8 pain for $2^2$ days.
> S3:  In which you endure level 7 pain for $2^3$ days.
> S10:  In which you endure level 0 pain for $2^{10}$ days.

You prefer S0 to S1. Though your pain in S0 is palpably more intense (you certainly can tell the difference between level 10 and level 9 pain), there is only half as much of it. If you are going to suffer terribly (as you will, in either case), you would rather *get it over with quickly.* And, for similar reasons, you prefer S1 to S2, S2 to S3, . . . etc. But you do not prefer S0 to S10. In S0 you suffer terribly, in S10 you suffer very mildly indeed. A hangnail is just a hangnail, no matter how long it lingers. So your preferences are intransitive.[5]

### Intensity vs the Numbers

Consider, now, these states of affairs:

> S0:  In which one person endures level 10 suffering for a day.
> S1:  In which 10 people endure level 9 suffering for a day.

[5] This sort of example first appeared in print in Temkin (1996). Temkin credited Stuart Rachels for the example, and Rachels later discussed it in detail in Rachels (1998).

S2:   In which $10^2$ people endure level 8 suffering for a day.

S3:   In which $10^3$ people endure level 7 suffering for a day.

S10:   In which $10^{10}$ people endure level 0 suffering for a day.

You prefer S0 to S1. Though the pain in S0 is palpably more intense than the suffering in S1, there is ten times as much of it in S1. And, for similar reasons, you prefer S1 to S2, S2 to S3, ... etc. But you do not prefer S0 to S10. In S0 someone suffers sustained agony. In S10 there are a bunch of hangnails. It does not matter how many hangnails. They are just hangnails. So your preferences are intransitive.[6]

What generates the intransitive preferences in these sorts of cases? Take the Intensity vs Numbers case. Here your preferences between states of affairs are again determined by their values along two dimensions: the number of people who will all suffer, and the level at which they will all suffer. When differences in the levels are small, then you take differences in the numbers to matter. But, when differences in the levels become large, then you take differences in the numbers to cease to matter. So, for any level of suffering $x$, there is what we may call a *zone of comparability* for $x$ (see Fig. 8.9).

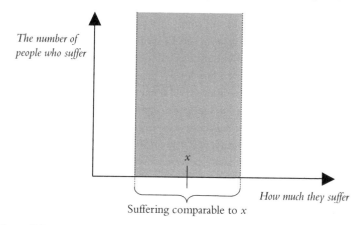

**Figure 8.9**

And for any given number of people who suffer, $y$, the beats boundary for $<x,y>$ will look broadly as shown in Fig. 8.10. And the boundary will

[6] One philosopher's modus ponens is often another's modus tollens. This sort of example was used by Alistair Norcross in Norcross (1987) to argue for the result that, if the many are many enough, it is worse that many suffer mild harms than that few suffer terrible harms. Clearly, says Norcross, each state of affairs in the series is better than its successor. And clearly, says Norcross, the relation *better than* is transitive.

be exhaustive. Points to the south-west of the boundary beat <x,y>. Points to the north-east do not.

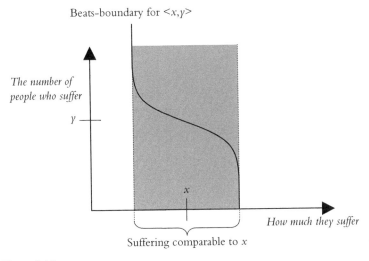

Figure 8.10

So, if we concentrate again on a north-west to south-east diagonal (representing a decreasing number of people, suffering ever more) (see Fig. 8.11), the exhaustive beats-boundaries for points along this diagonal form a thick braid (see Fig. 8.12). Because their boundaries cross, you have intransitive preferences.

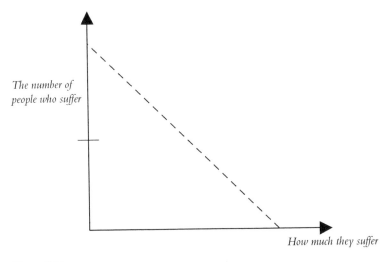

Figure 8.11

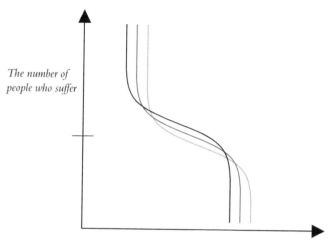

The number of people who suffer

How much they suffer

**Figure 8.12**

And there are other sorts of cases in which people take it that differences along one dimension cease to matter at all when one of the things being compared has an unusual value along that dimension. Consider:

The Procreator

The Procreator has one child, Danny, and is considering whether to have another. When he compares a future in which he has two children with a future in which he leaves Danny sibling-less, he always prefers the future in which Danny is better off: 'The measure of whether I ought to have another child is whether I make Danny better off by doing so.' But when he compares futures in which he has two children, he would rather that his two children, on average, be better off: 'If I am going to have two children in any case, I am not going to favoritize Danny.'

The Procreator's preferences between states of affairs are intransitive. Consider the states of affairs:

S1:     In which Danny has welfare 6, and his younger sibling George has welfare 1.

S2:    In which Danny has welfare 4, and George has welfare 4.

S3:    In which Danny has welfare 5, and George never exists.

The Procreator prefers S2 to S1 and S3 to S2. But he prefers S1 to S3.

In this case, the Procreator's preferences between states of affairs are again sensitive to how they are along two dimensions—Danny's welfare and George's welfare (which we can think of as a function that yields a value of some real number, measuring how well off he is, when George exists, and gives value $\Omega$ when George does not exist). And the exhaustive beats-boundary for an ordered pair $<x,y>$, where $x$ and $y$ are real numbers and $x$ is Danny's welfare, $y$ George's, looks as in Fig. 8.13.

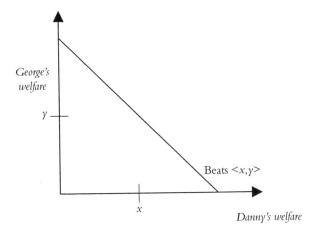

**Figure 8.13**

For any $i,j$, $<i,j>$ beats $<x,y>$ only if $i + j > x + y$. If the Procreator is comparing states of affairs in which he has two children, he prefers the one in which they have the highest average well-being.

But the exhaustive beats-boundary for an ordered pair $<z,\Omega>$, where $z < x + y$, is vertical (see Fig. 8.14).

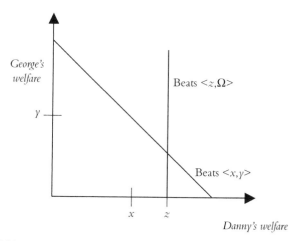

**Figure 8.14**

When the Procreator is comparing worlds in which he has a second child with worlds in which he does not, he cares only about Danny's welfare in those worlds. So, because the exhaustive beats-boundaries intersect, he has intransitive preferences.[7]

## 8.3. Arguing for R3–R5

So it is possible for you to fail to satisfy R3–R5. Why does this make you irrational?

One true observation is that, if you do not satisfy R3–R5, then you cannot make use of expected utility theory as a guide to how to proceed under conditions of uncertainty.[8] Might this be the basis of an argument that rationality demands of you that you satisfy R3–R5? It does not seem

---

[7] John Broome describes an example close to this in Broome (2004: sect. 4.1). It was adapted from examples in Temkin (1996).

[8] As you may recall from Chapter 3, it is also true that, if your preferences are negatively transitive, then you cannot make use of standard expected utility theory as a guide to how to proceed under conditions of uncertainty. But we saw that, in that case, there is a way to extend standard expected utility theory to do the job—we represent your conative attitudes with a set of utility functions, and work from there. If your preferences are intransitive, then there is no obvious way to extend standard expected utility theory to do the job. It is a much harder problem.

promising to me. If expected utility theory cannot help you, then so much the worse for expected utility theory.

Another true observation is that, if you do not satisfy R3–R5, then you may be vulnerable to exploitation. Under certain circumstances a clever bookie may be able to game you to his advantage (roughly: you have A, he offers you the opportunity to pay a dollar to swap it for B, then he offers you the opportunity to pay a dollar to swap that for C, then he offers you the opportunity to swap that for A, then he walks away chuckling and counting his money). Might this be the basis of an argument that rationality demands of you that you satisfy R3–R5? There is a big literature on this question. I will not summarize it here,[9] but I will note, in passing, that I do not find the argument promising. You will be exploited in these situations only if you lack foresight or self-control. The fault may be attributed to your lack of foresight or self-control, not to the structure of your preferences.

I think the best we can do by way of an argument is this. Reasons for desiring that a state of affairs obtain (a level-one conative attitude, notice) can be *stronger* or *weaker*, where the relations *stronger than* and *weaker than* are transitive. And you have all-things-considered reason to prefer state of affairs $x$ to state of affairs $y$ (a level-two conative attitude, notice) if and only if your reasons to desire that $x$ obtain (a level-one attitude) are stronger than your reasons to desire that $y$ obtain. And you have all-things-considered reason to prefer of $x,y,z$ that $x$ obtain (a level-three attitude) if and only if your reasons to desire that $z$ obtain (a level-one attitude) are stronger than your reasons to desire that $y$ obtain and stronger than your reasons to desire that $z$ obtain. And so on . . .

Now suppose that you do not satisfy one of R3 to R5. Suppose, for example, that you prefer $a$ to $b$, but have a level-three preference for $b$, from $a,b,c$—thereby violating R3. It follows that, if your level-three preference is supported by reason (you have all-things-considered reason to have it), then your level-two preference is opposed by reason (you have all-things-considered reason to have a different level-two preference), and vice versa. So either both attitudes are unsupported by reason (you do not

⁹ The literature goes back to Frank Ramsey's seminal 1928 paper "Truth and Probability," printed in Ramsey (1931). Ramsey claimed that someone who did not satisfy his "axioms of probability and preference" was systematically exploitable. Nowadays this is known as a "money pump" argument.

have all-things-considered reason to have them) or one is opposed by reason. And you are in position to know this—because it follows from facts about the structure of your attitudes. But this makes you irrational. Rational people do not sustain attitudes that they know to be unsupported or opposed by reason.[10]

I say this is "the best we can do by way of an argument" because it is unlikely to persuade people who were not antecedently sympathetic to its conclusion. The argument rests on these claims about how reasons-to-prefer work. Why accept them? Take, in particular, the claim that the relation *stronger than*, over sets of reasons to prefer, is transitive. Why accept that? I said, back in Chapter 3, that I do not consider it a requirement of rationality that our preferences be negatively transitive. So I must think that it is not true that the relation *stronger than*, over sets of reasons to prefer, is negatively transitive (otherwise, by the same argument, it would be a requirement of rationality that our preferences be negatively transitive). Why concede that the relation may be negatively intransitive, but insist that it be transitive? I do not have anything very enlightening to say in response. It seems to me, whenever I think about cases, that this is how reasons-to-prefer work. In particular, when I think about cases in which people have intransitive preferences, it always seems to me that they are making some kind of mistake.

Take the Blue Carpet case, for example. The idea is that your preferences between the ten carpets are governed by only two sorts of consideration—considerations having to do with the way the carpets look, and considerations having to do with how much the carpets cost. Because each carpet and its predecessor are pairwise-indistinguishable-to-the-naked eye, considerations to do with the way the carpets look do not tell in favor of preferring any carpet to its predecessor. Because each carpet is $10 cheaper than its successor, considerations to do with how much the carpets cost tell

---

[10] If you are familiar with recent work in the theory of practical rationality, this may remind you of arguments by Niko Kolodny (2008a, b). Kolodny argues that the *fault* that comes with having a collection of incoherent attitudes can always be traced to a fault in some particular attitude in the collection. I have argued that, if your attitudes fail to satisfy R1–R3, then one particular attitude of yours is unsupported or opposed by reason. But please note that I am not saying that just having an attitude unsupported or opposed by reason makes you irrational. What makes you irrational is the fact that the structure of your attitudes commits you to having an attitude unsupported or opposed by reason, and you are in a position to know that.

in favor of preferring each carpet to its successor. It follows that you have all-things-considered reason to prefer each carpet to its successor.

But it is a mistake to think that whenever two carpets are pairwise-indistinguishable-to-the-naked-eye, considerations to do with the way the carpets look do not tell in favor of preferring either. In this case it cannot be that the way the first carpet looks *is* (the *is* of numerical identity) the way the second carpet looks, and the way the second carpet looks *is* the way the third carpet looks, . . . , and the way the ninth carpet looks *is* the way the tenth carpet looks. The way the first carpet looks is not the way the tenth carpet looks, and numerical identity is a paradigmatically transitive relation. So there must be some adjacent pair of carpets in the series, pairwise-indistinguishable-to-the-naked-eye, such that the way the one looks is not the way the other looks. If you care about the way carpets look, then you have a looks-based reason to prefer one to the other.[11]

Maybe you feel the same way, maybe you do not. If you do not, then you may take what follows as conditional: supposing that R3–R5 are requirements of rationality, some interesting things follow about what decent and rational people do in morally portentous situations.

## 8.4. Rational Constraints on Behavior

R1 to R5 tell us a good deal about what rational people will desire. But notice that they do not tell us anything, directly, about how rational people will be disposed to *behave*. Consider, for example, dispositions to make choices between items. Let us define some terms.

*Dispositional Expansion Consistency*
Your dispositions-to-choose are expansion consistent when, for any items A,B,C, if you have a stable disposition to choose A, given a choice between A and B, then you have stable disposition to choose A or C, given a choice between A,B, and C.

*Dispositional Contraction Consistency*
Your dispositions-to-choose are contraction consistent when, for any items A,B,C, if you have a stable disposition to choose A, given a choice

---

[11] I thank Shelly Kagan for discussions that advanced my thinking about phenomenal sorites examples. He works over the examples thoroughly in Kagan (2011).

between A, B, and C, then you have a stable disposition to choose A, given a choice between A and B.

*Dispositional Transitivity*
You have transitive dispositions-to-choose when, for any items A,B,C, if you have stable disposition to choose A, given a choice between A and B, and you have a stable disposition to choose B, given a choice between B and C, then you have a stable disposition to choose A, given a choice between A and C.

R1–R5 do not tell us that rational people will have transitive, expansion, and contraction consistent dispositions-to-choose. It is possible to have conative attitudes that conform to R1–R5 (henceforth: *structurally consistent preferences*) and yet fail to have expansion consistent, contraction consistent, and transitive dispositions to choose.

One not-so-interesting way to do this is to have structurally consistent preferences, but be stably disposed to act against them. Your preferences make sense, but your behavior is not guided by your preferences. But this is not the only way. It is possible to have structurally consistent preferences and yet *willingly* fail to have expansion and contraction consistent dispositions to choose. Consider:

Respecting the Dying Wish
Given a choice between Bovril and jam on your bread, you always choose jam. Why? Because it tastes better. Given a choice between jam and Marmite on your bread, you always choose Marmite. Why? Because it tastes better still. But given a choice between Bovril and Marmite on your bread, you always choose Bovril. Why? Because your grandfather worked for Bovril inc. all his life and, on his deathbed, made you promise that you would take Bovril over its upstart rival, Marmite, if you were ever given the choice. Promises to a dying ancestor are more important to you than good-tasting bread.

Or (this example is from John Broome[12]):

Fear of Cowardice
Given a choice between an adventurous holiday and a culturally enlightening holiday, you will choose the enlightenment. Why? Because

---

[12] See Broome (1991: sect. 5.4).

adventure is risky and physically demanding. Given a choice between a culturally enlightening holiday and the comforts of home, you will choose the comforts of home. Why? Because holidays are tedious and stressful. But, given a choice between an adventurous holiday and the comforts of home, you will choose the adventure. Why? Because choosing comfort over adventure is *cowardly*. You would rather subject yourself to risk and physical demand than be a coward.

In both of these cases, your intransitive dispositions-to-choose are the product of structurally consistent preferences between maximal states of affairs. In the first case there are six distinct states of affairs in play (see Fig. 8.15). You prefer S1 to S2, S3 to S4, and S6 to S5.

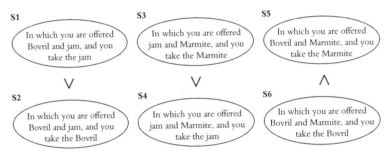

**Figure 8.15**

In the second case there are again six distinct states of affairs in play (see Fig. 8.16). You prefer S7 to S8, S9 to S10, S12 to S11.

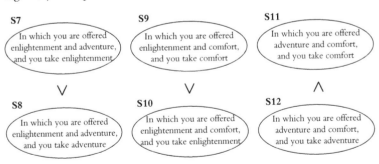

**Figure 8.16**

Are you rational in these cases? It certainly appears so. But in some other cases failures of dispositional expansion and contraction consistency seem like marks of irrationality. How do we distinguish the good cases from the bad ones? We need a couple more claims about rationality.

The first concerns the relation between preference and behavior. If you are rational then, for any states of affairs $a,b,c$:

(R9) *Preferences Guide Action*
Suppose that you have two options open to you, that you can bring about $a$ by taking one option, $b$ by taking the other, and that you face no epistemic or physical impediments to your will (you know that you are in a position to bring about just $a$ or $b$, and you know how to bring about $a$, and you know how to bring about $b$, and there is nothing standing in your way.) Under these conditions:
　You have a stable disposition to bring about $a$ iff you prefer $a$ to $b$.
Suppose that you have three options open to you, that you can bring about $a,b,c$ respectively, and that you face no epistemic or physical impediments to your will. Under these conditions:
　You have a stable disposition to bring about $a$ iff
　　from $a,b,c$, you have a level-three preference for $a$.

In the absence of impediment, rational people act on their all-things-considered preferences. If you do not do so, then the mechanism that translates desire into action is not working as it should. You have a *screw loose*, practically speaking.

The next claim concerns the relation between preferences and acknowledged reasons. If you are rational then, for any maximal states of affairs, $a,b,c$:

(R10) *Conative Attitudes Follow Acknowledged Reasons*
If you take yourself to have all things considered reason to prefer $a$ to $b$, then you prefer $a$ to $b$. If you take yourself to have all-things-considered reason to have a level-three preference for $a$, from $a,b,c$, then you have a level-three preference for $a$, from $a,b,c$.

Rational people regulate their conduct in light of reasons. They do not do things that they take themselves to have all-things-considered reason not to do. They do not have preferences that they take themselves to have all-things-considered reason not to have.

R1–R10 entail another principle that figures prominently in the literature on rational choice theory. Say that states of affairs $a$ and $b$ are *relevantly just like* states of affairs $a^*$ and $b^*$ when, to put it roughly, you see no evaluatively relevant differences between them. To put it precisely: when you take it that every reason to prefer $a$ to $b$ is a reason to prefer $a^*$ to $b^*$, every reason to prefer $b$ to $a$ is a reason to prefer $b^*$ to $a^*$, every reason to prefer $a^*$ to $b^*$ is a reason to prefer $a$ to $b$, and every reason to prefer $b^*$ to $a^*$ is a reason to prefer $b$ to $a$. If you are rational, then for any maximal states of affairs $a,b,c$, $a^*,b^*$:

(R11) *The Practical Insignificance of Irrelevant Alternatives*
If you have a stable disposition to bring about $a$, when knowingly in a position to bring about $a$ or $b$ or $c$, and $a^*$ and $b^*$ are states of affairs relevantly just like $a$ and $b$, but in which you are never in a position to bring about $c$, then you have a stable disposition to bring about $a^*$, when knowingly in a position to bring about $a^*$ or $b^*$.

In light of these principles, there are some useful questions that can be asked to diagnose whether expansion inconsistent, contraction inconsistent, or intransitive dispositions-to-choose are symptoms of irrationality on the part of the so disposed.

First, do you really have structurally consistent preferences between maximal states of affairs? Sometimes the prima facie odd dispositions-to-choose may be the expression of structurally inconsistent preferences between maximal states of affairs. For example, someone with the dispositions-to-choose among holidays of John Broome's holiday-maker may prefer S7 to S8 ("forget what choices I am offered—enlightenment beats adventure"), S9 to S7 ("forget what choices I am offered—comfort beats enlightenment"), and S8 to S9 ("forget what choices I am offered—adventure beats comfort—it would be cowardly to think otherwise"). By R1–R5, this person would be irrational.

Second, is your behavior consistent with your preferences between maximal states of affairs? It could be that your preferences are consistent, but you are stably disposed to act contrary to your preferences. Someone with the dispositions-to-choose among holidays of John Broome's holiday-maker may (unlike Broome's character) prefer S12 to S11, but be stably disposed to act contrary to that preference whenever he is in a position to bring about S11 or S12. By R9, this person would be irrational.

Third, do you take yourself to have reasons for preferring as you do? It could be that your preferences are well ordered, and you are stably disposed to behave in a manner that is consistent with your preferences, but you do not take there to be reasons for preferring as you do. Someone with the dispositions-to-choose among holidays and preferences of John

Broome's holiday-maker may (unlike Broome's character) see no reason to prefer S12 to S11 ("Why prefer S12 to S11?—Fear of cowardice is no reason.") Such a person is at least *arational*. If he also takes himself to have reason to prefer S11 to S12, then, by R10 he is *irrational*.

Let us see how these diagnostic questions might be helpful by looking at an anecdotally true story:

Sidney Morgenbesser Orders Dessert

"Have you any pie?" said Morgenbesser to a waitress.

"We have apple pie and blueberry pie," said the waitress.

"I'll have the apple," said Morgenbesser.

"Sure . . . " said the waitress " . . . oh, wait, we also have cherry pie."

"In that case I will have the blueberry!" said Morgenbesser.

Morgenbesser's dispositions-to-choose among pies were not expansion consistent. Was he irrational? It certainly appears so. The set-up encourages us to think that either his preferences were inconsistent or he did not take his preferences to be supported by reasons. But we need to delve more deeply into the story to see what was really going on. Maybe (variants of this point have been made several times) Morgenbesser knew that the restaurant employed two different chefs on different days. One chef made delicious apple pie, poor blueberry pie, and no cherry pie. The other chef made poor apple pie, delicious blueberry pie, and moderate cherry pie. So Morgenbesser really had structurally consistent preferences like those shown in Fig. 8.17. And maybe he took himself to have reason to prefer delicious pies to moderate pies to poor pies.

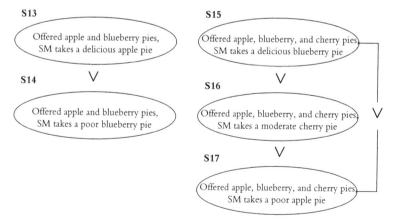

Figure 8.17

Indeed, on a realistic reconstruction of the case, something of this general kind was exactly what was going on. Morgenbesser had structurally consistent preferences like those shown in Fig. 8.18. And he took himself to have reason for so preferring, because he cared more about his reputation as a wit for the ages than about the taste of pie.

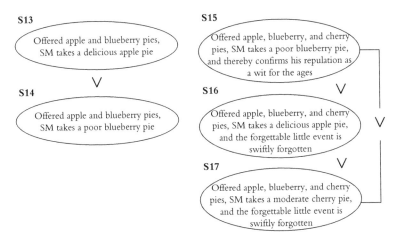

**Figure 8.18**

So the best we can say of funny dispositions-to-choose is this: if you are rational, then your dispositions to make choices among items will be transitive, expansion consistent, and contraction consistent, *unless* those dispositions are the product of structurally consistent preferences that you take to be supported by reason.

## 8.5. Rationality and Accordance with Reason

Can we not say something more? Can we not say that it is not enough to *take* yourself to have reasons to prefer as you do? Can we not say that you must also have reason to prefer as you do?

(R12) *Preferences Accord with Reason*
You are more or less rational to the extent that your preferences more or less closely reflect the reasons you have.

Derek Parfit has defended something close to R12 as a principle of practical rationality. Consider someone who would rather that he suffer agony next Tuesday than mild pain next Wednesday. Why? Because it is a *Tuesday*! Pain on Tuesdays does not matter. This person takes himself to have reasons for preferring as he does. But he is wrong. And he is irrational. To be rational is to be guided, in action and desire, by the reasons you have.

If we adopted this principle, then we might want to think again about whether some of our characters are rational. Take Broome's holiday-maker, for example. He takes himself to have reasons to prefer S12 to S11—in S12, by choosing adventure over comfort, he is *brave*, while in S11, by choosing comfort over adventure, he is *cowardly*. But are these really reasons to prefer S12 to S11? In both S11 and S12 he likes comfort far more than he likes adventure. Why is it so cowardly to act on his liking? What is so bad about that?

But I do not want to assume R12 here. It is not that I want to claim ownership of the notion of rationality. There is certainly a good, ordinary sense of the term in which someone who is indifferent to pain on future Tuesdays is irrational  bizarre, loopy, taking things to be reasons that just … are not. It is rather that I am in the business of deriving a theory of normative ethics from, in part, principles of rationality. If this project is to work, the principles will need to be such that we have a firm grip, before we commit ourselves to any particular view of the normative, on exactly when they are violated. R1–R11 do the job. We can easily tell whether someone is violating R1–R11 just by looking at his preferences, looking at whether he takes himself to have reason to prefer as he does, and looking at his dispositions to behave in different ways in different circumstances. Indeed, just so long as we are sufficiently self-aware, we can easily enough tell whether we ourselves are violating R1–R11 by performing the same checks. But R12 does not do the job. To tell whether someone is violating R12, we need to know whether the considerations that he takes to be reasons really are reasons, and that will involve knowing whether this or that view of the normative is correct.

## 8.6.  Generalizing the Picture

So there we go. I have sketched the background of a picture of how you need to be, if you are to be rational. The picture can immediately be generalized, in two ways.

First, to keep things simple, I made claims only about the relation between a rational person's second- and third-order conative attitudes. But the claims can immediately be generalized to apply to the relations between all of a rational person's higher-order conative attitudes. So, for example, generalized Contraction Consistency would entail that if, from maximal states of affairs $a,b,c,d$, you have a level-four preference for $a$, then, from $a,b,c$, you have a level-three preference for $a$. I will not bore you by restating the principles in the more general form.

Second, to keep things simple, I made claims only about a rational person's preferences between maximal states of affairs. But the claims can immediately be generalized to cover preferences between other sorts of things. In particular, the claims apply to *maximal prospects*. A maximal prospect is a collection of ordered pairs of maximal states of affairs and numbers, the numbers representing the probability that the maximal state of affairs will come about in a given scenario. So, for example, $\{<a,.7>,$ $<b,.3>\}$ is a maximal prospect, representing a scenario in which there is a 0.7 chance that $a$ will come about and a 0.3 chance that $b$ will come about. Everything that I have said about maximal states of affairs applies to prospects. So, for example, generalized Transitivity would entail that, if you prefer maximal prospect $\{<a,.7>, <b,.3>\}$ to maximal prospect $\{<a,.1>, <b,.9>\}$, and you prefer maximal prospect $\{<a,.1>, <b,.9>\}$ to maximal prospect $\{<a,.01>, <b,.99>\}$, then you prefer maximal prospect $\{<a,.7>, <b,.3>\}$ to maximal prospect $\{<a,.01>, <b,.99>\}$.

# 9

# Morphing

Here is where we are. Back in the first chapter of the book I made a claim: decent people are at least minimally considerate of, and benevolent toward, others. In the last two chapters I have made two more claims: all people have minimally robust essences. Rational people have coherent conative attitudes. My aim, in this chapter, is to put all these claims together and tease out their implications.

## 9.1. States of Affairs and Counterpart Theory

Recall that I characterized minimal consideration and minimal benevolence in terms of preferences between maximally specific states of affairs. A minimally considerate person will take the consideration "this same person is better off in S than in S*" to be a reason to favor S over S*. A minimally benevolent person will prefer, all other things being equal, a maximally specific state of affairs in which another person is better off over a maximally specific state of affairs in which that same person is worse off. What does my claim about essence entail about when individuals in distinct maximal states of affairs are the same or different? Well, to spell this out in an accurate way we will have to make some assumptions about what maximally specific states of affairs are, and about what sameness and difference across maximally specific states of affairs amounts to. Philosophers have offered some very different ways of thinking about this.

I will explain the difference by using a word—"identity"—about whose meaning it pays to be clear. There are different relations we may be interested in when, outside of a philosophy class, we talk about things being "the same" or "identical." On the one hand, there are relations of qualitative similarity. Things can be quite similar, very similar, very similar in some ways but not in others . . . and so on. When two things are very similar in ways that are important to us (think of two 5mm ball bearings from the same box), we may say that they are "the same" or that they are "identical." On the other hand, there is the relation that obtains between each thing and itself and nothing else. This relation does not obtain between two 5mm ball bearings from the same box. Indeed, it does not obtain between any *two* things. Some philosophers call the relation "numerical identity" for this reason. On being told that a thing "*a*" stands in the relation to a thing "*b*," I can infer something about the number of things referred to by the expressions "*a*" and "*b*." The expressions refer to one thing, not two.[1] Other philosophers call it "strict identity," because whether or not it is right to say that things are identical in this sense depends only on whether the relation obtains, while whether or not it is right to say that things are identical in the very-qualitatively-similar sense is a more loosey-goosey matter—it depends on what relations of qualitative similarity are important to us at the time. Other philosophers call it "real identity," implying that, when we use the word in its very-similar sense, we are making a sort of mistake, or engaging in a sort of pretence. "You may say that the two ball bearings are identical, but of course they are not *really* identical." I will just call it, the relation that obtains between a thing and itself and nothing else, "identity."

Now, *Counterpart Theorists*[2] say that there is no identity across maximally specific states of affairs.

A natural way to flesh out the background ontology of counterpart theory is to think of a state of affairs as an ordered collection of things, a certain way. Here is one state of affairs: Mike, John, and Julia (an ordered collection of things) are fighting (a way for things to be). Here is another state of affairs: Horton and Maisie (an ordered collection of things) are such that the first is larger than the second (a way for things to be.) A maximally specific state of affairs, then, is a collection of things, a certain, maximally specific way. Here is a maximally specific state of affairs: shatom and batom (a collection of things) are two iron atoms, a meter apart, in an otherwise empty Euclidean universe (a maximally specific way for things to be.)

---

[1] Thanks to Steve Yablo for convincing me that this is the etymology of the term "numerical identity." Prior to his convincing me I had assumed that the relation got that name because it was familiar to us from math: when I write " = " between "2 + 2" and "4," I convey to my readers that the relation obtains between the number picked out by the expression on the left and the number picked out by the expression on the right.

[2] For classic expositions of the theory, see Lewis (1968, 1971) and Stalnaker (1976, 1986).

With this background ontology in place, the counterpart theorists' central claim is that, for any two maximal states of affairs, the collections of things associated with them have empty intersection. Nothing figures in more than one maximal state of affairs.

*Identity theorists*,[3] on another hand, say that, sometimes, there is identity across maximally specific states of affairs. A natural way to flesh out identity theory is to think, once again, of a maximally specific state of affairs as a collection of things, a certain way, but this time to allow that one thing may figure in more than one maximal state of affairs. Here is one maximally specific state of affairs: shatom and batom (an ordered collection of things) are two iron atoms, a meter apart, in an otherwise empty Euclidian universe (a maximally specific way for things to be.) Here is another: shatom (a singleton collection of things) is an iron atom, alone in an otherwise empty Euclidian universe. *Shatom* figures in both states of affairs.

*Property theorists*,[4] on yet a third hand, say that, strictly speaking, the question of whether there is or is not identity across maximally specific states of affairs makes no sense. A maximally specific state of affairs is just a maximally specific way for things to be, qualitatively speaking—a special kind of property. Here is one maximally specific state of affairs: being two iron atoms, a meter apart, in an otherwise empty Euclidean universe. Here is another: being one iron atom in an otherwise empty Euclidean universe. There is no sense in asking: "is the one thing in the second state of affairs identical to anything in the first state of affairs?" There are no things in properties. Properties are instantiated by things.

I certainly do not want to presume in favor of any of these ways of thinking about identity across states of affairs in this book. Nonetheless, I think it will be helpful, for the purposes of explaining what follows from the fact that personal essence is not perfectly fragile, initially to frame the discussion in terms of counterpart theory. We will get to framing the discussion using identity theory and property theory later in this chapter.

Suppose, with the counterpart theorist, that there is no identity across states of affairs. How, then, are we to understand the claim that personal essence is not perfectly fragile? And how are we to make sense of the minimally benevolent person's preference for states of affairs in which individuals are better off over states of affairs in which those same

---

[3] For classic early defenses of the view, see Kripke (1972) and Plantinga (1973, 1974).

[4] I like this view. But it would be a wild digression to defend it here.

individuals are worse off? How can someone be better off in one state of affairs than in another if nobody exists in both?

This is where counterparts come in. Counterpart theorists observe that, while there is no identity across states of affairs as they construe them (counterpart theorists typically call them *possible worlds*, I will follow suit), things in distinct worlds may nonetheless be more or less qualitatively similar in various ways. Their idea is that we can make sense of *de re modal claims*, claims about what could have happened to particular things, in terms of relations of qualitative similarity between things. So, for example, according to counterpart theory, to say:

"It could have been the case that A had property *p*."

is to say that A is counterpart-related to something, in some world, that has property *p*. When are things counterpart-related? When they are appropriately qualitatively similar. When are things appropriately qualitatively similar? In the paradigmatic versions of the theory, David Lewis and Robert Stalnaker take appropriate similarity to be a highly context-sensitive matter. What precisely we say, when we utter a de re modal sentence, is highly sensitive to our interests, to background standards and expectations... etc. But counterpart theorists are not obliged to take this view. They can think that what we say when we utter a de re modal sentence is relatively insensitive to context. No matter.

Some examples: I say:

"John McCain could have won the 2008 election."

and what I say is true, not because there is a possible world in which John McCain wins the 2008 election, but rather because a counterpart of John McCain, in a nearby world, wins the 2008 election. I say:

"CJH could have been a mighty tennis player."

and what I say is true, because a counterpart of me, in a sadly distant world, is a mighty tennis player. I say:

"John McCain could have been a truck."

and what I say is false, because none of John McCain's counterparts is a truck.

So on this way of thinking claims about personal essence, general claims about the ways in which people could and could not have been different, are understood as claims about the extension of the counterpart relation. Psychological Essentialism is the claim that no person has a counterpart with a psychological history significantly different from his or her own. Parental Essentialism is the claim that no two people are counterparts whose parents are not counterparts. And Personal Essence is Not Perfectly Fragile, the claim we are assuming here, is the claim that, for any natural dimension of similarity and difference, any person, in any world, has counterparts in other worlds who are ever so-slightly different along that dimension. Any person who is 6 feet 5 inches tall on December 4, 2009 has a counterpart who is 6 feet 6 inches tall on December 4, 2009, any person who is born at 20:43:21 on December 4, 2009 has a counterpart who is born at 20:43:22 on December 4, 2009 . . . and so on.

## 9.2. Morphing

Now think back to Mary (the Mary who was trying to get pregnant but was advised to hold off a couple of months), and consider two worlds, a world that might come about if she plunges ahead:

> $W_{Jack}$: In which she ignores her doctor's advice, and soon conceives an unhealthy baby boy, baby Jack.

and a world that might come about if she waits:

> $W_{Jill}$: In which she heeds her doctor's advice, and three months later conceives a healthy baby girl, baby Jill.

Suppose that Jack in $W_{Jack}$ and Jill in $W_{Jill}$ are as different, physically and psychologically, as typical non-twin siblings,

On no plausible view of personal essence are Jack and Jill counterparts. We would clearly be blundering if we said to Jack—"if your parents had heeded the doctor, waited six months and conceived a girl, physically and psychologically quite different from the way you actually are, then you would have been younger than you actually are, and you would have been better off."

But notice that, because essence is not perfectly fragile, there exists a world, call it $W_2$, just like $W_{Jack}$ in all respects except this: Jack's counterpart in $W_2$ is just a little bit more like Jill than Jack is (born a fraction later, a fraction blonder . . . etc.). Fig. 9.1 shows the three worlds.

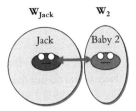

**Figure 9.1**

The shading represents qualitative similarity. The arrow represents the fact that Jack is counterpart-related to the baby in $W_2$, but Jill is not counterpart-related either to the baby in $W_2$ or to Jack.

Indeed, because essence is not perfectly fragile, there exists a *morphing sequence* of intermediary worlds, $W_2, \ldots, W_n$ such that:

*Morphing*
In each of $W_2$ to $W_n$ a counterpart of Mary has one baby, and Jack in $W_{Jack}$ is a counterpart of the baby in $W_2$, who is a counterpart of the baby in $W_3, \ldots$, who is a counterpart of the baby in $W_n$, who is a counterpart of Jill in $W_{Jill}$.

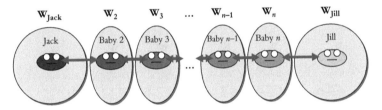

**Figure 9.2**

Fig. 9.2 shows the morphing sequence.

As we move along it so we encounter babies who are born increasingly later, increasingly less like Jack, increasingly more like Jill.

How many intermediary steps will there need to be? What will the transitions need to be like? How you answer these questions will depend on your views about personal essence. Vis-à-vis the number of steps: the more fragile you take personal essence to be, the longer you will think the sequence needs to be. The more robust you take personal essence to be, the shorter you will think the sequence needs to be. Vis-à-vis transitions: if, for example, you take gender essentialism to be true (no determinately male baby has a determinately female baby as a counterpart), then you will think that there needs to be some gender ambiguity at some world in the sequence. You will think that there needs to be a gradual transition, midway through the sequence, from determinately male babies to determinately female babies. But, if you take gender essentialism to be false, then you will think that there can be a clean jump from male to female babies. No matter. Just so long as you do not think that essence is perfectly fragile along some dimension, you will take it that some kind of morphing sequence can be constructed.

## 9.3. Upslope Morphing

Now suppose that Jill in $W_{Jill}$ is significantly better off than Jack in $W_{Jack}$. Suppose that Jill has a great life in $W_{Jill}$, while Jack has a terrible life in $W_{Jack}$.

I will assume here, plausibly enough, that well-being is *fine-grained*. Between a terrible life like Jack's and a great life like Jill's, there are ever so many intermediaries, enough to construct a morphing sequence with the following feature:

*Upslope Morphing*
Jack in $W_{Jack}$ is worse off than his counterpart in $W_2$, who is worse off than his counterpart in $W_3, \ldots$, who is worse off than her counterpart in $W_n$, who is worse off than her counterpart in $W_{Jill}$, Jill.

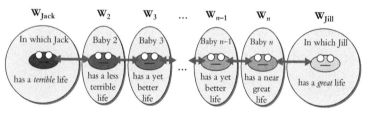

**Figure 9.3**

Fig. 9.3 shows an upslope morphing sequence.

Each world contains a baby, and is succeeded by a world in which a counterpart of that baby is better off.

## 9.4. Generalized Morphing

Of course, what holds for $W_{Jack}$ and $W_{Jill}$ holds for many other worlds too. How many? To answer that question precisely I need to define some more terms.

*Pareto-Dominance*

For any worlds W, W*, and kind K, say that W* K-pareto-dominates W iff

all K-people in W* have counterparts in W, and vice versa

and no K-person in W* is worse off than his or her counterpart in W

and some K-person in W* is better off than his or her counterpart in W.

*Anonymous Pareto-Dominance*

For any worlds W, W*, and kind K, say that W* anonymously K-pareto-dominates W iff there is a correspondence relation between the K-people in W and the K-people in W* such that

no K-person in W* is worse off than his or her pair in W

and some K-person in W* is better off than his or her pair in W.

Now here is the answer:

*Generalized Morphing*

For all worlds W, W*, kind K, if W* anonymously K-pareto-dominates W, then there exists a morphing sequence of worlds W, $W_1$, ..., $W_n$, W*, such that each world in the sequence K-pareto-dominates its predecessor.

Why is this? Well, suppose that W* anonymously K-pareto-dominates W. So there is a correspondence relation between W and W* with the properties above. The relation might look like Fig. 9.4 (lines indicate pairings).

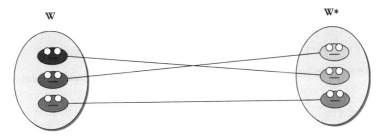

Figure 9.4

Because personal essence is not perfectly fragile we can then construct a sequence of intermediary worlds linking each individual in W to his or her pair in W* via a chain of counterparts. The sequence might look like Fig. 9.5 (as before, arrows indicate counterpart relations).

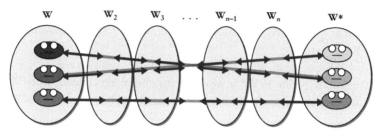

**Figure 9.5**

And, because well-being is fine-grained, we can construct the sequence in such a way that chains of counterparts connecting people in W to no-better-or-worse-off people in W\* are *flat* (each person on the chain is no better or worse off than his or her successor) and chains of counterparts connecting people in W to better-off people in W\* are *upslope* (each person on the chain is better off than his or her successor.) By construction, each world in such a sequence is K-pareto-dominated by its successor.

## 9.5. Anonymous Benevolence

Now we are in a position to get an important result.

*Anonymous Benevolence*
If decency requires of you that you be benevolent toward people of kind K (to prefer, other things being equal, K-pareto-dominant worlds), then decency and rationality together require of you that you be anonymously benevolent toward kind K-people (to prefer, other things being equal, anonymously K-pareto-dominant worlds).

Why? Well, suppose that world W\* anonymously K-pareto-dominates world W, and that decency requires of you that you prefer K-pareto-dominant worlds. By Generalized Morphing, there is an upslope morphing sequence from W to W\*. By Minimal Benevolence, if you are decent, then you will prefer each world in the sequence to its predecessor. If you are rational, then your preferences will be transitive. So, if you are decent and rational, then you will prefer the last to the first.

So, for example, if Mary is decent and rational, then she will prefer $W_{Jill}$ to the world that it anonymously pareto-dominates, $W_{Jack}$. Why? Focus on the worlds in the morphing sequence from $W_{Jack}$ to $W_{Jill}$. If Mary is decent, then she will prefer each world to its predecessor. If she is rational, then her preferences will be transitive. So, if she is decent and rational, then she will prefer $W_{Jill}$ to $W_{Jack}$. She will prefer that she bring Jill into existence, rather than Jack.

## 9.6. A First Worry: Is Essence Really so Robust?

That is my central claim. You might worry that I have argued for it using a particular, controversial picture of sameness-across-maximal-states-of-affairs: counterpart theory. I will get to how to frame the argument using different pictures of sameness-across-states of affairs in the next section, but first I want to pause a moment and address some other worries that may have occurred to you. I think that these worries are instructive. By understanding why they are mistaken we can get a better understanding of how morphing works.

First, you might worry that our essences may turn out to be much more fragile than we think. Maybe the science of genetics will demonstrate this. Maybe it will turn out that there is a gene—call it the *E-gene*—that plays an enormously important role in our physical and psychological development. Maybe it will turn out that some people have this gene and some people do not. Maybe it will turn out that the developmental role played by this gene is so important that it is plausible to say of any person with the E-gene that, if his or her mother had conceived a child genetically just like him or her, but without the E-gene, then he or she would never have existed, and vice versa. And maybe it will turn out that the having of this gene is an all-or-nothing matter. We are all either E-people or not-E-people. There are no half-E-people.[5]

I have quite permissive views about personal essence, so I think it unlikely that science will uncover any such genes, but put this to one side. Maybe there are indeed genes like the E-gene. So what? Why is this a problem for Generalized Morphing? Well, I take it that we are supposed to infer that E-people are essentially E-people, they could not have been not-E-people. No E-person has a not-E counterpart, and vice versa. And we are supposed to infer that, since all possible people are either E-people or not-E-people, we cannot construct a morphing sequence containing a chain of counterparts linking an E-person to a not-E-person.

But these are bad inferences. We can readily construct such a sequence. Here is one way to do it: in the first intermediary world in the sequence, the relevant person has the E-gene, but it is not expressed for ten seconds of his life (think of the E-gene being "switched off" for those ten seconds).

---

[5] Thanks to Alistair Norcross for conveying the spirit of this worry to me.

In the second intermediary world in the sequence, the relevant person has the E-gene, but it is not expressed for twenty seconds of his life . . . In the final intermediary world in the sequence, the relevant person has the E-gene, but it is not expressed for all of his life. Each person is a counterpart of his predecessor and successor.

"But wait!", you might say, "Science has shown us that the E-gene plays a tremendously important developmental role. There is no mechanism in nature that 'switches off' the E-gene in the way you are describing." Maybe so. In that case the intermediary worlds in the morphing sequence are, nomologically (that is to say: *with respect to physical law*), unlike our world. But that is no problem. We can have counterparts in worlds that are nomologically unlike our own. Uri Geller did not bend a spoon with his mind on the Johnny Carson Show, but, if Uri Geller had bent a spoon with his mind on the Johnny Carson Show, then I would still have existed. Why? Because I have a counterpart in the closest world in which a Uri Geller-counterpart bends a spoon with his mind on a show run by a counterpart of Johnny Carson, even though that world is in one small respect nomologically unlike our own.

My general point is that the worry vastly underestimates the diversity of possible states of affairs. They are very diverse indeed. Because this is so it does not follow from:

(1) Gary does not have the E-gene. If his mother had conceived a baby genetically just like him, but with the E-gene, then he would not have existed.

that

(2) Gary could not have had the E-gene.

Thinking counterpart theoretically, (1) is true, because Gary has no counterpart in the closest world in which a counterpart of his mother conceives a baby genetically just like him, but with the E-gene. But (2) is false, because Gary has counterparts in more distant worlds in which counterparts of his mother conceive babies genetically like him, but with the E-gene—worlds in which the expression of the E-gene is inhibited.

## 9.7. A Second Worry: Can Things Always Get Better?

Second, you might worry that, where we can construct a morphing sequence, we cannot always construct an *upslope* morphing sequence.

Take the morphing sequence connecting $W_{Jack}$ to $W_{Jill}$. Suppose that gender essentialism is true. No determinately male baby has a determinately female counterpart, and vice versa. Some worlds in the sequence must then contain people of indeterminate gender. It is an unfortunate fact that, in our imperfect world, gender indeterminacy brings with it a host of special trials and tribulations of which the determinately gendered have only the faintest understanding. So, as we move along the sequence into and through worlds in which the children are indeterminately gendered, the children will start getting worse off for a while, before getting better off again. There will not be a smooth upslope.[6]

I think it odd to suppose that gender essentialism is true. We ordinarily think that boys can become girls, and girls boys. People survive sex-change operations. So why think that boys could not have been born girls, and girls boys? But put that to one side. Suppose that gender essentialism is indeed true. The worry arises, once again, from vastly underestimating the diversity of metaphysically possible states of affairs. There are many ways to construct an upslope morphing sequence from $W_{Jack}$ to $W_{Jill}$. One, rather clunky, way to do it is to fix the background social conditions in intermediary worlds, but compensate the indeterminately gendered for the trials and tribulations that they suffer. So, as we move along the morphing sequence, keeping track of the money in the children's bank accounts, the graph looks something like Fig. 9.6.

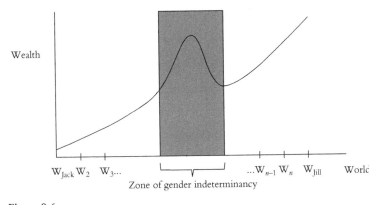

**Figure 9.6**

6 Thanks to Tom Dougherty for this worry.

I say that this is a *clunky* way of constructing the sequence because for us to get the result that there is a smooth well-being upslope we need to suppose quite precise commensurability between wealth and other aspects of well-being. As we move into the zone of indeterminacy, so we encounter people who suffer more discrimination than their predecessors, but are wealthier. We need to suppose that the numbers can be set in such a way that all such people are, on balance, a little bit better off than their predecessors.

A less clunky way of constructing the sequence is to vary the background social conditions. There is no need to compensate gender-indeterminate children in the intermediary worlds for the noxious effects of prejudice. They are spared these effects. Why? Because in this one respect the worlds in which they live are significantly different from our own. Nothing prevents us from having counterparts in worlds that are different from our own in this respect. It is not as if I would never have existed if one less child had been bullied in the playground this morning.

Again, the general point is that there are many, many metaphysically possible worlds. When you build morphing sequences, you have many, many bricks at your disposal.

## 9.8.  A Third Worry

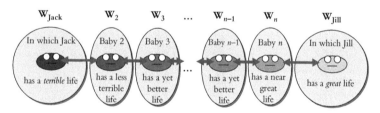

Figure 9.7

Third, you might worry that we have misconstrued what, on the counterpart-theoretic picture, decency requires of us. We supposed that, for certain kinds K, decency requires of you that you prefer (other things being equal) K-pareto-dominant worlds. But look again at the upslope morphing sequence from $W_{Jack}$ to $W_{Jill}$ (see Fig. 9.7) and think about what attitudes Mary might have *long after* she has acted. Suppose she actually brought about $W_{Jack}$, and she knows it. Suppose also that she loves Jack and wishes well for him. Then it would be very natural for her to wish that things had gone the way they go in $W_2$ ("because then Jack would have had a less terrible life") but to be happy that things did not go the way they go in $W_3$ ("because then Jack would never have existed"). Would this not amount to *preferring* $W_2$ to $W_3$? And would it not be consistent with her being a decent person that she prefer $W_2$ to $W_3$ in this way? And does this not show that the morphing argument fails, that decency does not commit us to preferring each world in the morphing sequence to its predecessor?

This worry raises some delicate issues concerning how to think about attitudes of retrospective satisfaction or regret. It may be helpful to coin a term here:

*Active Favoring*
Say that an agent actively favors world $W_x$ over world $W_y$ when she is disposed, upon coming to believe 'one of $W_x$ or $W_y$ is actual, but I don't know which',
- to be pleased to discover that $W_x$ is actual
- to be sad to discover that $W_y$ is actual
- to bring about $W_x$, given the choice.

Does Mary actively favor $W_3$ over $W_2$? We do not know. We know that, when she believes that $W_{Jack}$ is actual, she wishes that $W_2$ were actual and is glad that $W_3$ is not actual, but this does not tell us what attitudes she is disposed to have when she ceases to believe that $W_{Jack}$ is actual, and comes to believe "one of $W_2$ or $W_3$ is actual, but I don't know which."

Nonetheless I say this: if Mary is a decent, minimally benevolent person, then she will actively favor each world in the morphing sequence over its predecessor. Her pro-attitude toward $W_2$ over $W_3$ will be hostage to the belief that $W_{Jack}$ is actual. Why? Because, upon coming to believe that (for example) one of $W_2$ or $W_3$ is actual, Mary is in a position where she knows that she will have a child and she knows that her child is/will be better off if $W_3$ is actual (because the children in $W_2$ and $W_3$ are counterparts, if $W_3$ is actual then it will turn out that her child would be better off if $W_2$ were actual, and if $W_2$ were actual then it will turn out that her child would be better off if $W_3$ were actual). A decent, minimally benevolent person in this position will be pleased to discover that her child is better off, will be sad to discover that her child is worse off, and will choose to bring it about that her child is better off if she can.

What does this tell us about Mary's *preferences*? Is it right to say that decent, minimally benevolent Mary prefers $W_2$ to $W_3$, because (in virtue of her believing $W_{Jack}$ to be actual) she wishes that $W_2$ were actual and does not wish that $W_3$ were actual? Or is it right to say that she prefers $W_3$ to $W_2$, because she actively favors $W_3$ over $W_2$? I do not think that there is a right or wrong thing to say here. If one person chooses to identify the preference with the wishful thinking and another chooses to identify the preference with the active favoring, neither is abusing our inchoate notion of preference. But this is not the interesting question, for present purposes. The interesting question, for present purposes, is whether the transitivity constraint on rational preferring applies to rational active favoring. Should we accept this principle?

*Transitivity of Active Favoring*
If you are rational, then, for any worlds Wa, Wb, Wc, if you actively favor Wa over Wb, and you actively favor Wb over Wc, then you actively favor Wa over Wc.

If we should, then it follows that, if Mary is decent and rational, then she will actively favor $W_{Jill}$ over $W_{Jack}$.

I am inclined to think that, for the counterpart theorist, the arguments for the transitivity of rational active favoring are at least as strong as the arguments for the transitivity of rational preference. If the objects of our conative attitudes are Lewisian possible worlds, then any feature of Wa that counts in its favor when comparing it to Wb also counts in its favor when comparing it to Wc.

## 9.9. Doing without Counterpart Theory

But what if the "states of affairs" we are interested in here, the objects of our conative attitudes, the sorts of things that minimally benevolent people have preferences between, are not Lewisian possible worlds? I assumed they were because counterpart theory offers an exceptionally clear and precise way of setting out claims about essence. But, as I mentioned earlier, there are different ways of thinking about states of affairs—given by property theory and identity theory. Let me describe how to frame the argument making use of these different ways of thinking about states of affairs.

First, there is property theory. Properties are ways for things to be. When we represent the contents of conative attitudes with sets of "maximal states of affairs," the property theorist thinks of these things as properties of a special kind: fully precise ways for the world to be, qualitatively speaking. I will call them "world-properties." Since individuals do not exist in properties, the property theorist, like the counterpart theorist, will not say that Mary's minimal benevolence toward her future child consists in her preferring one maximal state of affairs to another when she has the very same child in both, and that child is better off in the one, and all other things are equal. The property theorist will instead say that her benevolence consists in her preferring one world-property to another whenever the world-properties bear a certain relation to one another (having to do with the well-being of children).

The argument now runs pretty much as before. Take the sequence of world-properties corresponding to worlds in the morphing sequence from $W_{Jack}$ to $W_{Jill}$ that I just described. Each world-property in this sequence bears the relevant relation to its predecessor, so minimally benevolent Mary will prefer each one to its predecessor. So, if she is rational, she will prefer the last to the first.

Second, there is identity theory. The identity theorist thinks that things figure in states of affairs, and that one thing may figure in more than one state of affairs. Mary's minimal benevolence toward her future child consists in her preferring, all other things being equal, MC-pareto-dominant states of affairs, where a state of affairs S* MC-pareto-dominates another state of affairs S when Mary's one child in S* is her one child in S, and that child is better off in S* than in S.

The reasoning is no longer quite so straightforward. Take $S_{Jack}$, the state of affairs that might come about if Mary ignores her doctor, and $S_{Jill}$, the state of affairs that might come about if she heeds her doctor's advice. Because identity is a transitive relation, we can construct a sequence of states of affairs beginning with $S_{Jack}$, ending with $S_{Jill}$, such that each state of affairs in the sequence MC-pareto-dominates its predecessor, only if Jack in $S_{Jack}$ is Jill in $S_{Jill}$. But Jack in $S_{Jack}$ is not Jill in $S_{Jill}$. Jack is nowhere to be found in $S_{Jill}$. Jill is nowhere to be found in $S_{Jack}$. So we cannot construct any such sequence. So we cannot directly appeal to the transitivity of rational preference to establish that, if Mary is decent and rational, then she will prefer $S_{Jill}$ to $S_{Jack}$.

But let us not jump to any hasty conclusions. Applying identity theory to morphing cases is a tricky, subtle business. I say that, if Mary is decent and rational, then she will prefer $S_{Jill}$ to $S_{Jack}$. I have two arguments to this conclusion.

My first argument appeals to the role that haecceitistic considerations (considerations to do with identity across states of affairs) play in shaping Mary's preferences. Consider a sequence of propositions, $P_{Jack}$, $P_1$, ..., $P_n$, $P_{Jill}$, that give full qualitative descriptions of the worlds in the morphing sequence I described earlier ($P_{Jack}$ fully describes how things are, qualitatively speaking, in $W_{Jack}$, $P_1$ fully describes how things are, qualitatively speaking, in $W_1$, ... etc.). Because our essences are not perfectly fragile, an identity theorist, not knowing which proposition is true, should think of each of them:

> "If *that* is true, then Mary will have a child, and it will turn out that, if the successor proposition had been true, then she would have had the same child, and that child would have been better off."

So, for any proposition in the sequence, there is a pair of states of affairs such that the proposition gives a full qualitative description of the first member of the pair, and its successor gives a full qualitative description of the second member of the pair, and Mary's child in the first state of affairs *is* Mary's child in the second state of affairs.

To represent what is going on, it may be helpful to introduce some notation: let $SP_i@P_k$ be the state of affairs that, supposing $P_k$ is true, would have come about if $P_i$ had been true. Because our essences are not perfectly fragile, there are states of affairs like that shown in Fig. 9.8. States in the same row contain the very same people. So, for example, Jack exists in both $SP_{Jack}@P_{Jack}$ and $SP_1@P_{Jack}$. States in the same column are qualitatively identical. So, for example, the qualitative features of $SP_1@P_{Jack}$ and $SP_1@P_1$ are both fully described by proposition $P_1$.

Because Mary's children are ever better off as we move along the morphing sequence, minimal benevolence commits her to having preferences as shown in Fig. 9.9.

$SP_{Jack}@P_{Jack}$     $SP_1@P_{Jack}$

        $SP_1@P_1$      $SP_2@P_1$

             $SP_2@P_2$     $SP_3@P_2$

                   $SP_3@P_3$ ...

                                 $SP_n@P_{Jill}$      $SP_{Jill}@P_{Jill}$

**Figure 9.8**

$SP_{Jack}@P_{Jack}$ $<$ $SP_1@P_{Jack}$

        $SP_1@P_1$    $<$    $SP_2@P_1$

             $SP_2@P_2$    $<$    $SP_3@P_2$

                  $SP_3@P_3$    $<$  ...

                                 $SP_n@P_{Jill}$    $<$    $SP_{Jill}@P_{Jill}$

**Figure 9.9**

Now suppose that these things, too, are true of Mary:

*Transitivity*
Her preferences between maximal states of affairs are transitive.

*Within this Domain, her Preferences Supervene on the Qualitative*
Within this domain, whether or not she prefers one state of affairs to another supervenes on the qualitative features of the states of affairs. There are no qualitatively identical states of affairs S1, S1*, qualitatively identical states of affairs S2, S2*, such that she prefers S1 to S2, but does not prefer S1* to S2*.

It follows that Mary must prefer any state of affairs described by $P_{Jill}$ to any state of affairs described by $P_{Jack}$. She must prefer that she have a happy child, rather than a numerically distinct, miserable child.

It is a condition on Mary's being rational that her preferences between maximal states of affairs be transitive. Is it a condition on her being decent or rational that her preferences between maximal states of affairs in this domain supervene on the qualitative? Not obviously so. We have already seen that Mary may, after coming to know that $P_{Jack}$ is true, have a preference for $SP_1@P_{Jack}$ over $SP_{Jill}@P_{Jack}$, on the grounds that $SP_1@P_{Jack}$ contains someone much beloved to her, *Jack*, and $SP_{Jill}@P_{Jack}$ does not. This preference will guide her attitudes of satisfaction and regret—she will wish that $P_1$ had been true (because then *Jack* would have been better off than he actually is), but she will not wish that $P_{Jill}$ had been true (because then *Jack* would never have existed). We have no grounds for thinking that she is thereby indecent or irrational.

Nonetheless, I say that, when we put aside preferences of the kind that guide retrospective attitudes of satisfaction and regret, and focus instead on preferences of the kind that guide action, decency requires of us that, in this domain, these preferences supervene on the qualitative. Imagine that Mary, before knowing what she will do, has preferences that fail to supervene on the qualitative. Imagine, for example, that she prefers $SP_2@P_1$ to $SP_1@P_1$ (because one person exists in both states of affairs, and is better off in the former) but she prefers $SP_1@P_{Jack}$ to $SP_2@P_{Jack}$ (because Jack exists in the former, but not the latter). She is then in an odd position. I describe to her a maximal state of affairs in complete, exhaustive qualitative detail: down to the position and trajectory taken by every atom throughout world history. I describe to her another state of affairs in complete, exhaustive qualitative detail: down to the inner thoughts of every turtle and newt. I ask her which she prefers, and she replies "I don't know. You have not told me enough about the states of affairs. You have told me, in glorious detail, all the qualitative facts about them, but I need to know some further, irreducibly haecceitistic facts about them in order to know which I prefer. These irreducibly haecceitistic facts matter to me." I am immediately inclined to ask why they matter to her. She has no special reason, at this stage, to want *Jack*, of all her possible future children, to exist. She has formed no special attachment to him, she does not know that he is her future child. I now feel about her the way that Derek Parfit feels about people who are future Tuesday indifferent. She takes things to matter that *just do not*. And this is not the behavior of a decent person. Decent people do not care about merely haecceitistic differences between states of affairs without grounds for so caring.

That is my first argument. It is limited in scope. It applies to someone in Mary's position, someone who is deciding whom to create. But it does not apply to someone who is dealing with already-created people—maybe this someone does have grounds for caring about merely haecceitistic differences between states of affairs in the morphing sequence, because she has grounds for caring (at least in the regret/satisfaction way) about whether the already-created people exist. To cover these people we need another, more general argument.

Let us begin by supposing that Mary is in a position to make any one of the propositions $P_{Jack}, P_1, \ldots, P_n, P_{Jill}$ (propositions that give full qualitative descriptions of worlds in the morphing sequence, remember) true, by pressing any one of a series of buttons, labeled $B_{Jack}, B_1, \ldots, B_n, B_{Jill}$. Suppose that she knows this. Suppose that she is mulling over what to do. Suppose that she is minimally benevolent and rational. Suppose she is an identity theorist. What will she do?

To help us see what is going on, let us simplify the case a bit, and suppose further that the morphing sequence has only two intermediary steps. By pressing $B_1$, Mary will bring a moderately miserable, moderately male child into the world, who will go by the name of "Janus." By pressing $B_2$, Mary will bring a moderately happy, moderately female child into the world, who will go by the name of "Jane."

If Mary believes that she will press $B_{Jack}$, then she believes that the actual state of affairs, $SP_{Jack}@P_{Jack}$, is one in which she conceives a child she calls "Jack," who has a miserable life. Let us go with Mary and call that child "Jack." Because essence is not perfectly fragile, she should then take it that the state of affairs that would have come about if she had pressed $B_1$, $SP_1@P_{Jack}$, is one in which that very same child, Jack, has a moderately miserable life under the name "Janus." And, because essence is somewhat fragile, she should take that the states of affairs that would have come about if she had pressed $B_2$ or $B_{Jill}$, $SP_2@P_{Jack}$ and $SP_2@P_{Jill}$, are ones in which different children have moderately good and good lives respectively. In a picture, she should take it that the states of affairs that would have come about if she had done one thing or another are as shown in Fig. 9.10.

Figure 9.10

Because Jack figures in both $SP_{Jack}@P_{Jack}$ and $SP_1@P_{Jack}$, Mary's minimal benevolence immediately commits her to preferring the latter. But it does not immediately commit her to having any further preferences. In a picture, she must have preferences like this:

$$SP_{Jack}@P_{Jack} < SP_1@P_{Jack} \quad SP_2@P_{Jack} \quad SP_{Jill}@P_{Jack}$$

So, when she presses $B_{Jack}$, she should take it that she would have brought about a preferable state of affairs by pressing $B_1$.

But, if Mary believes that she will press button $B_1$, then, by similar reasoning, she should take it that the states of affairs she would bring about by pressing one button or another are as shown in Fig. 9.11.

**Figure 9.11**

And minimal benevolence immediately commits her to having these preferences between them:

$$SP_{Jack}@P_1 < SP_1@P1 < SP_2@P_1 \quad SP_{Jill}@P_1$$

So, when she presses $B_1$, she should take it that she would have brought about a preferable state of affairs by pressing $B_2$, a less preferable state of affairs by pressing $B_{Jack}$.

And, if she believes that she will press button $B_2$, then, by similar reasoning, she should take it that the states of affairs she would bring about by pressing one button or another are as shown in Fig. 9.12.

And minimal benevolence immediately commits her to having these preferences between them:

$$SP_{Jack}@P_2 \quad SP_1@P_2 < SP_2@P_2 < SP_{Jill}@P_2$$

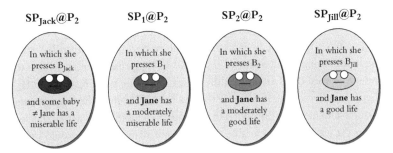

Figure 9.12

So, when she presses $B_2$, she should take it that she would have brought about a preferable state of affairs by pressing $B_{Jill}$, a less preferable state of affairs by pressing $B_1$.

Finally, if she believes that she will press button $B_{Jill}$, then, by similar reasoning, she should take it that the states of affairs she would bring about by pressing one button or another are as shown in Fig. 9.13.

Figure 9.13

And minimal benevolence immediately commits her to having these preferences between them:

$$SP_{Jack}@P_{Jill} \quad SP_1@P_{Jill} \quad SP_2@P_{Jill} < SP_{Jill}@P_{Jill}$$

So, when she presses $B_{Jill}$, she should take it that she would have brought about a less preferable state of affairs by pressing $B_2$.

The result of all this is that Mary is in a strange kind of situation—whether or not she believes that she would bring about preferable states of affairs by doing one thing or another depends on what she believes she will do. If, for example, she believes that she will press button $B_{Jack}$, then she believes that, if she were to press button $B_1$, then she would bring about a state of affairs ($SP_1@P_{Jack}$) that is preferable to the actual state of affairs ($SP_{Jack}@P_{Jack}$), and she believes that, if she were to press button $B_2$, then she would bring about a state of affairs ($SP_2@P_{Jack}$) that is not preferable to the actual state of affairs. But, if she believes that she will press button $B_1$, then she believes that, if she were to press button $B_2$, then she would bring about a state of affairs ($SP_2@P_1$) that is both preferable to the actual state of affairs ($SP_1@P_1$) and preferable to the state of affairs that she would bring about by pressing button $B_{Jack}$ ($SP_{Jack}@P_1$). Call this a situation in which *deliberatively relevant counterfactuals are actuality sensitive.*

What is it rational to do when deliberatively relevant counterfactuals are actuality sensitive? A great deal has been written about this question.[7] I will not propose a theory that tells us what to do *whenever* deliberatively relevant counterfactuals are actuality sensitive here. But I will propose and defend a partial theory, a theory that covers cases like Mary's. If she is rational, then she will press $B_{Jill}$.

One might be inclined to think that the key consideration in Mary's case is this: she knows that $B_{Jill}$ is the only button such that, if she presses it, then it will turn out to be the case that she would not have brought about a preferable state of affairs by doing something else. To put it another way:

---

[7] This is because a great deal has been written on Newcomb cases, and, on the standard interpretation of these cases, they give rise to situations in which counterfactuals are actuality sensitive. Take the classic Newcomb case (in brief: I stand before two boxes, one transparent and one opaque. I can take either or both home with me. I see that the transparent box contains $100. What does the opaque box contain? I know this: Some time ago a fantastically accurate predictor predicted what I would do. If it predicted that I would take the opaque box only, then it put $1,000,000 in the opaque box. If it predicted that I would take both boxes, then it put $0 in the opaque box.) On the standard interpretation, before playing the game it is right to think: "I am confident that the fantastic predictor has correctly predicted the choice I will actually make, so if I actually two-box then I will end up with $100, and if I actually one-box then I will end up with $1,000,000. But I am equally confident that my present decision has no influence over what is in the boxes, so if I actually two-box then it will turn out to be true that if I had one-boxed then I would have ended up with nothing, and if I actually one-box then it will turn out to be true that if I had two-boxed then I would have ended up with $1,000,100. What states of affairs I would bring about by doing one thing or another depends upon what I actually do."

Mary's problem is closely analogous to a modified Newcomb case, in which I get to pick one of four boxes. If the fantastically accurate predictor predicted that I would take Box 1, then it put something nice in Box 2. If it predicted that I would take Box 2, then it put something nice in Box 3, something nasty in Box 1. If it predicted that I would take Box 3, then it put something nice in Box 4, something nasty in Box 2. If it predicted that I would take Box 4, then it put something nasty in Box 3.

she knows that, if she presses $B_{Jill}$, then she will not harm her child (because it will turn out that she would not have made things better for Jill by pressing any other button), but if she presses any other button, then she will harm her child (if she presses $B_{Jack}$, for example, then it will turn out that her child, Jack, would have been better off if she had pressed $B_1$).

The implicit general principle is this:

*Avoid Regret*
If you are rational and there is exactly one option available to you such that, if you actually take it, then it will turn out that you would not have brought about a preferable state of affairs by taking any other option, then, absent epistemic or physical obstacles, you will take it.

But it is a dubious principle. Note that it gives strange results in other cases in which counterfactuals are actuality sensitive. Suppose that there is an endless series of levers, labeled 1, 2, 3, . . . , such that by pulling them Mary can have ever happier babies. And suppose that, if she pulls lever 1, then her baby would not have existed if she had pulled any other lever, but if she pulls lever 2 or higher, then her baby would have existed if she had pulled the next lever. If Mary prefers MC-pareto-dominant states of affairs, it follows from *Avoid Regret* that she rationally ought to pull lever 1. But that seems wrong.[8] To give a diagnosis of where it goes wrong: It may be a condition on our being rational that our actions be guided by our desires, but it does not follow that it is a condition on our being rational that our actions be, in retrospect, desirable.

Happily, there is a better principle in this vicinity. To state it I will need to introduce some terms. Say that one option is *pair-wise superior* to another when all of the following hold:

(i) Supposing you actually take the one, you would have brought about a less-preferable state of affairs by taking the other.

---

[8] Note also that *Avoid Regret* gives even stranger results in different cases in which counterfactuals are actuality sensitive. Consider a modified Newcomb case in which I get to pick one of three ottomans. If the fantastic predictor predicts that I will pick Ottoman 1, then it puts $1,000 in Ottoman 1, $1,001 in Ottoman 2, and nothing in Ottoman 3. If it predicts that I will pick Ottoman 2, then it puts $1,001 in Ottoman 1, $1,000 in Ottoman 2, and nothing in Ottoman 3. If it predicts that I will pick Ottoman 3, then it puts nothing in Ottoman 1, nothing in Ottoman 2, and $1 in Ottoman 3. It follows from *Avoid Regret* that I rationally ought to pick Ottoman 3. But that is wrong. No established version of causal or evidential decision theory yields this result. Nor should it.

(ii) Supposing you actually take the other, you would have brought about a preferable state of affairs by taking the one.

(iii) The state of affairs you will bring about, supposing you actually take the other, is not preferable to the state of affairs you will bring about, supposing you actually take the one.

Now consider a procedure:

(Step 1) Choose an option.

(Step 2) If there are pair-wise superior options, choose one, otherwise keep the option you have.

(Step 3) Continue, until there are no pair-wise superior options.

Say that an option is an *attractor* if, no matter how you apply this procedure (no matter which option you start off with, no matter which pair-wise superior options you choose along the way), you will always get to it.

Finally, say that an option is *stable* when both of the following hold:

(i) Supposing you actually take it, there is no other option such that you would bring about a preferable state of affairs by taking that other option.

(ii) There is no other option such that the state of affairs you will bring about, supposing you actually take that other option, is preferable to the state of affairs you will bring about, supposing you actually take this option.

Now here is the principle:

*Stable Attraction*
If an option is a stable attractor and you are rational, then, absent epistemic or physical obstacles, you will take it.

The motivating idea is that, if an option is a stable attractor and you are rational, then, no matter what your intentions are as you begin to think about what to do, you will end up with a settled intention to take it. Imagine yourself to be rational, surveying a range of options and trying to decide which to take. You form a tentative intention to take one of them. If there is another, pair-wise superior option, then this intention is self-weakening. With the intention comes a belief that this is the one you will take. With the belief comes another belief, that you would bring about a preferable state of affairs by taking the other option. So your tentative intention fades, and is replaced by an intention to take the other option. But this new intention is not self-weakening. It brings with it a new belief, that you will take the other option, but you still believe that you would bring about a less-preferable state of affairs by taking the original option, and you do not think that the state of affairs that will come about, supposing you actually do what you now intend to do, is less preferable to the state of affairs that will come about supposing you actually do what you originally intended to do. It is not self-weakening, unless, of course, there is yet another pair-wise superior option...And so you cycle through the options, arriving in time (as you must, because it is an attractor) at an intention to take the stable attractor. But this intention, at last, is stable. Supposing that you take the stable attractor, you would not bring about a preferable state of affairs by taking any other option, nor is the state of affairs that you suppose to be actual less preferable to the state of affairs that will come about, supposing you take any other option. So you stick with it, being rational.

Applying the principle to the cases we have been looking at...In the lever case, pulling-lever-1 is not a stable attractor, because it is not an attractor—if you start with a tentative intention to pull lever 2 and continually trade up to pair-wise superior options, then you will never arrive at an intention to pull lever 1.[9] But in Mary's case pressing-button-$B_{Jill}$ *is* a stable attractor. As she deliberates, no matter what her initial inclinations are, insofar as she is rational she will come to be inclined to press button $B_{Jill}$, and once she is so inclined her desires will not tell against her seeing through on her inclination.

So, in a four-option case, when Mary is in a position to make any of propositions $P_{Jack}$, $P_1$, ..., $P_{Jill}$ true, if she is decent (her preferences conform to *Personal Dominance*) and rational (she picks stable attractors), then she will make $P_{Jill}$ true.

All very well, but what if she does not have the intermediary options? What if she has only two options—bringing miserable Jack into the world or happy Jill into the world? Well, recall the final principle of practical rationality from Chapter 8:

---

[9] And note that, in the ottoman case I described in the last footnote, picking-O3 is not a stable attractor, because it is not an attractor—if you start with a tentative intention to pick O1 then you will never arrive at an intention to pick O3.

(R11) *The Practical Insignificance of Irrelevant Alternatives*
Say that states of affairs $a$ and $b$ are *relevantly just like* states of affairs $a^*$ and $b^*$ when, to put it roughly, you see no evaluatively relevant differences between them. To put it precisely: when you take it that every reason to prefer $a$ to $b$ is a reason to prefer $a^*$ to $b^*$, every reason to prefer $b$ to $a$ is a reason to prefer $b^*$ to $a^*$, every reason to prefer $a^*$ to $b^*$ is a reason to prefer $a$ to $b$, and every reason to prefer $b^*$ to $a^*$ is a reason to prefer $b$ to $a$.
If you are rational, then for any maximal states of affairs $a,b,c, a^*, b^*$,
> *if* you have a stable disposition to bring about $a$, when knowingly in a position to bring about $a$ or $b$ or $c$,
> *and* $a^*$ and $b^*$ are states of affairs relevantly just like $a$ and $b$, but in which you are never in a position to bring about $c$,
> *then* you have a stable disposition to bring about $a^*$, when knowingly in a position to bring about $a^*$ or $b^*$.

And notice that the states of affairs Mary is in a position to bring about by pressing $B_{Jack}$ and $B_{Jill}$ in the four-option case are relevantly just like the states of affairs she is in a position to bring about by pressing $B_{Jack}$ and $B_{Jill}$ in the two-option case. In the four-option case, no matter what she believes she will do, she believes that pressing $B_{Jack}$ and pressing $B_{Jill}$ would bring different children into the world—the former happier than the latter. In the two-option case that is true too. It follows that, if Mary is rational, then she will press $B_{Jill}$ in the two-option case.

And what goes for simple morphing sequences goes for the other "cross-morphing" sequences we have looked at too. So we have the general result:

*Anonymous Benevolence (for the Identity Theorist)*
If one maximal state of affairs anonymously K-pareto-dominates another, and decency requires of you that you prefer K-pareto-dominant states of affairs, then decency and rationality together require of you that you bring about the anonymously K-pareto-dominant state of affairs, given the chance.

Rational people will be anonymously benevolent where they are benevolent.

# 10

# Transparent Conflicts

Rational people will be anonymously benevolent where they are benevolent. What can we do with this result?

## 10.1. Closing the File on the Non-Identity Problem

The first thing we can do is cut down a worry that we left hanging at the end of Chapter 5. In that chapter I argued that, if Mary, the prospective mother, is both rational and minimally benevolent toward her children, then she will choose to conceive a healthier child earlier rather than a less healthy child later. My argument crucially relied on Mary's assuming it to be equally likely, for any child she might conceive, that she conceive that child if she plunges ahead or waits. The worry was that Mary should not make this assumption. Essentialism about months-of-conception is true. None of us could have been conceived a month before or after the moment we were actually conceived. If Mary recognizes this, then she will take it that the set of children she might conceive by plunging ahead and the set of children she might conceive by waiting have no intersection.

As I said back in Chapter 5, I find essentialism about months-of-conception to be a funny view. But to reply to the worry we need not deny it. We need only observe that, for any precise genetic-profile G, Mary's credence in

$S_{Gnow}$: In which Mary conceives a child this month, with genetic-profile G, and the child's life is blighted by health problems.

conditional on her plunging ahead, is the same as her credence in

$S_{Glater}$: In which Mary conceives a child next month, with genetic-profile G, and the child has a life just like that of her child in $S_{Gnow}$, but not blighted by health problems.

conditional on her waiting. Whether or not $S_{Glater}$ pareto-dominates $S_{Gnow}$ (an essentialist about months of conception will say that it does not—because they are states of affairs in which she has different children), $S_{Glater}$ certainly does *anonymously* pareto-dominate $S_{Gnow}$. So we can construct an upslope morphing sequence from $S_{Gnow}$ to $S_{Glater}$. So, if Mary is minimally benevolent toward her children and rational, then she will prefer $S_{Glater}$ to $S_{Gnow}$. So, by the prospectist theory of practical rationality, if Mary is minimally benevolent toward her children and rational, then she will wait.

## 10.2. Constraints Redux

A second thing we can do is extend the central argument from Chapter 6. I argued there that my preferring to respect constraints against killing in some cases in which I do not know whom I am in a position to kill would involve a kind of selfishness on my part. We can now argue that the same kind of selfishness would be involved in my preferring to respect constraints against killing in some cases in which I do know whom I am in a position to kill. We began with such a case:

Human Fuel
By quickly, painlessly killing Amy, I can prevent Brian and Celia from being killed in protracted, painful ways. I know this, and I know everything about the lives Amy, Brian, and Celia will lead if I do one thing or the other.

In this case the two states of affairs I am in a position to bring about are as shown in Fig. 10.1.

$S_{Kill}$ anonymously pareto dominates $S_{Refrain}$, so we can construct an upslope morphing sequence from $S_{Refrain}$ to $S_{Kill}$, a sequence looking like that shown in Fig. 10.2 (as before, I will represent states of affairs in the sequence as Lewisian possible worlds, and use arrows to indicate counterpart relations between individuals in those worlds):

Figure 10.1

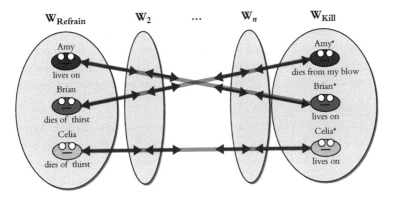

Figure 10.2

Each world in the sequence pareto-dominates its predecessor. So, if I am rational and (preferring not to violate the constraint against killing-one-to-save-others) I do not prefer the last to the first, then I must not prefer some world to another that it pareto-dominates. How can I explain my failing to prefer a pareto dominant world?

The best I can say is this: "Notice that I kill-someone-to-save-others in $W_{Kill}$ and do not in $W_{Refrain}$, so there must be a transition, somewhere in the sequence, from worlds in which I kill-someone-to-save-others to worlds in which I do not. Suppose for simplicity, that this transition is abrupt. There is a first world in which I kill-someone-to-save-others: $W_J$. Then I do not prefer $W_J$ to $W_{J-1}$, because in $W_J$ I kill-to-save-others and in $W_{J-1}$ I do not."

But this leaves me open to the familiar charge of selfishness: "You do not prefer $W_J$ to $W_{J-1}$, even though *everybody*, including the person you kill in $W_J$, is better off in $W_J$! Why? Because in $W_{J-1}$ *you* do no killing. That is just selfishness on your part."

A willing constraints theorist who wishes to avoid this charge must revert to the position I discussed in Chapter 6—"True, when I am in a position to bring about the states of affairs $S_{Kill}$, $S_{Refrain}$, I do willingly bring about $S_{Refrain}$. But I am not thereby expressing an indecent preference for $S_{Refrain}$ over $S_{Kill}$. I prefer, in the relevant way, that $S_{Kill}$ come about." As I said in Chapter 6, I do not see much future in this position.

## 10.3. Rescue Cases Redux

A third thing we can do is extend the arguments from Chapter 4, the arguments that in certain cases in which we do not know whom we are in position to rescue by doing what, rationality and decency together commit us to rescuing some people rather than others, to cover certain cases in which we do know whom we are in a position to rescue by doing what. Consider:

Transparent Big Differences

Atticus is on an island to my west, Barry on an island to my east. Atticus has food and water, but he is sick. He needs the medicine on my boat. Without it he will live for a few months, with it he will live for a few years. Barry is healthy, but he has no food or water. He needs the food and water on my boat. Without it he will die immediately, with it he will live on for many years. I know everything there is to know about these people, and about the lives they will lead if I go west or east.

In this case the two states of affairs that I am in a position to bring about as shown in Fig. 10.3.

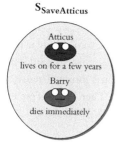
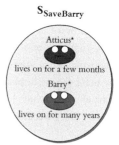

Figure 10.3

Because S$_{SaveBarry}$ anonymously pareto-dominates S$_{SaveAtticus}$, we can construct an upslope morphing sequence from the one to the other (see Fig. 10.4).

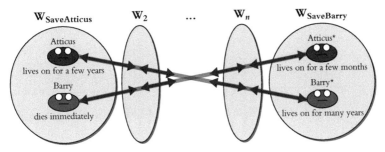

**W$_{SaveAtticus}$**     **W$_2$**   ...   **W$_n$**     **W$_{SaveBarry}$**

Atticus — lives on for a few years — Barry — dies immediately

Atticus* — lives on for a few months — Barry* — lives on for many years

Figure 10.4

So, by the arguments from before, if I am decent and rational, then I will head east, and save Barry.

Does the same go when the differences are small? Consider a case we discussed before:

Transparent Small Differences
I can save Andy in 3 hours by heading west, Ben in 2.5 hours by heading east. Again, I know everything there is to know about them.

In this case the states of affairs that I am in a position to bring about are as shown in Fig. 10.5.

**S$_{SaveAndy}$**                 **S$_{SaveBen}$**

Andy — is saved in 3 hours — Ben — dies

Andy — dies — Ben — is saved in 2.5 hours

Figure 10.5

I said that, on reflection, when I thought about all the ways in which it would be terrible if Andy died, and all the quite different ways in which it would be terrible if Ben died, I would have no preference for S$_{SaveBen}$ over

$S_{SaveAndy}$. Can we show that I am thereby indecent or irrational? Well, we certainly can construct a morphing sequence from $S_{SaveAndy}$ to $S_{SaveBen}$, a sequence like that shown in Fig. 10.6.

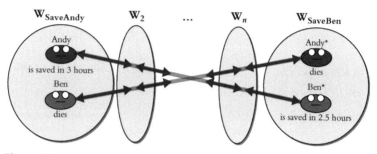

**Figure 10.6**

Can we construct an *upslope* morphing sequence—a sequence in which each world pareto-dominates its predecessor? This is a tricky question. Focus, in particular, on the Andy-to-Ben* chain of counterparts. We can construct an upslope morphing sequence only if we can construct a sequence in which each person on that chain is better off than his predecessor on that chain. Assuming that the relation *better off than* is transitive, we can do this only if Ben* in $W_{SaveBen}$ is better off than Andy in $W_{SaveAndy}$. Is Ben* in $W_{SaveBen}$ better off than Andy in $W_{SaveAndy}$? The answer to this turns on whether the relation *better off than* is negatively intransitive.

## 10.4. The Negative Intransitivity of *Better Off Than*

Let me explain what I mean. Sometimes, when we describe how one thing relates to another, the word "better" naturally creeps into our description. We may say that one person is "better off" than another, or that one person is a "better basketball player" than another, or that one tool is "better for opening tins of beans" than another. Philosophers call the relations that we thereby pick out different "betterness relations" or, more colloquially, "different ways of being better."

Where *better$_W$ than* is a betterness relation, say that *better$_W$ than* is *negatively intransitive* when there are items $x$, $y$, $z$ such that it is not the case that $x$ is better$_W$ than $y$, not the case that $y$ is better$_W$ than $z$, but it is the case that $x$ is better$_W$ than $z$. On one view, many betterness relations are negatively intransitive. Take, for example:

### Three Athletes and the Relation *Better Athlete Than*

Kenenisa Bekele: A runner with extraordinary endurance but (relatively!) poor top speed.

Usain Bolt: A runner with extraordinary top speed, but (relatively!) poor endurance.

Kenenisa Bekele+: A fictional runner just like Kenenisa Bekele, but with a fractionally higher top speed.

It is not the case that Bekele+ is a better athlete than Bolt. The most we can say of them is that they are each extraordinary athletes, in very different ways. Nor is it the case that Bolt is a better athlete than Bekele. The most we can say of them is that they are each extraordinary athletes, in very different ways. But Bekele+ is a better athlete than Bekele. Bekele+ is just like Bekele, but a bit faster. Another example:

### Three Careers and the Relation *Better Career Than*

Investment Banking: In which you earn a great deal of money for doing something you find only moderately interesting.

Philosophy: In which you earn a moderate amount of money for doing something you find very interesting.

Investment Banking+: A career just like Investment Banking, but in which you earn a further $1,000 a year.

It is not the case that Investment Banking+ is a better career than Philosophy. The most we can say of them is that they are good and bad in very different ways. Nor is it the case that Philosophy is a better career than Investment Banking. Again, they are good and bad in very different ways. But Investment Banking+ is a better career than Investment Banking. Investment Banking+ is just like Investment Banking, but a bit more lucrative.

These putative examples of negatively intransitive betterness relations have a common structure. In each case there is a way of being better, better$_W$, (call this a *covering value*[1]), and certain other ways of being better or worse (call

---

[1] I borrow the terminology from Ruth Chang's very helpful discussions of the structure of negatively intransitive betterness relations—summarized in the introduction to Chang (1997).

these *contributory values*) that determine whether things are better or worse in this way. Focus, for simplicity's sake, on the cases where there are just two contributory values. The idea is that, for an item that instantiates the first contributory value to degree $x$, the second to degree $y$, the space of items that are better$_W$ or worse$_W$ than the item is as shown in Fig. 10.7.

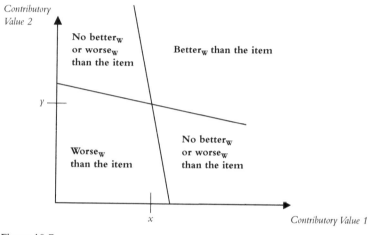

**Figure 10.7**

Roughly: when we compare the item with another, better in one contributory respect, worse in another, we sometimes find that the contributory values balance, so that neither item is better$_W$, though the balance is not perfectly delicate, so that the addition of any drop of value on either side will tip it. The contributory values are, to use slightly confusing philosophical jargon, "incommensurable."[2] Their incommensurability can be more or less extreme. Maximally extreme incommensurability would look as in Fig. 10.8. There is no trading off the contributory values. One item is better$_W$ than another only if it dominates with respect to both.

---

[2] I say "slightly confusing" because the term gets used by different philosophers in different ways. Some, like Chang, think that incommensurability of values leads to negatively intransitive betterness relations. Others think that it leads to indeterminacy about what is better than what. Some think that incommensurability of values leads to things being strictly speaking incomparable. Others think that it does not.

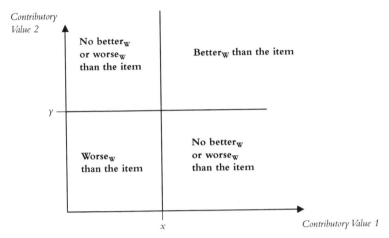

Figure 10.8

Mild incommensurability would look as in Fig. 10.9.

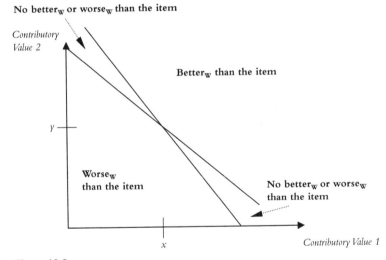

Figure 10.9

In a substantial range of cases in which contributory values conflict, one outbalances the other.

In any case, whether mild, moderate, or extreme, the incommensurability gives rise to a negatively intransitive betterness relation. Within the range of items that are neither better$_w$ nor worse$_w$ than the item that instantiates the contributory values to degrees $x$ and $y$, some are better$_w$ than others.

Now, is the relation *better off than* negatively intransitive? I am inclined to think that it is. On all interesting accounts of well-being, there are many contributory values that determine who is better off than whom (even the simplest, hedonistic thories of well-being have it that there are many contributory values: the intensity of pain, the duration of pain, the intensity of pleasure, the duration of pleasure . . . and so on). When we trade these values off against each other, we will find that they are to some greater or lesser degree incommensurable.

So, in the Transparent Small Differences case, when I focus on these states of affairs:

> S$_{SaveBen}$: in which I save Ben in two and a half hours, and leave Andy to die.
>
> S$_{SaveAndy}$: in which I save Andy in three hours, and leave Ben to die.
>
> S$_{DawdletoBen}$: in which I dawdle, save Ben in three hours, and leave Andy to die.

I am inclined to think that, while Ben in S$_{SaveBen}$ certainly is better off than Ben in S$_{DawdletoBen}$, Andy in S$_{SaveAndy}$ is neither better nor worse off than Ben in S$_{SaveBen}$, neither better nor worse off than Ben in S$_{DawdletoBen}$. Indeed, this partly explains why I would have negatively intransitive preferences between these states of affairs.

If this is correct, then we cannot construct an upslope morphing sequence from W$_{SaveAndy}$ to W$_{SaveBen}$. We cannot use the morphing arguments to show that decency and rationality compel me to save Ben in the Transparent Small Differences Case.

## 10.5. Pareto Dominance Reconsidered

Could we not apply the morphing arguments to a similar sort of case? Consider:

### Transparent Small Differences Having to Do with Other People

I can save Aaron in 3 hours by heading west, Beebee in 3 hours by heading east. But Cedric (who is unacquainted with either Aaron or Beebee) has left his wallet on the east island. If I head over there, I can retrieve it for him. Again, I know everything there is to know about these people.

In this case the states of affairs I am in a position to bring about are as shown in Fig. 10.10.

**Figure 10.10**

Cedric is better off getting his wallet than losing his wallet. Aaron, living for many years, is no better or worse off than Beebee, living for many years. Aaron, dying immediately, is no better or worse off than Beebee, dying immediately. So it looks as if we can construct an upslope morphing sequence from $S_{\text{SaveAaron}}$ to $S_{\text{SaveBeebee}}$ (see Fig. 10.11).

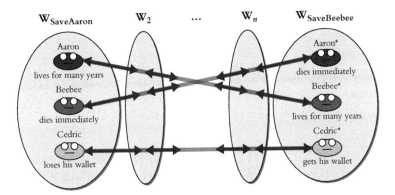

**Figure 10.11**

Each person on the Aaron-in-$W_{\text{SaveAaron}}$-to-Beebee*-in-$W_{\text{SaveBeebee}}$-chain is neither better nor worse off than his or her predecessor. Each person on the Aaron-in-$W_{SaveAaron}$-to-Beebee*-in-$W_{SaveBeebee}$-chain is neither better nor worse off than his or her predecessor. Each person on the Cedric-in-$W_{SaveAaron}$-to-Cedric*-in-$W_{SaveBeebee}$-chain is neither better nor worse off than his predecessor. So each world in the sequence pareto-dominates its predecessor. So surely, if I am decent and rational, then I must save Beebee.

But this argument is too quick. If we allow that the relation *better off than* may be negatively intransitive, then we must think again what sort of benevolence decency demands of us.

Let us distinguish (using Ruth Chang's terminology, again) between the relations of *parity* and of *equal goodness*. It follows from two things being on a par$_W$ that neither is better$_W$ than the other. It follows from two things being equally good$_W$ that neither is better$_W$ than the other and that anything better$_W$ than one is better$_W$ than the other. So, in the examples we looked at earlier, Kenenise Bekele and Usain Bolt are on a par with respect to athleticism, but they are not equally good athletes, Philosophy and Investment Banking are on a par career-wise, but they are not equally good careers.

Now let us distinguish two sorts of pareto-dominance. For any states of affairs S, S* involving the same people:

*Loose Pareto-Dominance*
S loosely pareto-dominates S* when there is somebody better off in S than S*, nobody better off in S* than S.

*Tight Pareto-Dominance*
S tightly pareto-dominates S* when there is somebody better off in S than S*, and everybody not better off in S than S* is equally well off in S and S*.

Does decency demand of us that, other things being equal, we prefer loosely pareto-dominant states of affairs? If the relation *better off than* is negatively intransitive, then I say it does not. Consider:

The Gifts
I have gifts A+, A, B to give away to Tom, Dick, and Harry. Each of them is better off with A+ than A, no better or worse off with A+ than B, no better or worse off with A than B. To whom should I give what?

In this situation there are six states of affairs that I am in a position to bring about. Three are particularly interesting (see Fig. 10.12).

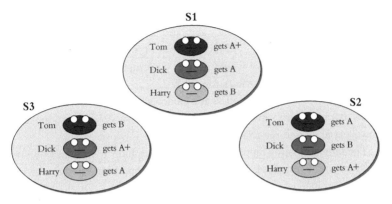

Figure 10.12

S1 loosely pareto-dominates S2 (Tom is better off in S1, nobody is worse off in S1). S2 loosely pareto-dominates S3 (Harry is better off in S2, nobody is worse off in S2). S3 loosely pareto-dominates S1 (Dick is better off in S3, nobody is worse off in S3). So, if decency demands of me that I prefer loosely pareto-dominant states of affairs, then decency demands of me that I have intransitive preferences. But it is a condition on our being rational that our preferences be transitive. Decency cannot demand of us that we be irrational.

So I suggest that, to capture the idea that decency demands of us that we be minimally benevolent, we should think of decency as demanding of us that we prefer, all other things being equal, *tightly* pareto-dominant states of affairs. This tells us two important things.

First, it tells us something about the significance of the parity relation. There is a temptation to think that when a person is no better or worse off in one state of affairs than another then that person's interests have no bearing on the attitudes that we ought to take toward those states of affairs. This is not right. Dick and Harry are no better or worse off in S1 and S2. If they were equally well off in S1 and S2, or if they did not exist in S1 and S2, then decency would demand of me that I prefer S1 (it is better for Tom). But decency does not demand this of me. The differences in how things are for Dick and Harry in S1 and S2 influence the attitude I ought to take toward those states of affairs, even though neither Dick nor Harry is better off in either.

Second, it tells us something about limits to the power of morphing arguments. To show that decency and rationality commit us to preferring $W_{SaveAaron}$ over $W_{SaveBeebee}$ in the <u>Transparent Small Differences Involving Other People</u> case we would need to construct a morphing sequence such that each person on the Aaron-in-$W_{SaveAaron}$-to-Beebee*-in-$W_{SaveBeebee}$-chain is equally well off as his predecessor. But no such sequence exists, because Aaron-in-$W_{SaveAaron}$ and Beebee*-in-$W_{SaveBeebee}$ are not equally well off and the relation *equally well off as* is transitive.

The same limitations apply when we put morphing arguments to work on transparent rescue cases in which I am in a position to save one or many. Consider again:

### 1 or 2? – Transparent Interpersonal Conflict
Astrid is on an island 3 hours to my west, Beth and Chris on an island 3 hours to my west. Again, I know everything there is to know about them.

In this case (supposing that Astrid is no better off if I save her, than Beth or Chris will be if I save them, and Astrid is no worse off if do not save her, than Beth and Chris will be if I do not save them), it is certainly possible to construct a morphing sequence from the state of affairs in which I save Astrid to the state of affairs in which I save Astrid and Chris such that each state of affairs in the sequence *loosely* pareto-dominates its predecessor. The sequence may look like the one shown in Fig. 10.13, or like the one shown in Fig. 10.14.

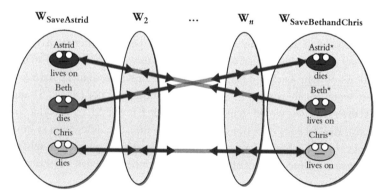

Figure 10.13

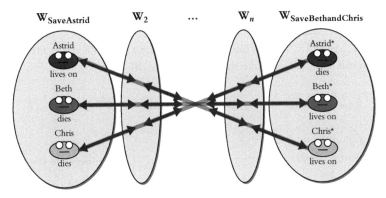

**Figure 10.14**

But it is possible to construct a morphing sequence in which each world *tightly* pareto-dominates its predecessor only if one of Beth or Chris will be equally well off, if he or she dies, as Astrid will be, if she dies, and one of Beth or Celia will be equally well off, if he or she lives, as Astrid will be, if she lives. If there is significant incommensurability in the contributory values that make Astrid, Beth, and Celia better or worse off then this may not be so.

## 10.6. Semi-Transparent Rescue Cases

Nonetheless, the morphing arguments do enable us to make progress in rescue cases in which we know *some* things about the people we are in a position to save. Consider:

### 1 or 2? – Semi-Transparent Interpersonal Conflict

I know that a person called 'Astrid' is on an island 3 hours to my west, while people called 'Beth' and 'Chris' are on an island three hours to my west. I have photographs of these people. I know their height, weight, and age. But I do not know anything that bears directly on how well off they are.

As a way of getting a grip on what it might be rational to do in a case like this, partition the space of different ways for a life to go into *life-properties*, such that all individuals with the same life-property are equally well off, all individuals with different life-properties are not equally well off (they are either merely on a par with respect to well-being, or one is better off than the other). Now note that in this case, for any life-properties L1, L2, such that individuals with life-property L1 are better off than individuals with life-property L2, decency and rationality commit me to taking an attitude towards states of affairs like that shown in Fig. 10.15.

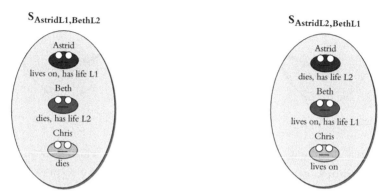

**Figure 10.15**

I must prefer $S_{AstridL2,BethL1}$, because we can construct a morphing sequence from $S_{AstridL1,BethL2}$ to $S_{AstridL2,BethL1}$ in which each world tightly pareto-dominates its predecessor (see Fig. 10.16).

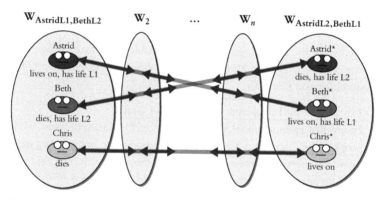

**Figure 10.16**

(All people on the Astrid to Beth* chain are equally well off. All people on the Beth to Astrid* chain are equally well off. Each person on the Chris to Chris* chain is better off than his predecessor.) Note also that in the <u>1 or 2? Semi-Transparent Interpersonal Conflict</u> case, because I know nothing that bears directly on the different ways in which Astrid, Beth, and Chris will be well or badly off if I head west or east, for all life properties L1, L2, my credence that $S_{AstridL2,BethL1}$ will come about if I head east will be the same as my credence that $S_{AstridL1,BethL2}$ will come about if I head west.

It follows, by the prospectist theory of rationality, that, if I am decent and rational, then I will head west.

## 10.7. Wrapping up on Rescue Cases

The general moral to draw from this is that what decency and rationality require of you in rescue cases may depend on what you know about the people you are in a position to save and where they are. If you know that your heading in one direction anonymously *tightly* pareto-dominates your heading in the other direction, then, other things being equal, decency and rationality require of you that you head in the one direction, however much you know about the people you are in a position to save by doing one thing or another. If you know that your heading in one direction merely anonymously *loosely* pareto-dominates your heading in the other direction, then, other things being equal, decency and rationality require of you that you head in the one direction in *fully opaque cases* (cases in which you do not know anything more about who you are in a position to save by doing one thing or another) and in *semi-transparent cases* (cases in which you know more about the people you are in a position to save by doing one thing or another, but nothing that pertains to their well-being) but not in *fully transparent* cases (cases in which you know everything about the people you are in a position to save by doing one thing or another).

This is as it should be. It is a laborious way of confirming a piece of folk wisdom: sometimes the more we know, the messier our decisions become, the less clear it becomes that there is a right decision to be made.

# 11

# Morphing, Infinity, and the Limits of Good Will

To whom must we be minimally considerate and benevolent, on pain of moral indecency? *To everyone, always*—is one response. I said, back in Chapter 1, that this response, noble as it may sound, is not quite right. It is time to explain why.

## 11.1. Infinite People

There are around seven billion people on Earth. Might there be more than around seven billion people in the universe? Modern astrophysics does not give us grounds for dismissing this possibility. All serious astrophysical theories agree that the universe is very big indeed. Large portions of it are entirely invisible to us. Large portions of it are invisible in detail.

Might there be *infinitely* many people in the universe? Some astrophysical theories rule this out. They say that space is finite. The topology is that of a four-dimensional object with unbounded surface—like a hypersphere or a hypertorus. To picture how things are for us in the universe (not always the best way of understanding physical theories, it must be said), imagine a two-dimensional creature living on the surface of a three-dimensional object with unbounded surface—like a sphere or a torus. Just as this creature will find that "straight" paths lead back to her eventually, so we three-dimensional creatures, living on the surface of a four-dimensional object with unbounded surface, find that "straight" paths lead back to us eventually. To picture the expansion of the universe following the Big Bang, imagine the unbounded surface of a three-dimensional object expanding very rapidly. Expansion is the four-dimensional analogue of that.

Other astrophysical theories do not rule it out. They say that space is infinite. To picture how things are for us in the universe, imagine a two-dimensional creature on the surface of an infinite sheet of rubber. Our condition is the three-dimensional analogue of that. To picture the expansion of the universe following the Big Bang, imagine an infinite sheet of rubber stretching very rapidly in all directions at once. Expansion is the three-dimensional analogue of that.

If space is infinite, then matter may be infinite, and there may be infinitely many people. How seriously should we take this possibility? Well, likelihoods that can be represented by numbers are hard to come by in situations like this, but it is safe to say that astrophysicists currently regard the question of whether space and matter are infinite as very much open.[1] And it is safe to say that, if space and matter are infinite, then the possibility that there are infinitely many people looms real and large.

## 11.2. Extending Good Will to Infinite Worlds

Call states of affairs that contain infinitely many people *infinite worlds*. Given that our world may be an infinite world, it behooves me to form preferences between infinite worlds. One thing I might try to do, moved by a sense of all-encompassing bonhomie, would be to extend my minimal good will toward all the inhabitants of these worlds. I might say this: "If one infinite world tightly pareto-dominates another (they contain all the same people, at least one of whom is better off in the one than the other, all of whom are better off or equally well off in the one), then, other things being equal, I will prefer it."

But then I would face a problem: I prefer all tightly pareto-dominant infinite worlds. It follows from the result of Chapter 9 that I must, on pain of irrationality, prefer all anonymously tightly pareto-dominant infinite worlds. But many infinite worlds anonymously tightly pareto-dominate themselves!

---

[1] Though Einstein famously postulated that the universe was a hypersphere (see Einstein 1917), the theory of relativity is consistent with both finite and infinite space. There are currently many, quite different, research programs that aim to settle the question of whether space is finite or infinite. Some are disarmingly simple—they involve looking for patterns that would show that some of the galaxies we see when we point our telescopes north are one and the same as galaxies we see when we point our telescopes south. See Luminer, Starkman and Weeks (1999) for an accessible introduction to the research.

How many? Well, it takes some effort to imagine an infinite world that does not do it. Here's one: *Equable World* contains infinitely many people, all equally well off. Here is another: *Isolated Inequity World* contains a group of infinitely many people, all equally well off, plus just one person, worse off than everybody else. Here is yet another: *Finite Inequity World* contains a group of infinitely many people, all equally well off, plus a large but finite group of people, each of whom is worse off than everybody in the infinite group. Generally: An infinite world will anonymously tightly pareto-dominate itself just so long as there is an infinite subgroup of the people in the world such that somebody in the group is worse off than somebody else in the group, and everybody in the group has infinitely many people in the group who are equally well off or worse off than him or her.

So, if I prefer all tightly pareto-dominant worlds, then I can avoid irrationality only by preferring worlds to themselves—which is to say that I cannot avoid irrationality.

That is quick. To get a more substantial grip on the idea, consider an example of an infinite world that anonymously tightly pareto-dominates itself: *Target World* contains a person (call him Person 0), another person better off than him (Person 1), another person worse off than either of those two (Person −1), another person better off than any of those three (Person 2), another person worse off than any of those four (Person −2)...and so on.

Take the function *f* such that *f*(Person 2) = Person 1, *f*(Person 1) = Person 0, *f*(Person 0) = Person −1...and so on. *f* is a correspondence relation between the people in Target World and the people in Target World such that no person in Target World is worse off than the person with whom he is associated in Target World, and somebody in Target World is better off than the person with whom he is associated in Target World (in fact they *all* are.) So Target World anonymously tightly pareto-dominates itself.

Because of this we can (I will put this in a counterpart-theoretic way) construct a morphing sequence from Target World to itself. Fig. 11.1 is a representation of such a sequence. (For figurative purposes I have made it short, with just four intermediary worlds. It may need to be longer, obviously—depending on how fragile you take essence to be.)

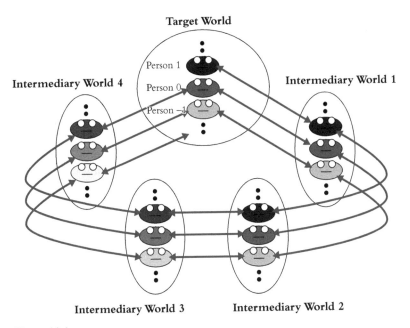

**Figure 11.1**

The ovals represent worlds, the arrows represent counterpart relations, the colors of the people represent their qualitative features (similar colors mean similar qualitative features).

Furthermore, we can construct the sequence in such a way that there is a *well-being up slope*. Intermediary World 1 tightly pareto-dominates Target World (because everyone in Intermediary World 1 is better off than his or her counterpart in Target World). Intermediary World 2 tightly pareto-dominates Intermediary World 1. Intermediary World 3 tightly pareto-dominates Intermediary World 2. Intermediary World 4 tightly pareto-dominates Intermediary World 3. Target World tightly pareto-dominates Intermediary World 4.

If I always prefer tightly pareto-dominant infinite worlds, then I prefer Intermediary World 1 to Target World, Intermediary World 2 to Intermediary World 1, Intermediary World 3 to Intermediary World 2, Intermediary World 4 to Intermediary World 3, Target World to Intermediary World 4. My preferences are either intransitive or reflexive. I am irrational.

We can dramatize the point by imagining that I am in a position to press any one of buttons $B_T, B_1, B_2, \ldots, B_n$. Pressing button $B_T$ will bring about a state of affairs qualitatively just like Target World. Pressing button $B_1$ will bring about a state of affairs qualitatively just like Intermediary World 1, ... and so on.

If I always prefer tightly pareto-dominant states of affairs, then, if I press button $B_n$, I will regret not pressing button $B_T$, and, if I press button $B_T$, I will regret not pressing button $B_1$ ... and so on. And, if I am willing to pay to bring about my preferences, I will pay to press $B_T$ rather than $B_n$, pay to press $B_1$ rather than $B_T$ ... and so on. This is not rational behavior.

## 11.3. What about the Boy in the Well?

What does this tell us about decency and our attitude toward strangers? Recall the boy who fell down a well back in Chapter 2:

*The Boy in the Well*
The newspapers report that, in northern India, a small boy has fallen down a deep, narrow well. Rescuers are frantically digging down in an effort to save him.

I said that Bertha and Ben, on reading the newspapers, will, on pain of moral indecency, hope that the boy be rescued. It does not matter that they have no interesting connection to the boy. If they are decent, they will wish him well. But now we see that we cannot *always* wish *everybody* well and remain rational. So what gives?

One proposal: decency and rationality come apart in these cases. If Bertha and Ben are decent, then they will prefer, other things being equal, pareto-dominant worlds, even when those worlds are infinite. If they are decent, then they will be irrational. Irrationality is the price they pay for decency.

This seems to me a desperate proposal, a proposal of the last resort. Let us see if there is anything better to say.

Another proposal: it is not true that Bertha and Ben must, if they are decent, wish the boy well. He is just another stranger to them. They cannot always, everywhere, wish well of all strangers, on pain of irrationality. So they are off the hook.

This seems to me an equally desperate proposal. If there is any area of firm-footing on this unstable normative terrain, it is this: there is a moral failing in Bertha and Ben when they do not wish the boy well.

Another proposal: Bertha and Ben must, if they are decent and rational, wish the boy well, because (on the assumption that they are like us) they do not know whether the world is finite or infinite. To put this in a more precise way, there are four relevantly different states of affairs that might, so far as they know, come about:

*Rescue with an Infinite Backdrop*:    The world is infinite, and the boy is rescued.

*Death with an Infinite Backdrop*:    The world is infinite, and the boy dies.

*Rescue with a Finite Backdrop*:    The world is finite, and the boy is rescued.

*Death with a Finite Backdrop*:    The world is finite, and the boy dies.

If Bertha and Ben are decent, then they will prefer *Rescue with a Finite Backdrop* to *Death with a Finite Backdrop*, and they will at least not prefer *Death with an Infinite Backdrop* to *Rescue with an Infinite Backdrop*. Given that they do not know what the pair of states of affairs that might come about is, it makes sense, then, for them to want the boy to be rescued. It makes sense for them to think something like this: "I hope he is rescued, because for all I know the world might be finite, and, if it is finite, I would much rather that he be rescued than not."

This is a step in the right direction, but it seems to me too fragile a basis for good will. We have very little idea about whether the world we inhabit is finite or infinite. What if astrophysicists were to make a strong case for its being infinite? If Bertha and Ben's good will toward the Indian boy were hostage to the thought "Because, for all we know, the world might be finite," then you would expect their good will to weaken. At the extreme, when they became convinced that the astrophysicists were right, then you would expect it entirely to disappear. But it should not disappear.

Another proposal: maybe, on pain of irrationality we cannot favor one infinite world over another whenever *infinitely* many people are better off in the one than the other and all other things are equal. But still, maybe we can favor one infinite world over another whenever *finitely* many people are better off in the one than the other and all other things are equal. And maybe that is the basis of proper benevolence toward others. You prefer that, for example, I not be knocked over by a car today because you take the world in which I am not knocked over to be preferable to the world in which I am. Both worlds may be infinite, but the former *finitely* tightly pareto-dominates the latter. That is what matters.

But this does not solve the problem, because some infinite worlds anonymously *finitely* tightly pareto-dominate themselves. We can construct morphing sequences from these worlds to themselves such that each world in the sequence finitely tightly pareto-dominates its predecessor. If you prefer all finitely tightly pareto-dominant worlds, then your preferences are intransitive.

To see the idea, consider Target World 2, which, like Target World, contains infinitely many people, with the integers as names. In Target World 2, all the people with positive integer names are equally well off, all the people with negative integer names are equally well off, and all the people with positive integer names are better off than all the people with negative integer names. Target World 2 anonymously finitely tightly pareto-dominates itself. The function that associates each person in Target World 2 with the person numbered below him in Target World 2 is a correspondence relation such that everyone in Target World 2 is better off than, or equally well off as, the person with whom he or she is associated in Target World 2, and finitely many people in Target World 2 are better off than the people with whom they are associated in Target World 2. So we can construct a morphing sequence from Target World 2 to Target World 2 (the picture will look just like Fig. 11.1), such that each world in the sequence finitely tightly pareto-dominates its predecessor.

A last proposal: notice that, although worlds in the morphing sequence may only finitely tightly dominate one another, they nonetheless differ at infinitely many places—infinitely many people in $W_T$ are qualitatively different from their counterparts in $W_1$, for example. So maybe we can say that proper benevolence consists in preferring one world to another whenever the one finitely tightly dominates the other, and intrinsic qualitative differences between them are limited to a finite region of space.

There remains something a little bit odd about this attitude. Zeus constructs an infinite world and offers it to you as a gift. "Thank you Zeus," you say. "But, to be honest, there are better worlds." So he improves the life of one person, person number 0. "Better!" you say. "But it could be still better." So he improves the life of another person, person number 1. "Still better!" you say. "But it could be still–still better." So he improves the life of person number −1. "Still–still better!" you say. "But it could be still–still–still better." And Zeus goes on and on, encouraged by you, faster and faster, creating ever better worlds... until his supertask is done, *everybody's* life has been improved, and you regard the world you are left with as no better than the world you started with!

But, odd or not, this attitude is the furthest we can go toward wanting of everyone that they be better off.

# PART III

# Introduction to Part III

I described three problems in the Introduction to this book. One had to do with killing people. Another had to do with creating people. Another had to do with weighing our own interests against the interests of needy strangers. I have addressed the first two problems. It is time to address the third. Those needy strangers will no longer be ignored.

# 12

# Distance and Need

Recall from the Introduction:

Oxfam

The charity Oxfam is soliciting donations for a program that will vaccinate distant, impoverished children against disease. Craftily, the administrators of the program have arranged their finances in such a way that the marginal benefits of further donations are clear. For every $100 you give, around ten more children will be vaccinated. For every ten children vaccinated, around one of them will live through an epidemic of disease that would otherwise have killed him/her.

Do decency and rationality commit you to donating to the program?

In one way the case may be under-specified. Have you given money to this or to similar programs before? Maybe that matters. So let us for the moment specify that you have not given money to this or to similar programs before. Now, do decency and rationality commit you to donating to the program?

Obviously the assumption that decent people are at least minimally benevolent towards others (they prefer, when all other things are equal, that others be better off) will not directly give us an answer to this question, because all other things are not equal. You lose money by donating to the program. Nor will that assumption give us an indirect answer by way of morphing arguments. The state of affairs in which you give money does not anonymously pareto dominate the state of affairs in which you do not. So (another FLAG) to get any traction on the question we must make some stronger assumptions about the attitudes of decent people.

It certainly seems fair to suppose that, at least sometimes, decency commits us to being more than just minimally benevolent toward needy strangers. At least sometimes, decency commits us to preferring that they be much better off and we be slightly worse off than vice versa. Here's a famous example, due to Peter Singer (I have mildly altered some details):

Pond

While hurrying through a park, on your way to catch a train, you come across a boy desperately thrashing around in a muddy pond. If you save the boy, then you will miss the train—no *great* loss to you, there is another train soon, but your ticket is non-refundable, and a new one costs $100.

We all think that, if you are decent, then you will want to save the child, at a cost to you of $100, in this case.

Does it follow that, if you are decent, then you will want to save the child, at a cost to you of $100, in the Oxfam case? Not directly. There are some striking differences between the relationships between you and needy children in the Oxfam and Pond cases. Notably:

1. *Physical Proximity*

In the Pond case a needy child is physically close to you. Not so in the Oxfam case.

2. *Psychological Salience*

In the Pond case you are vividly confronted with a child and his need. Not so in the Oxfam case.

3. *Unique Responsibility*

In the Pond case there is a child who you, and only you, are in a position to save. If you do not help and the child dies, then you, and only you, are responsible. Not so in the Oxfam case. In that case, if you do not help, then, for any dead child who would have lived if you had helped, responsibility for the death is distributed across all people who could have donated a further $100 but did not.

4. *Rarity*

Cases like the Pond case are rare. A disposition to help in such cases is likely to be inexpensive to you. Cases like the Oxfam case are common. A disposition to help in such cases is likely to be ruinously expensive to you.

5. *Known Benefit versus Expected Benefit*

In the Pond case you know (pretty much) that by helping you will save one child. In the Oxfam case you don't know that. Maybe you will save no children. Maybe you will save a hundred children. All you know (pretty much) is that the mean number of children saved by an action like this is one.

## 6. *Identifiability*

In the Pond case you can identify the child you are in a position to save by some means other than the definite description "the child I am in a position to save." You can point to him with your finger. You can locate him in space. You can describe his appearance. Not so in the Oxfam case.

## 7. *Determinacy*

In the Pond case, if you do not help, there is a fact of the matter about precisely who would have been saved if you had helped. Not so in the Oxfam case. (I will explain what I mean by this in the next chapter.)

Maybe these differences collectively matter. That is what most people are inclined to think.[1] So for the moment the most we are entitled to assume is:

### Sacrifice for the Sake of the Near

If you are a decent person, then you will be disposed to make small sacrifices to save the lives of children in Pond-type cases, and you will be disposed to do so willingly—you will prefer, other things being equal, that in these cases you make a sacrifice and, as a result, a child lives, than that you do not and, as a result, that same near child dies.

In this chapter and the next I will argue that we can get from this uncontroversial assumption to the conclusion that, if you are decent and rational, then you will be similarly generous toward children in Oxfam-type cases, by way of a further, familiar assumption, which we have already (back in Chapter 6) given a big FLAG:

### Dominance

If you are decent and the only relevant-to-you differences between state of affairs S and state of affairs S* are:

(i) S *significantly pareto-dominates* S*. All the same people exist in S and S*. Everybody (including yourself, remember) is at least as well off in S as in S*. Somebody is significantly better off in S than in S*.

---

[1] But some famous philosophers have urged us to think otherwise. Peter Singer's strategy (in Singer 1972) is to appeal to moral principles that treat Pond and Oxfam cases the same. Peter Unger's strategy (in Unger 1996) is to go through the differences one by one and argue that they are of no moral importance.

(ii) You stand in different causal relations to the good and bad things
that happen to people in S and S*.

then you will prefer_wide S to S*.

## 12.1. Rationality and the Needy

Let us attend first, to differences (1), (2), (3), and (4). Do they collectively
matter? Consider a very unrealistic Oxfam-ish case that differs from the
Pond case in ways (1), (2), (3), and (4), but does not differ from the Pond
case in ways (5), (6), and (7), an Oxfam-ish case in which, if you do not
help, there is a fact of the matter about exactly which dead children would
have been alive if you had helped, and in which there is precisely one such
child, and in which you are in a position to identify that child by name:

Oxfam*

Still more craftily, Oxfam's administrators have arranged their finances
in such a way that you know this: your $100 donation will save the life
of precisely one child: "little Ned." But, unlike the Pond case, Ned is
physically distant from you. And, unlike the Pond case, many other
people have had the opportunity to save Ned's life at one time or
another (though you know they have not taken it—he will die if you
do not donate), so, if you do not donate, responsibility for Ned's death
will be spread across many people. And, although, as in the Pond case,
this sort of thing has not happened to you before, unlike the Pond case
you can expect this sort of thing to happen to you again and again. The
administrators will be calling upon you to save the life of "little
Sammy" tomorrow, "little Talloolah" the day after that.

I will begin by arguing that, if you are decent and rational, then you will
donate in this case.

Back in Chapter 8 we looked at several different ways in which intransitive preference structures might arise. Here is one more, in which intransitive preference structures arise from trading-off conflicts between values
along different dimensions differently, depending on what sorts of things
you are comparing. I will first describe its general structure.

Suppose that your preferences between items of a certain kind are
sensitive to their values along two dimensions—$x$ and $y$. And suppose
that, whenever one item of the kind beats another of the kind along both

dimensions, you prefer it. And suppose that, when one item of the kind beats another of the kind along the $x$ dimension, and the other beats the one along the $y$ dimension, whether you prefer the one item to the other or the other to the one depends on what sub-kind of item they are. In particular, there are extended regions R1, R2 such that you prefer any item of sub-kind 1 with $x,y$ values represented by a point in region R1 to any item of sub-kind 1 with $x,y$ values represented by a point in region R2, and you prefer any item of sub-kind 2 with $x,y$ values represented by a point in region R2 to any item of sub-kind 2 with $x,y$ values represented by a point in region R1 (see Fig. 12.1).

If all this is true of you then your preferences are cyclical—either reflexive or intransitive. Look at points A,B,C,D on Fig. 12.2:

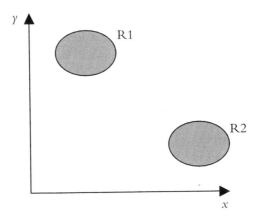

Figure 12.1

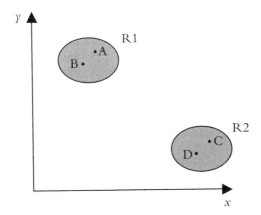

Figure 12.2

Let item *a2* be a sub-kind 2 item with *x,y* values represented by A.
Let item *b1* be a sub-kind 1 item with *x,y* values represented by B.
Let item *c1* be sub-kind 2 item with *x,y* values represented by D.
Let item *d2* be a sub-kind 2 item with *x,y* values represented by C.

You prefer *a2* to *b1*, *b1* to *c1*, *c1* to *d2*, and *d2* to *a2*. Your preferences are cyclical—either reflexive or intransitive.

That is very abstract characterization of the preference structure. To get a grip on what is going on, it may helpful to look at a particular example, involving a fellow named James, and his preferences between cars:

### The Autophile

James looks for two things in a car: *practicality* and *style*. He measures these things on scales of 1 to 100. Whenever one car (of whatever make) is both more practical and more stylish than another (of whatever make), then he would prefer to own it. But when he must trade off practicality and style, how he arrives at an all-things-considered preference depends upon what kinds of car he is comparing. When he is comparing Maseratis, he places overwhelming weight on style: "Maseratis are about style," says James. When he is comparing Hondas he places overwhelming weight on practicality: "'Hondas are about practicality,'" says James.

James's preferences between cars are cyclical. Consider:

### The Four Cars

James is offered any one of the following cars:

| | |
|---|---|
| A *Honda S2000* (an agile sportscar) | **Practicality: 26 Style: 76** |
| A *Maserati Birdcage* (another agile sportscar) | **Practicality: 25 Style: 75** |
| A *Maserati Quattroponte* (a barge-like saloon) | **Practicality: 75 Style: 25** |
| A *Honda Civic* (another barge-like saloon) | **Practicality: 74 Style: 24** |

James would prefer to own the Honda S2000 than the Maserati Birdcage (the former is both more stylish and more practical). He would prefer to own the Maserati Birdcage than the Maserati Quattroponte ("Maseratis are all about style"). He would prefer to own the Maserati Quattroponte than the Honda Civic (the former is both more stylish and more practical).

And yet he would prefer to own the Honda Civic than the Honda S2000 ("Hondas are all about practicality").

Here is another example, more relevant to matters at hand, involving you and your preferences between states of affairs that differ with respect to how well off you are, and how well off a needy child is.

### You, Embedded in a World of Need

When you are considering whether to aid a needy child, you care about two things, *your well-being* and *the well-being of the child*. When both you and the child are better off in one state of affairs than another, then you prefer the one to the other. But when you must trade off your well-being against the child's, how you make the trade-off depends on your relation to the child. When the child is physically near, psychologically salient to you, such that only you are in a position to save him, and in a rare relation to you (for short: *near etc.*), you place greater weight on the child's interests—"I can't have nearby children dying for want of help," you say. When the child is physically far, not salient to you, such that others are in a position to save him, and in a common relation to you (for short: *far etc.*), you place greater weight on your own interests—"I can't solve all the world's problems myself," you say.

Your preferences are cyclical. Contrast the Oxfam* case with this case

### Pond*

While hurrying through a park, on your way to catch a train, you come across little Ned desperately thrashing around in a muddy pond. As before, if you save him then you will miss the train. As before, that is no *great* loss to you, there is another train soon, but your ticket is non-refundable, and a new one costs $100. But his death in this case, if you leave him in this case, will be better than his death in the Oxfam* case, if you leave him in the Oxfam* case. Furthermore, you will not be in any interesting sense worse off in this case, if you leave him in this case, than you will be in the Oxfam* case, if you leave him in the Oxfam* case (nobody will find out either way, and you will be no more or less plagued by guilt either way). And his life in this case, if you save him in this case, will be worse than his life in the Oxfam* case, if you save him in the Oxfam* case. Furthermore, you will not be in any interesting sense better off in this case, if you save him in this case, than you will be in the Oxfam* case, if you save him in the Oxfam* case (nobody will find out either way, and you will get no more or less satisfaction from your charity either way).

The states of affairs you are in a position to bring about in the Oxfam* case are:

$S_{SaveDistant}$   In which you save distant etc. Ned, and he has a slightly better life.

$S_{LeaveDistant}$   In which you leave distant etc. Ned to die a slightly worse death.

The states of affairs you are in a position to bring about in the Pond* case are:

$S_{SaveNear}$   In which you save near etc. Ned, and he has a slightly worse life.

$S_{LeaveNear}$   In which you leave near etc. Ned to die a slightly better death.

What preferences do you have among them? You prefer $S_{SaveDistant}$ to $S_{SaveNear}$ (it is better for Ned and worse for nobody). You prefer $S_{SaveNear}$ to $S_{LeaveNear}$ ("I can't have nearby children dying for want of help"). You prefer $S_{LeaveNear}$ to $S_{LeaveDistant}$ (it is better for Ned and worse for nobody). And yet you prefer $S_{LeaveDistant}$ to $S_{SaveDistant}$ ("I can't solve all the world's problems myself").

You can render your preferences transitive, and thereby avoid irrationality, easily enough by dropping any one of these preferences. But it is not so easy to do so in a way that is consistent with your being a decent person. If you are decent, then (by *Dominance*) you must prefer $S_{SaveDistant}$ to $S_{SaveNear}$, and (by *Sacrifice for the Sake of the Near*) you must prefer $S_{SaveNear}$ to $S_{LeaveNear}$, and (by *Dominance*) you must prefer $S_{LeaveNear}$ to $S_{LeaveDistant}$. So, if you are decent and rational, then you must prefer $S_{SaveDistant}$ to $S_{LeaveDistant}$. You must all-things-considered want to save Ned's life, at a small cost to you, when he is distant etc. And what goes for Ned goes for all needy children. If you are decent and rational, then you will all-things-considered want to save their lives, at a small cost to you, when they are distant etc.

Let us go over this argument again, very slowly. There are four states of affairs to focus on (see Fig. 12.3).

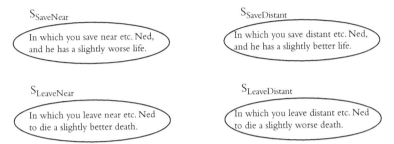

Figure 12.3

By *Sacrifice for the Sake of the Near* you must, if you are decent, prefer $S_{SaveNear}$ to $S_{LeaveNear}$. We can represent that preference with an inequality sign (see Fig. 12.4).

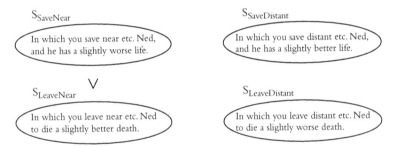

Figure 12.4

By *Dominance* you must, if you are decent, prefer $S_{SaveDistant}$ to $S_{SaveNear}$, and $S_{LeaveNear}$ to $S_{LeaveDistant}$ (see Fig. 12.5).

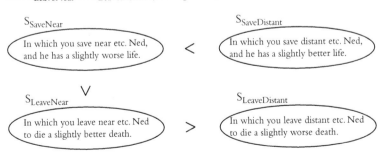

Figure 12.5

So, by *Transitivity*, you must, if you are decent and rational, prefer $S_{SaveDistant}$ to $S_{LeaveDistant}$ (see Fig. 12.6).

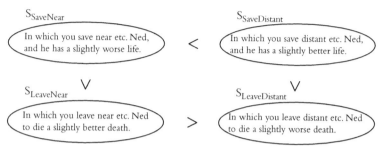

Figure 12.6

Which is to say that, if you are decent and rational, you must prefer to save Ned in the Oxfam\* case.

## 12.2. Dominance Redux

The controversial move in this argument is the appeal to *Dominance*—you must, if you are decent, prefer $S_{SaveDistant}$ to $S_{SaveNear}$, and prefer $S_{LeaveNear}$ to $S_{LeaveDistant}$.

First, an objector might note that these are not action-guiding preferences. You cannot be in a position to bring about both $S_{SaveDistant}$ and $S_{SaveNear}$. You cannot be in a position to bring about both $S_{LeaveNear}$ and $S_{LeaveDistant}$. Indeed, it is hard to imagine a situation in which both $S_{SaveDistant}$ and $S_{SaveNear}$ are both open epistemic possibilities for you, hard to imagine a situation in which both $S_{LeaveNear}$ and $S_{LeaveDistant}$ are both open epistemic possibilities for you. Does this matter? I say it does not. Sometimes decency demands of us that we have preferences that are not action-guiding, between states of affairs that we do not take to be open epistemic possibilities. Remember Bertha and Ben from Chapter 1. After that little boy has been rescued from the well, I say that they will, if they are decent, be glad that he was rescued from the well, even though that preference is not action guiding for them, even though the state of affairs in which he dies in the well is no longer an open epistemic possibility for them.

Second, an objector might note that there are other things at stake in these comparisons than your well-being and Ned's. Take $S_{LeaveNear}$ and

$S_{LeaveDistant}$. Yes, Ned is better off in $S_{LeaveNear}$ than in $S_{LeaveDistant}$, and nobody (including you) is worse off in $S_{LeaveNear}$ than in $S_{LeaveDistant}$, but there is a further, maybe significant difference between the two states of affairs. In $S_{LeaveNear}$ you leave a near etc. child to die—by ordinary moral standards a *terrible* thing to do. In $S_{LeaveDistant}$ you leave a distant etc. child to die—by ordinary moral standards a *not so terrible* thing to do. Might a decent person not care about that? Might a decent person not say: "I would rather that we both be worse off, and I do a not-so-terrible thing, than that we both be better off and I do a terrible thing."?

The issue here is closely related to the issue that arose with respect to side constraints back in Chapter 6. Recall the Fuel in a Gorilla Suit example. We saw that, if decency commits you to preferring (e.g.)

$S_{ShoveAmy}$:  In which you kill Amy, and Benjamin and Celia live.

to

$S_{LeaveCelia}$:  In which others kill Amy and Benjamin, and Celia lives.

then decency and rationality together commit you to killing one person to save two others. But might a decent person not say: "I would rather that we all (and particularly Benjamin) be worse off, and I do a by-ordinary-moral-standards-not-so-terrible thing (failing to kill one person so as to save two others), than that we all (and particularly Benjamin) be better off, and I do a terrible thing"?

I argued back in Chapter 6 that such an answer would evince an unseemly self-preoccupation (not *selfishness*, I repeat, because it is not concern for your welfare that would be driving you), and that decent people are not self-preoccupied in this way. The same goes for The Well. Being decent involves caring about people's interests, not caring about the way in which you contribute to their interests. If you care about people's interests, then you will prefer $S_{LeaveNear}$ to $S_{LeaveDistant}$.

It might seem as if this claim is too strong to serve as a premise in an interesting argument to the conclusion that a decent and rational person will prefer $S_{SaveDistant}$ to $S_{LeaveDistant}$. If (like most people) you are antecedently inclined to deny the conclusion of the argument, why not just deny this premise? If you are antecedently inclined to think that it is okay to want a needy child to be substantially worse off for the sake of your keeping $100, why not also think that it is okay to want a needy child to be substantially worse off for the sake of your not having done a terrible thing?

The difference lies in the way in which the preferences can be justified. Why prefer $S_{LeaveDistant}$ to $S_{SaveDistant}$? You are better off in $S_{LeaveDistant}$. Being no moral saint, you give special weight to your own interests, projects, bank accounts. Maybe it is okay for you to be that way. Maybe a decent person can be moved by non-moral concerns. Why prefer $S_{LeaveDistant}$ to $S_{LeaveNear}$? Given that everybody (including yourself) is better off in $S_{LeaveNear}$, the only grounds you have are *moral*—you do a morally worse thing in $S_{LeaveNear}$. Your preference is an expression of moral concern. But it is just a mistake to want, on moral grounds, that everybody be worse off. That is not an appropriate expression of moral concern.

An analogy may be helpful. We care about money, but there are different ways to care about money. Consider:

The Sealed Envelopes
Going through your mail, you throw away one sealed envelope and keep another. Later you learn that things are one of two ways:

S+:   The envelope you threw away contained $100, the one you kept contains $100.

S−:   The envelope you threw away contained $0, the one you kept contains $10.

One way of caring about money will yield a preference for S− over S+. You damaged your financial situation in S+, but not in S−. Another way will yield a preference for S+ over S−. You have more money in S+. The idea is that someone properly moved by moral concern cares about people's interests in the second kind of way. She wants people to be better off, irrespective of the relation she stands in to the good or bad things that happen to them.

# 13

# Ignorance and Indeterminacy

I have argued that, if you are decent and rational, then you will give your money away in the Oxfam* case. But that case was artfully unrealistic. In that case you know that by donating $100 to Oxfam you will save the life of exactly one child—"little Ned." In real life, when we have the opportunity to donate money to charity, we do not know exactly who or how many will benefit from our donation. Indeed sometimes, in real life, it may be that there is no precise fact of the matter about who or how many will benefit from our donation. Do these things matter? Let us go over them one by one.

## 13.1. Not Knowing Precisely *who* you are in a Position to Save

Suppose (as I have argued) that decency and rationality commit you to wanting to save distant etc. Ned, when you are knowingly in a position to do so at a small cost to yourself, and to wanting to save distant etc. Nellie, when you are knowingly in a position to do so at a small cost to yourself. To put it in a laborious way, of

$S_{LeaveDistantNed}$:    In which distant etc. Ned dies for want of your help (and you knew that he, in particular, would die).

$S_{SaveDistantNed}$:    In which you save distant etc. Ned (knowing that you would save him, in particular).

you prefer, other things being equal, $S_{SaveNed}$, and likewise for Nellie. What, then, can we say about a situation like this?:

### Which Distant etc. Person are you in a Position to Help?

You know this: Ned and Nellie are in trouble. One of them will die whatever you do. You can save the other by donating $100. But you do not know who you can save—you have credence 0.5 that it is Ned, credence 0.5 that it is Nellie.

Here the prospect associated with not donating is 0.5 each of

$S_{LeaveDistantNed}*$: In which distant Ned dies for want of your help (and you did not know that he, in particular, would die for want of your help).

$S_{LeaveDistantNellie}*$: In which distant Nellie dies for want of your help (and you did not know that she, in particular, would die for want of your help).

And the prospect associated with donating is 0.5 each of

$S_{SaveDistantNed}*$: In which you save distant Ned (not knowing that you would save him, in particular).

$S_{SaveDistantNellie}*$: In which you save distant Nellie (not knowing you would save her, in particular).

By the prospectist theory of practical rationality, just so long as you prefer $S_{SaveDistantNed}*$ to $S_{LeaveDistantNed}*$, and $S_{SaveDistantNellie}*$ to $S_{LeaveDistantNellie}*$, you must, if you are rational, donate.

Decency and rationality commit you to preferring, for example, $S_{SaveDistantNed}$ to $S_{LeaveDistantNed}$. Do they also commit you to preferring, for example, $S_{SaveDistantNed}*$ to $S_{LeaveDistantNed}*$? Perhaps you could say this: "Decency commits me to preferring $S_{SaveDistantNed}$ to $S_{LeaveDistantNed}$, because in $S_{LeaveDistantNed}$ I do something very wrong—knowingly leaving distant Ned to die. But decency does not commit me to preferring $S_{SaveDistantNed}*$ to $S_{LeaveDistantNed}*$, because in $S_{LeaveDistantNed}*$ I do not do anything wrong. I do not know that I am leaving distant Ned to die. I just know that I am leaving one of them to die."

I do not find this very persuasive. Why does it matter so much whether you know precisely who the distant child is? In any case we have independent reason to think that it can't be right. Consider

## Which Nearby etc. Person are you in a Position to Help?

While again hurrying through a park on the way to catch your train, you come across two children, Ned and Nellie, in a muddy pond. One is clearly dead. The other is thrashing around in desperate need of your help. What with all that mud and all that thrashing, you cannot tell who is who.

I take it that decency commits you to helping the child, willingly, in this case. So, supposing you are acting rationally, given your preferences, it must be that of, for example,

$S_{LeaveNearNed}$*:  In which near Ned dies for want of your help (and you did not know that he, in particular, would die)

$S_{SaveNearNed}$*:  In which you save near Ned (not knowing that you would save him, in particular).

you prefer $S_{SaveNearNed}$*. So (by the argument from the previous chapter—I won't repeat the details) by *Dominance* and *Transitivity*, if you are decent and rational then you must prefer $S_{SaveDistantNed}$* to $S_{LeaveDistantNed}$*.

## 13.2. Not Knowing Precisely *how many* you are in a Position to Save

What about a situation like this:

### Will Your Help be Effective?
You know this: Distant Nellie and Ned are in trouble. They will die unless you donate $100. But you do not know whether your donation will be effective. You have credence 0.5 that it will save them both, credence 0.5 that it will make no difference.

Do decency and rationality commit you to helping? This question is not quite so easy. If we were entitled to assume that decency and rationality committed you to regarding two deaths as twice as bad as one, or something like that, then perhaps we would have an answer. But we are not entitled to make any such assumptions.

To simplify things, let us suppose that Ned and Nellie's interests are substantially independent. They have no meaningful relationship. Neither is better or worse off with the other dead or alive.

Now here is an argument for thinking that decency and rationality commit you to helping. Note that in the old, Which Distant Person are you in a Position to Help? case, the relative strengths of three desires

*your desire that Ned, in particular, be better off*
*your desire that Nellie, in particular, be better off*
*your desire that you keep your $100*

will lead you, if you are decent, to favor the prospect associated with donating over the prospect associated with not donating—in spite of the $100 loss to you. But, so far as those desires go, you have no grounds for distinguishing the prospects associated with donating/not donating in that case and in the new, <u>Will Your Help be Effective?</u> case. In both cases, as far as wanting Ned, in particular, to be better off goes, you have 0.5 credence that he will die if you donate, certainty that he will die if you do not. In both cases, as far as wanting Nellie, in particular, to be better off goes, you have 0.5 credence that she will die if you donate, certainty that she will die if you do not. In both cases, as far as wanting to keep your $100 goes, you are certain you will lose it if you donate, keep it if you do not. It is not just that, as far as these desires go, you have no preference, all things considered, between these prospects. It is that you have no grounds at all for distinguishing them. So I take it that, unless you have some other grounds (not having to do with Ned's interests, Nellie's interests, or the contents of your wallet) for distinguishing them, if you are rational then you will favor the prospect associated with donating in the <u>Will Your Help be Effective?</u> case.

## 13.3. Counterfactual Open-ness

So to the last, and I think most interesting, way in which real-life situations in which we are in a position to donate to charity differ from the Oxfam* and Pond* cases. In real life it may be that, if we do not donate, there is no fact of the matter about who would have lived or died if we had donated.

Some vocabulary: say that a process is *counterfactually open* when, supposing that we initiate it, there is no fact of the matter about what its outcome would have been if we had not initiated it. To be precise: let P be the proposition that we initiate the process, and $O1, \ldots, Ok$ be exclusive propositions concerning the relevantly different outcomes of the process. The counterfactual

(CF0)   If it had been that P, then it would have been that O1 or O2 or . . . or Ok

is true, but none of the counterfactuals

(CF1)   If it had been that P, then it would have been that O1
. . .
(CF2)   If it had been that P, then it would have been that Ok

are true.

So, for example, a process governed by indeterministic laws may be counterfactually open. Suppose that, in an optics lab, I have the opportunity to fire a photon through a narrow slit. Suppose I do not do it. Now this counterfactual is true:

(CF3)   If I had fired the photon, then it would have deflected left or deflected right.

But neither of these is true:

(CF4)   If I had fired the photon then it would have deflected left.
(CF5)   If I had fired the photon then it would have deflected right.

Why? Well, to put the point in the laborious vocabulary of possible worlds, no world in which I fire the photon and it deflects left is relevantly more similar to the actual world than all worlds in which I fire the photon and it deflects right, and vice versa. Why? Because the physical laws that govern the actual world are no more or less violated in a non-actual world in which the photon deflects left than in a non-actual world in which the photon deflects right.

And, for another example, a process governed by deterministic laws may be counterfactually open when its outcome is sensitive to differences in initiating conditions over which we have no control. I have a quarter in my pocket. I was mulling over whether to flip it onto the floor just now. I decided not to. This counterfactual is true:

(CF6)   If I had flipped the coin then it would have landed heads or tails.

And maybe, if the laws of nature that govern our world are sufficiently deterministic, some counterfactuals with very specific antecedents, like

(CF7)   If I had flipped the coin while its center of gravity was between 1.48318 and 1.48319 meters from the floor, applying between 2.899 and 2.900 Newtons of force to its upper edge at an angle of . . . then it would have landed heads.
(CF8)   If I had flipped the coin while its center of gravity was between 1.48320 and 1.48321 meters from the floor, applying . . . then it would have landed tails.

are true. But neither of these counterfactuals is true:

(CF9)   If I had flipped the coin then it would have landed heads.

(CF10)   If I had flipped the coin then it would have landed tails.

No world in which I flip the coin and it lands heads is relevantly more similar to the actual world (in which I do not flip it, remember) than all worlds in which I flip it and it lands tails, and vice versa. The antecedent of counter-factuals (CF9) and (CF10), "If I had flipped the coin..." is *under-specified*.[1]

When there is no fact of the matter about precisely what would have happened if a process had been initiated, there may, nonetheless, be precise counterfactual conditional probabilities. So for example, in the coin case this counterfactual is true:

(CF11)   If I had flipped the coin, then it might, with probability 0.5, have landed heads.

Say that a counterfactually open process is *evenly weighted* when, supposing that it is not initiated, for each of the relevantly different outcomes, the counterfactual conditional probability of the process having that outcome, if it had been initiated, is the same. Typical coin-flips are indeed evenly weighted, counterfactually open processes.

Vocabulary settled, we are in a position to observe that it may be that the processes by which we come to benefit particular, distant people through charitable donations are counterfactually open. Our best dynam-ical models of global weather exhibit extreme sensitivity to initial condi-tions—small differences in earlier states tend to magnify rapidly in later states. Just as whether I get a head or tail depends on precisely how I flip the coin, so whether a hurricane strikes Bermuda in November depends on precisely how things are in Massachusetts in May. If our world is as these models represent it to be, then it may be, for some pairs of counter-factuals like this:

---

[1] I should note that there is some disagreement about how, precisely, to put this point. On one canonic treatment of counterfactuals offered by David Lewis, (CF9) and (CF10) are false. See Lewis (1973: sect. 3.4). On another canonic treatment of counterfactuals offered by Bob Stalnaker, (CF9) and (CF10) are neither determinately true nor determinately false. They have indeterminate truth value. See Stalnaker (1984: ch. 7). I side with Lewis on this matter, and I will talk accordingly. (Briefly: because it seems to me that a counterfactual claim is analogous to a claim concerning a story—a story whose details are fixed by the antecedent of the counterfactual and the nature of the actual world. But if the story does not specify, e.g., whether the coin lands heads or tails, it is just false to say that, according to the story, the coin lands heads.) But nothing of importance for present purposes turns on this.

(CF11)   If I had donated $100 to Oxfam in 1986, then, five years later, distant Ned would not have died of Typhus.

(CF12)   If I had donated $100 to Oxfam in 1986, then, five years later, distant Ned would have died of Typhus.

neither is determinately true—because the condition "If had donated $100 to Oxfam in 1986" is under-specified.

Of course, our world is not exactly the way that these models represent it to be. For one thing, these models represent a world in which relatively simple laws govern the behavior of a relatively small number of things. In our world relatively complex laws govern the behavior of a relatively large number of things. For another thing, these models represent a world governed by deterministic laws. The laws that govern our world may not be deterministic. Fine, but we have no reason to think that the extra complexity and nomological determinism renders counterfactuals like (CF11) and (CF12) determinately true or false.

Does counterfactual open-ness matter? Consider:

Open Benefit
Nellie and Ned are in trouble. If you keep your $100, then they both will die. If you donate, then one of them will live—an evenly weighted, counterfactually open process will determine which one.

In this new case, the prospects associated with your donating and not donating may not appear to have changed much (you still think it 0.5 likely that you will save Nellie, 0.5 likely that you will save Ned, if you donate, and you are still certain that they both will die if I you keep your $100), but the effects that your actions may have on individuals have changed a great deal. In the old, Which Person am I in a Position to Help? case, if Ned is the person you are in a position to help, then donating will turn out to be great for Ned, not donating will turn out to be terrible for Ned. If Nellie is the person you are in a position to help, then donating will turn out to be great for Nellie, not donating will turn out to be terrible for Nellie. Either way, you know that, if you donate, then it will turn out that you have done something great for somebody, while if you do not donate, then it will turn out that you have done something terrible for somebody. But in this new, Open Benefit case, things are not so simple. Suppose you keep your money. Nellie and Ned die. How bad was your action for Nellie? That would seem to depend on whether Nellie would have lived or died if you had donated.

But there is no fact of the matter about whether Nellie would have lived or died if you had donated! All that can truly be said is that, if you had donated, then Nellie might, with probability 0.5, have lived.

We have to make a strategic decision here. We could say that in a case like this, when you act and there is no fact of the matter about whether Nellie would have been better off if you had acted differently, there is no fact of the matter about whether your action was good or bad for Nellie. Or we could say that it depends on the counterfactual conditional probabilities. If the probability that she would have been better off is very high, if this is true:

(CF13)    If you had donated, then she might, with probability 0.9999, have lived.

then your action was terrible for Nellie. But if it is lower, if this is true:

(CF14)    If you had donated, then she might, with probability 0.5, have lived.

then your action was less terrible for Nellie. And, if it is very low, if this is true:

(CF15)    If you had donated, then she might, with probability 0.0001, have lived.

then your action was not very bad at all for Nellie.

I say that, if we ever want to be able to talk about the effects of actions on people in realistic cases, we had better go down the second route. This means that in the new, Open Benefit case, if you keep your money for yourself, then, rather than doing something terrible for one person, you have done something less terrible for two people.

Does this matter? It is still quite terrible to be denied a 0.5 chance of living, and maybe it is morally objectionable to do something quite terrible for two people. But we can inflate the numbers:

Open Benefit 2
100,000 people are in trouble. If you keep your $100, then they will all die. If you donate, then one of them will live—an evenly weighted, counterfactually open process will determine which one.

In this case, if you keep your money for yourself, then you have done something good for you, and only very, very slightly bad for each of 100,000 people. And surely this makes a difference. Surely it is not so morally objectionable to do something that is only very, very slightly bad for each of 100,000 people—recall Scanlon's World Cup example. So surely a decent person may keep his money in this case, knowing that by doing so he does not significantly harm anybody.

There certainly is something attractive about this reasoning. A confession: I gave much less money to charity last year than I could have. I think it likely that, if I had given more money, then somebody would have been significantly better off than he or she actually is. But I do take consolation in the thought that there is no person who would have been significantly better off if I had given more money. There is nobody, sick now, who would have been healthy if I had given more money. There is nobody, dead now, who would have been alive if I had given more money. My not giving more money was just very, very slightly bad for each of a vast multitude of people.

Maybe a decent person can find consolation, after the fact, in such thoughts. But will a decent person be moved by them, before the fact? I am inclined to think not. Consider:

One Counterfactually Open, or Two Counterfactually Closed?
1,000,000 people are in trouble. You can save one of them or two of them. If you choose to save the one, then the one will be selected by way of a fair, counterfactually closed process. If you choose to save two, then the two will be selected by way of a fair, counterfactually open process.

In this case there is something to be said for your saving the one. If you save the one, then you will have done something only mildly bad for each of 999,999 people—it will be true of each one of them that he/she is dead, but might, with probability close to 2/1,000,000, have survived if you had acted differently. If you save the two, on the other hand, then almost certainly (with probability close to 998/1,000,000) you will do something terrible for one person—it will be true of one person that he/she would have survived if you had acted differently. But in this case there is also something to be said for your saving the two. If you do so, then, for each person, your expectation that that person will survive is close to 2/1,000,000. If you save the one, on the other hand, then, for each person, your expectation that that person will survive is 1/1,000,000. Saving the two maximizes, for each person, your expectation that that person will survive.

So, if you care only about not doing terrible things for people, then you will save the one, while (by the arguments from Part I), if you care only about people, then you will save the two. What will you do if you are decent? I am inclined to think (appealing, once again, to *Dominance*) that a decent person, in this situation, will save the two. A decent person's concern for people is stronger than her concern for her not doing terrible things for people.

This suggests to me that, in the sort of situation we began with, in which you can save a life or keep your resources to yourself, a decent person will not be significantly moved by the thought that "If I keep my resources to myself then I will not have done anything terrible for anybody." Again, her concern for people is stronger than her concern for her not doing terrible things for people.

## 13.4. No Escape

So it seems to me that there is no escaping it. The short answer to the question with which I began Chapter 12 is yes. Decency and rationality do commit you to giving away your $100 in the Oxfam case.

We specified that, in that case, you have not given money to Oxfam before. What if you have? What if you have already given away 10 percent of your income for this year? What if you have given 50 percent? What if you have given 90 percent? When does it stop?

By the arguments from this chapter and the last, if decency commits you to saving the child, at a cost to you of $100, in a Pond-type case in which you have already made certain sacrifices in the past, then decency and rationality together commit you to giving $100 in an Oxfam-type case in which you have already made those same sacrifices in the past. So the question is when, in Pond-type cases, it stops. After how much sacrifice may you, as a decent person, throw up your hands and ignore the drowning child in a Pond-type case?

I am inclined to think that it stops a long way short of complete devotion to the needy. Suppose, for example, you have been dragging children out of ponds for a hundred days straight. Suppose you look ahead of you and see a string of further ponds stretching off to the horizon, each with its own drowning child. Suppose you realize that there will always be a further pond, that you could spend every second of your waking life flailing in the mud and still have no realistic hope of saving them all. I would not then judge you harshly if you were to say "To hell with this!" and go catch your train.

But we should not take too much from this. I have not spent the last hundred days dragging children from ponds, and nor have you.

# 14

# Commitment

We are nearly done, and you may feel haggard. In the last two chapters I have argued that, if you care more about people's well-being than about the way in which you affect people's well-being, and you are disposed willingly to save the life of a stranger, at a small cost to yourself, when he is drowning in a pond beside you or bleeding on your couch, and you are rational, then you will willingly give money to charities to save the lives of distant strangers. Worse, I have argued that it is a condition of your being decent that you be this way. You may feel as if you are being asked to inhabit the condition of a mother bird who returns to her nest to find a thousand upturned beaks.

I want to close on a more optimistic note. Being rational involves, at least sometimes, having a kind of commitment to the well-being of particular people, and ignoring the upturned beaks of needy strangers.

## 14.1. Sticking by a Decision

Remember Andy and Ben, my friends. I said that, if I were in a position to save either of them, but not both of them, then, other things being equal, I would rather save Andy more quickly than Andy less quickly, I would rather save Ben more quickly than Ben less quickly, but I would have no preference between my saving Andy more or less quickly and my saving Ben more or less quickly.

One puzzling question that this preference structure gives rise to has to do with what I ought, rationally, to do under conditions of uncertainty. I discussed that in some detail in Chapter 4. Another puzzling question has to do with the relationship between the rational permissibility of composite actions (actions with actions as proper parts—like *my making a cup of tea*, which has *my turning on the kettle* and *my putting a tea bag in the cup* and *my pouring boiling water into the cup* as proper parts) and the rational permissibility of actions of which they are composed. Consider another example:

Stick or Switch?

Again I am in a position to save one and only one of Andy and Ben. But this time I am driving. I see clearly ahead of me the arrangement of roads shown in Fig. 14.1. By heading north at Junction 1 and north again at Junction 2 I will save Andy quickly. By heading south at Junction 1 and south at Junction 3 I will save Ben quickly. By heading north and then south I will save Ben less quickly. By heading south and then north I will save Andy less quickly.

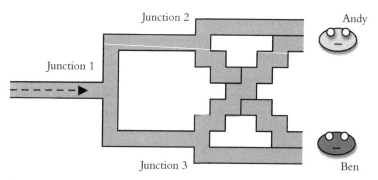

Figure 14.1

What ought I, rationally, to do—go north–north, south–south, north–south, or south–north? The theories of decision I discussed in Chapter 4 say that it is rationally impermissible for me to go north–south—because I prefer the outcome of my going south–south. And they say that it is rationally impermissible for me to go south–north—because I prefer the outcome of my going north–north. And they say it is rationally permissible for me to go north–north—because I prefer no other outcome. And they say that it is rationally permissible for me to go south–south—because I prefer no other outcome.

Well and good. But now suppose (without loss of generality) that I head south at Junction 1. I arrive at Junction 3 (see Fig. 14.2).

What ought I, rationally, to do—go north or south? The theories say that it is rationally permissible for me to go north, rationally permissible for me to go south—because I have no preference between those outcomes.

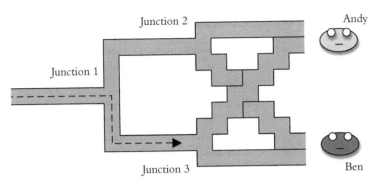

**Figure 14.2**

This is, I think, the right thing to say, but it may seem mysterious. If it is rationally permissible for me to head south at Junction 1, and rationally permissible for me, having headed south at Junction 1, to head north at Junction 2, then how can it be rationally impermissible for me to head south-at-Junction-1-then-north-at-Junction-2?

To dispel the mystery we need to focus, carefully, on what we mean by saying that an option is *rationally impermissible*, and how this differs from saying, more loosely, that an option is *irrational*. I take it that for an option to be rationally impermissible for me is for me to have decisive reasons to favor some alternative to it. Heading south-and-then-north is rationally impermissible because I have decisive reasons to favor an alternative—by heading north-and-then-north I will save Ben more quickly. Heading south at Junction 1 is not rationally impermissible, because I do not have decisive reasons to favor the one alternative, heading north at Junction 1. Heading north at Junction 3 is not rationally impermissible, because I do not have decisive reasons to favor the alternative, heading south at Junction 3 (I am, remember, wildly torn between saving Ben and Andy). But if I head north at Junction 3 then I will have done something rationally impermissible—not heading north at Junction 3, but heading south-at-Junction-1-then-north-at-Junction-3. There is a sense, then, in which heading north at Junction 3, though rationally permissible, may fairly be described as "irrational." It is the sort of thing that a rational person will not do, because doing it involves doing something (else) that is rationally impermissible, and rational people do not do rationally impermissible things.

## 14.2. What Moves the Rational Person?

An interesting question now arises. Roughly: given my preferences, heading-south-and-then-north is rationally impermissible. But what prevents me from doing it? When I arrive at Junction 3 I have no preference for heading south!

One way to interpret this question is as a question about human psychology. The world contains rational people, the sorts of people who do not do rationally impermissible things. In cases like this they head south at Junction 3. But how do they manage it, given that they do not have a preference for heading south or take themselves to have all things considered reason to head south?

Another way to interpret it is as a practical question. Before I enter into any situations of this kind I have an interest in being the sort of person who does not head south and then north, or north and then south, in a case like this. So what steps can I take to ensure that I am that sort of person? What mechanisms can I put it into place that will prevent me from performing rationally impermissible composite actions?

## 14.3. One Strategy: Avoiding the Problematic Situations

Your first thought may be that no trickery is needed, because these sorts of situations are rare or avoidable. Rational people stay rational by never visiting places like Junction 3. There is no need for me to put mechanisms into place that will prevent me from performing rationally impermissible composite actions, like heading-south-and-then-north, because situations in which I have an opportunity to do so are very unlikely to arise.

This is not right. We all find ourselves in situations like this all the time. A mundane example:

Restaurants Redux
Recall (from Chapter 4) that I lack a preference between going to the Indian or the Chinese restaurants, each a mile away from me, in opposite directions, for dinner this evening. Nor will mildly sweetening or souring either prospect give me a preference. So when I attend to the states of affairs

A+: My walking 1 mile to the Chinese restaurant.
  A: My walking 1.2 miles to the Chinese restaurant.
B+: My walking 1 mile to the Indian restaurant.
  B: My walking 1.2 miles to the Indian restaurant.

I find that, though I prefer A+ to A, B+ to B, I have no preference between A+ or A and B+ or B. Arbitrarily I decide to walk to the Indian restaurant. After 0.1 miles I arrive at a road. I can cross it, and continue, or turn back and walk to the Chinese restaurant.

What should I do? I have arrived at the point on a decision tree shown in Fig. 14.3. Turning around and walking back to the Chinese restaurant is not rationally impermissible, because I have no preference for B+ over A. But if I do it then I will have done something rationally impermissible—walking 1.2 miles to the Chinese restaurant when I could have walked 1 mile to the Chinese restaurant.

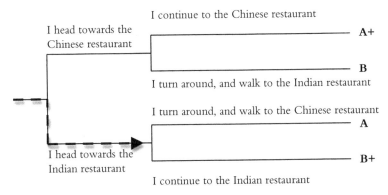

Figure 14.3

Nor is this the end of it. In all the examples we have seen so far the problematic situations arise because we have negatively intransitive preferences between maximal states of affairs, yielding a certain kind of imprecision in our conative attitudes—our conative attitudes cannot be represented by a utility function, U, that assigns numbers to maximal states of affairs in such a way that for all maximal states of affairs $x$, $y$, $U(x) \rangle U(y)$ iff we prefer $x$ to $y$. But they also commonly arise when we have negatively intransitive preferences between *gambles*, due to a certain kind of imprecision in our cognitive attitudes—our cognitive attitudes cannot be represented by a credence function, E, that assigns numbers to propositions in such a way that for all propositions $x$, $y$, $E(x) \rangle E(y)$ iff we think $x$ more likely than $y$. A contrived example of this general kind:

### Which Ticket?

Let $M$ be the proposition that Marco Rubio will secure the Republican nomination for President in 2020, $P$ be the proposition that Paul Ryan will, $D$ the proposition that Donald Trump will. When I consider these gambles:

A+:    I win \$100 if $M \vee D$, nothing otherwise.
A:    I win \$100 if $M$, nothing otherwise.
B+:    I win \$100 if $P \vee D$, nothing otherwise.
B:    I win \$100 if $P$, nothing otherwise.

I have a preference for A+ over A, B+ over B, because I think $M \vee D$ more likely than $M$, $P \vee D$ more likely than $P$. But I have no preference between either A+ or A and either B+ or B, because I do not think either $M \vee D$ or $M$ more or less likely than either $P \vee D$ or $P$. Why? Well, I take myself to have some reasons to think $M$ more likely than $P$—Rubio is more personable than Ryan, less overtly ideological, he has Florida behind him; and I also take myself to have some reasons to think $P$ more likely than $M$—Ryan has wider support among the fabled Republican base, his relentless fiscal conservatism will appeal to big-money donors. Overall I do not take either set of reasons to be decisive, so I do not think $M$ more or less likely than $P$. But it is not as if I take the reasons to be perfectly evenly balanced, so that a tiny extra consideration, like 'if Trump wins then the proposition will be true', will tip the balance.

A less contrived example:

### Which Highway?

I am heading up to Vermont from Boston this evening. Should I take Route 3 or US-93? For me it is just a matter of which will be faster. But I have no idea which will be faster. Route 3 is a bit further, US-93 usually has more traffic. But it is a Thursday, so that is good for US-93. But then again there was construction on US-93 earlier in the summer. Has it gone? I don't know. When I consider these gambles:

A+:    My taking Route 3 in the normal way.
A:    My heading towards US-93 for a short while, then doubling back and taking Route 3.

B+: My taking US-93 in the normal way.

B: My heading towards Route 3 for a short while, then doubling back and taking US-93.

I prefer A+ to A, because I am confident that Route 3 with no detour will be faster than Route 3 with a detour. I prefer B+ to B, because I am confident that US-93 with no detour will be faster than US-93 with a detour. Yet I have no preference between A+ or A and B+ or B. I have no idea whether taking US-93, detour or no, will be faster than taking Route 3, detour or no.

I had to choose between these gambles yesterday. I headed towards US-93. Soon I had the opportunity to double back (though I had no more evidence about which was the faster route). It was not rationally impermissible for me to double back, but if I had doubled back then I would have done something rationally impermissible.

## 14.4. A Second Strategy: Thoughtless Obedience to a Plan

Maybe rational people, when they are choosing between composite actions, form plans and then execute them *thoughtlessly*. Maybe that is a good strategy for avoiding performing rationally impermissible composite actions.

It is a good strategy, and one we make use of a lot. Yesterday, when I headed up US-93 and came to the first exit, the thought of turning around and heading up Route 3 never crossed my mind. I had a plan. It never occurred to me to depart from the plan.

But the strategy has its limitations. Sometimes, mid-plan, I cannot help but think about the options before me. Sometimes, for example, somebody asks me "What do we do now and why?" I have to answer. If I am consistently to avoid performing rationally impermissible composite actions, then I will need a back-up strategy.

## 14.5. A Third Strategy: Sharpening up your Preferences

Maybe rational people, in situations like this, willfully sharpen their preferences between A+, A, B+, and B, so that their preferences between these items are no longer negatively intransitive. Later, when (for example) they are choosing between A+ and B, they are no longer helpless. They prefer A+.

This is another good strategy, another one that I make use of a lot. Last time I had to choose between Indian and Chinese restaurants, I fixated, more or less arbitrarily, on one of the attractive features of one of the restaurants—the delicious mango lassi at the Indian restaurant. I dwelt on that mango lassi, sipped it in my imagination, until I had formed an all things considered preference for the Indian restaurant, sweetened or not over the Chinese restaurant, sweetened or not. My decision to walk to the Indian restaurant no longer seemed arbitrary. If I had paused when I arrived at the first road, if I had asked myself "should I keep going or turn back?" I would have found a clear preference for keeping going.

But this strategy, too, has its limitations. It is not always so easy to alter your preferences in a controlled way. I find myself to have some control when food is involved, much less control when other things are involved. In the Stick or Switch? case, for example, I very much doubt that I would be able willfully to form a settled preference for saving Andy, quickly or slowly, over saving Ben, quickly or slowly, and vice versa. And it gets worse when my intransitive preferences between items derive from imprecise cognitive attitudes. I find that I have almost no control over my cognitive attitudes, almost no ability to sharpen them at will. In the Which Highway? case, for example, I am quite unable, in the absence of good evidence, to persuade myself that Route 3, small diversion or not, is likely to be faster than US-93, small diversion or not, and vice versa.

## 14.6. A Fourth Strategy: Caring about your own Choices and Plans

Maybe rational people, though they retain their negatively intransitive preferences between the original items in question, care about things other than the original items, in such a way as to render their preferences between the outcomes in which they get the items sharp. One way to implement this strategy is to care about your not having chosen an item that you dis-prefer to some other item that you were once in a position to choose. Another way to implement this strategy is to make a decision and then care about your own decisiveness.

This is a good strategy. I use both versions of it. Last time I walked towards the Indian restaurant and arrived at the first road, if the thought of turning back had occurred to me, and if I had not already fixed on the mango lassi as a decisive reason to go ahead, I would still have gone ahead, on the grounds that it would frustrate me to have walked an unnecessary extra few hundred meters to the Chinese restaurant, and that I do not want to be a wishy-washy sort of person, the sort of person who does not stick to his decisions.

But (no surprise) this strategy, too, has limitations. Sometimes, when we make these sorts of choices, matters of vast import are at stake. Sometimes, when matters of vast import are at stake, our preferences are insensitive to very powerful sweetening (a further orphaned child here ... a further orphaned child there ... these things will not tip the balance). In these cases I will not take the consideration "if I do this, then I will have been indecisive" to be a balance-tipping consideration, to be a decisive reason to prefer one outcome to another, unless I have an outrageously skewed vision of the significance of my own decisiveness. I do not take (for example) the consideration that a further child will be orphaned if I head south to be a decisive reason to prefer the outcome of my heading south, but I do take the consideration that I will have been indecisive if I head north to be a decisive reason to prefer the outcome of my heading south!

## 14.7. A Last Strategy: Letting a Consideration be Decisive without Taking it to be of Decisive Significance

So it seems to me that we have need of one last, less limited strategy for assuring that we do not perform rationally impermissible composite actions. We develop a disposition to make plans or decisions and later be moved by the consideration "this was what I planned/decided to do" without taking that consideration to be a decisive reason to regard one outcome as better than another, or taking that consideration to be a decisive reason to prefer one outcome to another.

My implementing this strategy in the <u>Stick or Switch?</u> case would involve my thinking, as I arrive at Junction 3: "I decided to help Ben, and I see that revisiting the issue now, considering all the pros and cons (including those that have to do with my now being closer to Ben, and those that have to do with my having decided to help Ben), will leave me ambivalent and confused, so I will just stick with my decision."

You might see this as a kind of illicit partiality on my part—"Why do you consider Ben to be the more worthy of your help? Why are you continually favoring him in your decision-making?" But that would be a mistake. I am committed to Ben, but I do not consider him to be the more worthy of my help. And my disposition to commit to people in this way is not the relic of an uncivilized evolutionary past, the sort of thing for which I must give mumbling apologies. It is a mechanism that prevents me from doing rationally impermissible things when dropped into a world in which people's interests conflict and people's interests are significantly incommensurate.

## 14.8. In the End: The Decent and the Alien

I hope this goes some way toward showing that the demands of decency and rationality are not too alien. It would be very surprising if they were. Throughout the book I have made assumptions about what decent people want. The big assumption early on was that decent people are minimally benevolent towards others—roughly, they want, other things being equal, for other people to be better off. The big assumption later on was that decent people's preferences conform to *Dominance*—roughly, they care more about people than about how their own actions affect people. I have then argued that rational people with such wants will do certain things in morally portentious situations.

But I have not just been describing the behavior of a curious species of creature. We all have at least some of the desires I have attributed to the decent person. It does not take very much to be minimally benevolent toward others (conforming to *Dominance* is another matter—I am not sure I manage it). So, for us, coming to believe that a rational person with these desires will do this or that should feel like discovering that this or that is *the thing to do*.

Here is to discovering *the thing to do*.

# References

Amis, M. (1996). "First Lady on Trial," *Sunday Times*, March 17, 1996.

Benetar, D. (1997). "Why it is Better Never to Come into Existence," *American Philosophical Quarterly*, 34: 345–55.

Boonin, D. (2008). "How to Solve the Non-Identity Problem," *Public Affairs Quarterly*, 2: 127–57.

Broome, J. (1984). "Selecting People Randomly," *Ethics*, 95/1: 38–55.

——(1991). *Weighing Goods*. Oxford: Oxford University Press.

——(1998). "Kamm on Fairness," *Philosophy and Phenomenological Research*, 58: 955–61.

——(2004). *Weighing Lives*. New York: Oxford University Press.

Chang, R. (1997) (ed.). *Incommensurability, Incomparability and Practical Reason*. Cambridge, MA: Harvard University Press.

Clinton, H. (1996). *It Takes a Village: And Other Lessons Children Teach Us*. New York: Simon and Schuster.

Doggett T. (2009). "What is Wrong With Kamm and Scanlon's Arguments Against Taurek?," *Journal of Ethics and Social Philosophy*, 3/3: 1–15.

——(2013). "Saving the Few," *Noûs*, 45/2: 302–15.

Einstein, A. (1917). "Kosmologische Betrachtungen zur allgemeinen Relativitätstheorie" (Cosmological Considerations in the General Theory of Relativity), *Sitzungsberichte der Königlich Preussische Akademie der Wissenschaften*, 6–7: 142–52.

Foot, P. (1985). "Utilitarianism and the Virtues," *Mind*, 374: 196–209.

Goodman, N. (1955). *Fact, Fiction and Forecast*. Cambridge, MA: Harvard University Press.

Hamilton, Alan M. (1910). *The Intimate Life of Alexander Hamilton*. C. New York: Scribner's Sons.

Harman, E. (2004). "Can We Harm and Benefit in Creating?," *Philosophical Perspectives*, 13, *Ethics*, 89–113.

Hume, D. (1740). *A Treatise of Human Nature*. London.

Kagan, S. (2011). "Do I Make a Difference?," *Philosophy and Public Affairs*, 39/2: 105–41.

Kamm, F. (1984). "Equal Treatment and Equal Chances," *Philosophy and Public Affairs*, 14/2: 177–94.

——(1993). *Morality, Mortality*, i. *Death and Whom to Save from it*. Oxford: Oxford University Press.

——(2005). "Aggregation and Two Moral Methods," *Utilitas*, 17/1: 1–123.

Kolodny, N. (2008a). "The Myth of Practical Consistency," *European Journal of Philosophy*, 16/3: 366–402.

——(2008b). "Why be Disposed to be Coherent?," *Ethics*, 118/3: 437–63.

Korsgaard, C. (2008). "The Normativity of Instrumental Reason," in her *The Constitution of Agency*. Oxford: Oxford University Press, 26–68.

Kripke, S. (1972). "Naming and Necessity," in D. Davidson and G. Harman (eds.), *Semantics of Natural Language*. Dordrecht: Reidel Press, 253–355.

Lewis, D. (1968). "Counterpart Theory and Quantified Modal Logic," *Journal of Philosophy*, 65/5: 113–26.

——(1971). "Counterparts of Persons and their Bodies," *Journal of Philosophy*, 68/7: 203–11.

——(1981). "Causal Decision Theory," *Australasian Journal of Philosophy*, 59/1: 5–30.

Luminer, J., Starkman, G., and Weeks, J. (1999). "Is Space Finite?," *Scientific American* (April), 90–7.

McCloskey, H. (1963). "A Note on Utilitarian Punishment," *Mind*, 288: 599.

Norcross, A. (1997). "Comparing Harms: Headaches and Human Lives," *Philosophy and Public Affairs*, 26/2: 135–67.

Nozick, R. (1974). *Anarchy, State and Utopia*. New York: Basic Books.

Parfit, D. (1976). "Rights, Interests and Possible People," in S. Gorowitz (ed.), *Moral Problems in Medicine*. New York: Prentice Hall, 369–75.

——(1983). *Reasons and Persons*. Oxford: Oxford University Press.

——(1986). "Comments," *Ethics*, 96/4: 832–72.

——(2011a). *On What Matters Vol. 1*. Oxford: Oxford University Press.

——(2011b). *On What Matters Vol. 2*. Oxford: Oxford University Press.

Pettit, P. (1991). "Consequentialism," in P. Singer (ed.), *A Companion to Ethics*. Oxford: Blackwell, 230–40.

Plantinga, A. (1973). "Transworld Identity or Worldbound Individuals?," in M. K. Munitz (ed.), *Logic and Ontology*. New York: New York University Press.

——(1974). *The Nature of Necessity*. Oxford: Oxford University Press.

Quinn, W. (1990). "The Puzzle of the Self-Torturer," *Philosophical Studies*, 59/1: 79–90.

Rachels, S. (1998). "Counterexamples to the Transitivity of Better Than," *Australasian Journal of Philosophy*, 76/1: 71–83.

Ramsey, F. (1931). *The Foundations of Mathematics and Other Logical Essays*, ed. R. Braithwaite. London: Routledge.

Rawls, J. (1971). *A Theory of Justice*. Cambridge, MA: Harvard University Press.

Roberts, M. (1998). *Child versus Childmaker: Future Persons and Present Duties in Ethics and the Law*. Lanham, MD: Rowman & Littlefield.

Scanlon, T. (1999). *What Do We Owe to Each Other?* Cambridge, MA: Harvard University Press.

Scheffler, S. (1982). *The Rejection of Consequentialism*. Oxford: Oxford University Press.

Shiffrin, Seana (1999). "Wrongful Life, Procreative Responsibility, and the Significance of Harm," *Legal Theory*, 5/2: 117–48.

Singer, P. (1972). "Famine, Affluence and Morality," *Philosophy and Public Affairs*, 1/1: 229–43.

Stalnaker, B. (1976). "Possible Worlds," *Nous*, 10/1, 65–75.

——(1984). *Inquiry*. Cambridge, MA: MIT Press.

——(1986). "Counterparts and Identity," in P. French, T. Uehling, and H. Wettstein (eds.), *Midwest Studies in Philosopy XI: Studies in Essentialism*. Minneapolis: University of Minnesota Press.

Steinbock, B., and McClamrock, R. (1994). "When is Birth Unfair to the Child?," *Hastings Center Report*, 24/6: 15–21.

Taurek, J. (1977). "Should the Numbers Count?," *Philosophy and Public Affairs*, 6/4: 293–316.

Temkin, L. (1996). "A Continuum Argument for Intransitivity," *Philosophy and Public Affairs*, 25/3: 175–210.

Thomson, J. (1993). "Goodness and Utilitarianism," *Proceedings and Addresses of the American Philosophical Association*, 67: 145–59.

——(2008). *Normativity*. Chicago: Open Court Publishing.

Timmerman, J. (2004). "The Individualist Lottery: How People Count, but not their Numbers', *Analysis*, 64: 106–12.

Unger, P. (1996). *Living High and Letting Die: Our Illusion of Innocence*. New York: Oxford University Press.

Van Inwagen, P. (1990). *Material Beings*. Ithaca, NY: Cornell University Press.

Velleman, D. (2008). "Persons in Prospect," *Philosophy and Public Affairs*, 36: 221–88.

Woodward, J. (1986). "The Non-Identity Problem," *Ethics*, 96: 804–31.

# Index

Printed in the USA/Agawam, MA
November 14, 2022

801212.001